Okereke and Agupusi provide a refreshing and forceful critique of external meddling in Africa under the guise of development. Going far beyond aid agency doublespeak about 'country ownership', they make clear that homegrown development is really about NOT having external agencies or experts in charge.
     William Easterly, *Professor of Economics at New York University,*
     Co-director of the NYU Development Research Institute,
     and author of The Tyranny of Experts.

Okereke and Agupusi's new book *Homegrown Development in Africa* is as timely as it is relevant. It comes at a moment of great deal of optimism surrounding development possibilities across Africa. A must read for development scholars and practitioners, the book speaks directly to those who value internally generated sustainable solutions through meaningful ownership of the national development agenda.
     Yacob Mulugetta, *Professor of Energy and Development Policy, and*
     Director of the MPA programme at the Department of Science,
     Technology, Engineering & Public Policy (STEaPP)
     at University College London.

This volume is a must read for scholars and practitioners interested in international development programing in Africa. It provides a rigorous and balanced assessment of 'homegrown' development initiatives in Africa, set up as alternatives to externally sponsored development. The key finding that most national development programmes in the continent continue to retain 'external character' through over inclination towards external expertise (rather than building endogenous capacity) is sobering, especially in the context of sustainable development in Africa. The observation that 'no country has ever managed to achieve sustainable development through externally driven strategies' is a truism that sadly continues to be ignored in many development planning exercises around the world.
     Professor Kevin Urama, *Managing Director of Quantum Global*
     Research Lab, Switzerland.

Homegrown Development in Africa

Internationally driven development programmes have not been entirely successful in transforming the economic status of African countries. Since the late 1990s many African countries have started to take initiatives to develop an integrated framework that tackles poverty and promotes socio-economic development in their respective countries.

This book provides a critical evaluation of 'homegrown' development initiatives in Africa, set up as alternatives to externally sponsored development. Focusing specifically on Ghana, Nigeria, South Africa and Kenya, the book takes a qualitative and comparative approach to offer the first ever in-depth analysis of indigenous development programmes. It examines:

- How far African states have moved towards more homegrown development strategies.
- The effects of the shift towards African homegrown socio-economic development strategies and the conditions needed to enhance their success and sustainability.

This book will be of interest to students and scholars of development studies, international politics, political economy, public policy and African politics, sociology and economics.

Chukwumerije Okereke is Associate Professor of Environment and Development at the University of Reading, UK.

Patricia Agupusi is a postdoctoral Fellow at the International Studies Watson Institute, Brown University, USA.

Routledge Studies in African Politics and International Relations

Edited by Daniel C. Bach, Emile Durkheim Centre for Comparative Politics and Sociology, Sciences Po Bordeaux

1. Neopatrimonialism in Africa and Beyond
Edited by Daniel Bach and Mamoudou Gazibo

2. African Agency in International Politics
Edited by William Brown and Sophie Harman

3. The Politics of Elite Corruption in Africa
Roger Tangri and Andrew M. Mwenda

4. Reconstructing the Authoritarian State in Africa
George Klay Kieh, Jr. and Pita Ogaba Agbese

5. Critical Perspectives on African Politics
Liberal interventions, state-building and civil society
Edited by Clive Gabay and Carl Death

6. Homegrown Development in Africa
Reality or illusion?
Chukwumerije Okereke and Patricia Agupusi

7. Real Governance and Practical Norms in Sub-Saharan Africa
The game of the rules
Edited by Tom de Herdt and Jean-Pierre Olivier de Sardan

Homegrown Development in Africa

Reality or illusion?

Chukwumerije Okereke and
Patricia Agupusi

LONDON AND NEW YORK

First published 2015
by Routledge
2 Park Square, Milton Park, Abingdon, Oxfordshire OX14 4RN

and by Routledge
711 Third Avenue, New York, NY 10017

First issued in paperback 2016

Routledge is an imprint of the Taylor & Francis Group, an informa business

© 2015 Chukwumerije Okereke and Patricia Agupusi

The right of Chukwumerije Okereke and Patricia Agupusi to be identified as
author of this work has been asserted by them in accordance with sections
77 and 78 of the Copyright, Designs and Patents Act 1988.

All rights reserved. No part of this book may be reprinted or reproduced or
utilised in any form or by any electronic, mechanical, or other means, now
known or hereafter invented, including photocopying and recording, or in
any information storage or retrieval system, without permission in writing
from the publishers.

Trademark notice: Product or corporate names may be trademarks or
registered trademarks, and are used only for identification and explanation
without intent to infringe.

British Library Cataloguing in Publication Data
A catalogue record for this book is available from the British Library

Library of Congress Cataloging in Publication Data
Okereke, Chukwumerije, author.
  Homegrown development in Africa : reality or illusion? / Chukwumerije
Okereke and Patricia Agupusi.
    pages cm. – (Routledge studies in African politics and international
relations ; 6)
  Includes bibliographical references and index.
  1. Sustainable development–Government policy–Africa, Sub-Saharan.
2. Sustainable development–Government policy–Ghana. 3. Sustainable
development–Government policy–Nigeria. 4. Sustainable development–
Government policy–Kenya. 5. Sustainable development–Government
policy–South Africa. 6. Economic development–Africa, Sub-Saharan.
7. Economic assistance, Domestic–Africa, Sub-Saharan. 8. Poverty–Africa,
Sub-Saharan. I. Agupusi, Patricia, author. II. Title. III. Series: Routledge
studies in African politics and international relations ; 6.
  HC800.Z9E5578 2015
  338.96–dc23
               2014039643

ISBN 13: 978-1-138-29199-7 (pbk)
ISBN 13: 978-0-415-52574-9 (hbk)

Typeset in Times New Roman
by Taylor & Francis Books

Contents

	List of illustrations	viii
	Acknowledgements	ix
1	African homegrown development: Renaissance or illusion?	1
2	Homegrown development in Africa: Historical and current perspectives	12
3	Conceptualizing homegrown development	29
4	Ghana: Vision 2020 and Poverty Reduction Strategy Papers	46
5	Nigeria: National Economic Empowerment and Development Strategy	70
6	Kenya: Economic Recovery Strategy and Vision 2030	91
7	South Africa: Reconstruction and Development Programme	108
8	Common trends and issues in African homegrown development efforts	130
	Conclusion	152
	Bibliography	162
	Index	186

List of illustrations

Figures

3.1 Essence and features of homegrown development   33
3.2 Dimensions of homegrown development   33
8.1 Pyramid of self-reliant growth   148

Table

8.1 Calibrating homegrown development in the four
    case-study countries   131

Acknowledgements

We have accumulated quite some debt in the process of writing this book. Firstly, we are most grateful to God Almighty for his infinite grace which made it possible for us to undertake and complete this project. We would also like to acknowledge many of our colleagues and friends who proofread draft chapters at various stages, provided intellectual stimulation, and offered insightful comments on the manuscripts. These include Ben Onyango, Briony O'Shea, Henry Alhassan, Karie Fisher, Megan Turnball, Nelson Oppong, Simon Mariwah and Sylvester Ajah.

Chukwumerije would like to express his deep appreciation to his long-suffering wife (Boma) and children (Chioma and Chukwuebuka) for their prayers, care and encouragement. For several months – including during their holidays – they gracefully put up with long hours without husband and dad being at home. Thanks are also due to wider family – dad, mum, Nneka, Uzo, Nnabugwu, Ifeyinwa, Amauche, Ngozi and Ogochukwu – for their support and motivation. It is also a pleasure to acknowledge Cynthia White for generous provision of tasteful coffee during the several long hours at the Oxford library. Prayers from Aaron Senanu's, Chima Mordi's, Dapo Akande's and David Aneju's families are warmly appreciated. Research funding from Leverhulme Trust (Grant Reference ECF/7/SRF/2010/0624) without which this work would not have been undertaken, is also deeply acknowledged.

Patricia would like to express her debt and gratitude to Glenn Loury who sponsored part of this project and for his intellectual contribution. Thanks also to Peget Henry who provided various rigorous and insightful discussions that have deeply contributed to this book and to Arjan Verschoor for moral support. Gratitude is due to friends and colleagues at Watson Institute and Population Studies, Brown University for their support during the process of this book. Profound thanks to friends Amaka, Solange, Niousha, Ayesha and John Mcdonough for their encouragement and belief in the message of this book. Finally special heart felt appreciation to Grace and Dona Agupusi and all my siblings for their unconditional love and unwavering support.

1 African homegrown development
Renaissance or illusion?

Observed patterns of development processes across time and space show that no country has ever managed to achieve sustainable development through externally driven strategies. Countries may borrow and adapt ideas, money, and human resources. For a period of time they may need tutelage, technology and technical assistance. In the end, however, truly sustainable economic growth and development can only come through self-reliant homegrown strategies. The alternative is perpetual dependency and servitude.

One of the notable tragedies of much of African development efforts is that for far too long they have been based on externally invented strategies that are not compatible with local conditions and realities. Just how much these externally led and oriented strategies are imposed, as opposed to being self-inflicted, has been the subject of much vitriolic debate. What is hardly contested is that, regardless of where the bulk of the blame lies, a fundamental shift in the approach to 'doing development' is required for political independence in Africa to translate to economic freedom and self-reliance.

Meanwhile, in the first decade of independence, most African countries made great strides in development through homegrown strategies. The struggle for independence had in fact carried with it a promise not simply of political freedom but also crucially of economic decolonization (Adedeji, 1981; Ake, 1991). Such was the strength of the recognition that President Kaunda of Zambia forcefully declared in 1965: 'Political independence without matching economic independence is meaningless. It is economic independence that brings in its wake social, cultural and scientific progress of man' (Kaunda, 1968).

Julius Nyerere in his famous Arusha Declaration speech in 1967 made the point even more forcefully, saying:

> It is stupid to rely on money as the major instrument of development when we know only too well that our country is poor. It is equally stupid; indeed it is even more stupid, for us to imagine that we shall rid ourselves of our poverty through foreign financial assistance rather than our own financial resources. It is stupid for two reasons. Firstly, we shall not get the money. It is true that there are countries which can, and which would

2 African homegrown development

like to, help us. But there is no country in the world which is prepared to give us gifts or loans, or establish industries, to the extent that we would be able to achieve all our development targets ... Secondly, even if it were possible for us to get enough money for our needs from external sources, is this what we really want? Independence means self-reliance. Independence cannot be real if a nation depends upon gifts and loans from another for its development.

(Nyerere, 1967)

Okoye (1980: 5) has aptly observed that slogans such as 'boycott the boycottables', 'African Personality', 'Negritude' and 'cultural authenticity' which provided the ideational thrust for independence struggle were all underpinned by, and expressive of the hope for African indigenous and self-reliant economic growth. It was with this mind-set – a desire to prove to the world that they were ripe for self-rule – that various governments at independence embarked on strategic development initiatives to accelerate the pace of socio-economic development.

For example, Ghana, inspired by the modernization theory, went for the 'big push' development based on rapid infrastructural growth – even though Nkrumah rather curiously called his approach 'scientific socialism' (Nkurumah, 1957a). Tanzania routed for a more 'pure' brand of African socialism based on Nyerere's famous concept of *Ujamaa* – with its emphasis on self-sufficient agriculture and local cooperative societies. Nigeria prioritized industrialization, taking the number of medium and large scale size plants in the industrial sector from 150 at independence (in 1960) to 380 by 1965. This was, as Iwuagwu, (2009: 157) rightly observed 'the era of the pioneer mills for palm oil processing, palm kernel and groundnut crushing, cotton ginning, leather tanning, power driven saw mills, beer brewing, and oil seed milling'.

Kenya for its own part, through *Harambee*, favoured a delicate combination of self-reliant economic development and the importation of factor input such as capacity and equipment from abroad. The approaches were all qualitatively different which gave credence to their authenticity. The common denominator, however, was that each country made concerted efforts to articulate and manage their own development plan based on their national priorities and with sensitivity to their history, culture and economic advantages. While many of the post independent economic policies had serious flaws and produced mixed results, they were widely characterized by a determined effort towards self-reliant development. Accordingly, they galvanized the people and led to a sense of national pride. But the euphoria did not last as many of the countries badly stumbled before they had the chance to firmly stand on their feet.

The period between 1980 and 1999 has been widely described as the two lost decades in Africa with regards to economic development (Easterly, 2001; Noman, *et al.*, 2012). During this period, Africa suffered real failure in economic development and much of the progress made in the years following independence was reversed. This era of woeful economic performance coincided with the time the Bretton Woods Institutions introduced and imposed the Structural Adjustment Programme (SAP). This was a set of conditionality stipulations on borrowing by developing countries in return for loans, debt reliefs and the financial aid they beggarly sought to help prop up their rapidly declining economies. The World Bank and the IMF's SAPs were introduced in over 40 African countries between 1980 and 1993 (Loewenson, 1993) and a total of 958 adjustment loans were made to developing countries from 1980 to 1998 (Easterly, 2001: 136).

Since the late 1990s, there have been renewed calls for African governments to (re)take responsibility for developing an integrated framework that tackles poverty and socio-economic development in their respective countries. The shift back towards African homegrown development (HGD) is based on a wide consensus (by scholars, African leaders and their development partners) that externally crafted and imposed development programmes have largely not been successful in transforming the socio-economic status of African countries. Across the spectrum, there is a widespread feeling that Africans must now (re) take full ownership of their development agendas and direct their own political social and economic destiny. Homegrown development for Africa has thus emerged as the new mantra in international development discourse.

'African Solutions to African Problems' is now the key refrain of the Organization of African Unity (OAU) – a philosophy trumpeted with regards to economic development, peace and security and the management of the continent's environmental challenges (Beswick, 2012). Since the turn of the Millennium, a number of African leaders notably Thabo Mbeki of South Africa and Olusegun Obasanjo of Nigeria have been talking up the idea of 'African Renaissance' and a 'new partnership' with the West based on self-management, policy autonomy, equality and mutual respect (UNECA, 2001; NEPAD, 2001). Hear them:

> The resources, including capital, technology and human skills, that are required to launch a global war on poverty and underdevelopment exist in abundance, and are within our reach. What is required to mobilise these resources and to use them properly, is bold and imaginative leadership that is genuinely committed to a sustained human development effort and poverty eradication, as well as a new global partnership based on shared responsibility and mutual interest.
>
> (NEPAD, 2001: 15)

Continuing, they vowed: 'Across the continent, Africans declare that we will no longer allow ourselves to be conditioned by circumstance. We will determine our own destiny and call on the rest of the world to complement our efforts' (NEPAD, 2001: 15).

Meanwhile about the same period the mood of donor countries and International Financial Institutions (IFIs) about African development was also changing. The 2005 Paris declaration on aid effectiveness is often quoted as a

4   *African homegrown development*

turning point. Here, over 100 donor agencies and receipt countries affirmed that henceforth country ownership would become the key pillar of a new aid paradigm. In the same year the eight most industrialized countries (G8) expressed their exasperation with the failure of African leaders to step up and take the lead in defining their national development strategies. In a call for bolder leadership they declared:

> It is up to developing countries themselves and their governments to take the lead on development. They need to decide, plan, and sequence their economic policies to fit with their own development strategies, for which they should be accountable to all their people.
>
> (G8 Statement on Africa, 2005)

'National ownership' of strategies is now the keyword for international donors' lending strategy as epitomized in the Poverty Reduction Strategy Papers (PRSPs). The PRSPs replaced SAP and currently guide the lending policy of the IMF and World Bank. They have provided the context for virtually all the aid-related national development strategies by African governments since 1999. HGD has also been rapidly acquiring a growing presence in the internet and blogosphere. A google search on the phrase 'African solution to African problem' shows 150,000 results in 0.2 seconds while 'homegrown development in Africa' search provides over a million hits.

It is curious, however, that despite rhetorical inflation within policy circles, there has so far been very little engagement with HGD strategies and their challenges in the academic scholarship. In fact, it is shocking to find, based on searches on Amazon, Google Scholar and Web of Knowledge, that the term 'homegrown development' does not appear to figure *even once* in the title of any book or journal article in print. By contrast, the term 'ownership' is much more widely used, if poorly defined and operationalized. The purpose of this book is to fill this gap.

The focus of the book

The general objective of the book is to contribute to the rapidly growing but poorly articulated HGD discourse in Africa. The specific aim is to provide a critical evaluation of a number of the development initiatives in Africa put in place between 1999 and 2009 to assess the extent of their *indigeneity* (how indigenous they are) as well as their effectiveness. In practice this is seen as a way of exploring the extent to which the clamour for HGD in Africa has resulted in truly self-reliant development. Focusing specifically on Ghana, Nigeria, Kenya and South Africa, the book takes a qualitative and comparative approach to offer an in-depth analysis of the 'new wave' of development programmes in Africa, which since the late 1990s have been presented as alternatives to externally driven development.

The book is concerned with two overarching questions. The first is to explore the extent to which these post-SAP developmental initiatives in sub-Saharan Africa could be truly described as homegrown. Fundamental to answering this question is a close and detailed exploration of various development programmes and the degree to which there has been a change in the aid relationship between African governments and donor countries and agencies. We are interested in knowing whether African governments have indeed extricated themselves from the paternalistic relationship with Western countries and donor institutions that characterized the era of colonialism as well as the Structural Adjustment Programmes in the 1980s and 1990s.

The second overarching question explored in the book is the extent to which these development initiatives have been effective and what factors account for their success, or lack of it. Here, we are interested in looking critically at these initiatives to see what works, what does not work and why? In other words, what makes these initiatives different from the previous externally prescribed programmes; what are the challenges that these programmes face; and what is needed to enhance the effectiveness of these initiatives?

The concept of HGD

A prior and critical requirement in analysing the quality of these strategies is a clear definition and robust conceptualization of HGD. This is necessary because while HGD and its cognates such as 'country-led', 'country-owned', 'self-reliant' and 'indigenous' growth have become emblems for new directions in the development process, precious little effort has so far been devoted to actually defining what these terms mean and how they may be conceptualized. Some of the many questions that have arisen about HGD in Africa, which give urgency to the need for a strong conceptualization of the concept relate to its relationship with existing development paradigms, its normative content (if it has any) and its utility as a vehicle for ushering in sustainable development (Apuuli, 2012; Beswick, 2010; Mays, 2003; Whitfield, 2009). Furthermore, does HGD include borrowing ideas from other successful countries or solely leveraging local knowledge and assets? Does it entail broad based participation that involves civil society organization in development planning or merely the more direct involvement of national parliaments?

Emerging scholarship on country ownership, aid politics and sustainable African development provide a discordant picture. There are some who appear to suggest that HGD for Africa implies going back to ancient cultures and institutions (see Oomen, 2000). Others however, suggest that the solution lies in generating 'organizational and disciplinary techniques for blending the past with the present' (Okoye, 1980: 5). Some scholars, notably Easterly (2006a; 2006b) have strongly linked HGD with 'the dynamism of individuals and firms in free markets' (Easterly, 2006a: 368) suggesting a very limited role for the state. On this account, HGD for Africa implies effective functioning free market capitalism as is the case in Western democracies. But this recipe

6 African homegrown development

for HGD has been criticized with strong arguments produced to indicate that HGD in Africa requires the effective role of the state (Stiglitz, 1998). Lastly, while some imply that embracing HGD warrants cessation of development aid to Africa (Easterly, 2006b; Moyo, 2009), others see increased aid flow as compatible with nurturing HGD (Kalinowski, 2009; Sachs et al., 2004; Whitfield and Fraser, 2009). Crucially, in the context of well-rehearsed technical and human capacity gaps in Africa, unequal relationship with donor agencies, institutional weakness and the 'extraversion' of African leaders (Whitfield and Fraser, 2009), there are questions about whether, and to what extent, Africans and their development partners can truly claim the existence of HGD development initiatives in the continent. And, if indeed HGD strategies are now taking root in Africa, what exactly do they look like and what results are they generating?

In this book, we have defined a HGD strategy as one that is initiated, crafted and implemented by a country without external control. By this definition, we suggest that the most important factor in HGD is policy ownership or autonomy. Our use of ownership is different from its common application in the mainstream aid discourse where it is often taken to mean the greater commitment of borrowing countries to implement polices agreed with or even forced upon them by donor agencies often in keeping with loan conditionality. We use ownership to mean absolute control by a country over its development agenda, plans and priorities.

Emphasis on local solutions and total policy autonomy does not imply that HGD is anti-aid. HGD is, however, inherently incompatible with the type of aid conditionality which imposes policy prescriptions on recipient countries. We argue that, at one level, HGD is normatively neutral in the sense that it does not presuppose commitment to any ideology, procedure or policy prescription. In other words, it can involve more or less market, big or small state, very active or minimal civil society participation, limited or extensive import of external ideas and technology. At this level, the simple test of a HGD is whether or not the country in question has the freedom to borrow, accept, or reject inputs from external sources.

But HGD does not automatically equal 'good' development – understood in terms of development that leads to optimum and sustainable improvement in the wellbeing of the greatest number of the population. While it is difficult to envisage sustainable development in Africa that is not homegrown, it is not hard to see that policy autonomy alone will not necessarily translate to sustainable self-reliant growth. HGD, as Ikoku (1980) makes clear does not equal autarky. Domatob (1998: 80) also emphasizes this, when he cautions that 'delinking, as once proposed by some scholars like Cees Hamelink (1983: 16) is not the answer'.

We suggest that HGD can better be understood as an effective development strategy by thinking of it as having a 'core' and 'periphery' or what we call 'features'. The core is the essential characteristic that defines whether or not a development approach is homegrown. The features are the components

African homegrown development 7

that need to be in place for the concept to produce successful or 'good' outcome, which in this case is sustainable socio-economic development. As already stated, policy autonomy is the core of HGD. In the book, we identify four components of effective HGD. These include: (i) economic diversification and attention to local imperatives; (ii) broad stakeholder consultation and participation; (ii) attention to human capacity and institutions; and (iv) social development rather than narrow focus on gross domestic product (GDP) growth. An alternative but mutually compatible way to conceptualize HGD is in terms of the 'who', 'what' and 'how' questions. The response to the 'who question' reveals who is actually in control of the development initiative and therefore whether the strategy is HGD or not. Answers to the 'why' and 'how' questions will provide indications of the normative content of the development strategy under examination. Although the focus of our conceptual development is on Africa, the analytical model proposed in this book, in our view has global application.

Is African bouncing back through homegrown development?

In the first decade of the twenty-first century, many African countries achieved and maintained a growth of between 5 per cent and 7 per cent GDP per year indicating that at last progress had started to be made. A popular report on African Development (*The Economist*, 2011) indicates that about one-third of Africa's countries have GDP growth rates of more than 6 per cent. According to the same source, Africa's collective GDP per capita reached US $953 in 2013 – an all-time high, while the number of middle income countries on the continent rose to 26, out of a total of 54. Six out of the fastest growing countries in the world are from Africa and according to various international statics Africa will be the fastest growing continent in the next seven years – surpassing China, India and other fast emerging economies. This surge in economic growth improvement has reinvigorated the idea that Africans have made fundamental shifts in their development strategies (Ajulu, 2001; Liebenberg, 1998).

However, a cursory analysis reveals that poverty remains quite deep and widespread in Africa. Most economies are still predominantly monocultural and rudimentary. There is wide infrastructural deficit and institutions are still hobbled with corruption and patronage. The percentage of unemployed is growing and poverty is still rampant. Education and health care services are still inefficient and electricity generation is irregular. For example, electricity generation capacity in Africa at 39 MW per million population is about one-tenth of the levels found in other low income regions of the world (Okereke and Yusuf, 2013). Per capita electricity consumption in Africa (excluding South Africa) averages only 124 kilowatt-hours a year, barely 1 per cent of the consumption typical in high income countries (Energy Information Administration, 2011). This is hardly enough to power one light bulb per person for six hours a day. On current trends less than half of African countries will

8 African homegrown development

reach universal access to electricity even by 2050. Clearly then, for Africa, it is not yet *Uhuru* (a Swahili word meaning 'complete freedom').

The mainstream interpretation for persistent poverty in Africa, despite over ten years of post-SAP reforms, is that the economic development problem on the continent was much deeper than generally thought at the turn of the new millennium. Accordingly, it is said that more time is needed for this new set of initiatives to bear fruit (cf. Devarajan, Dollar and Holmgren, 2001). However, concerns have been expressed that this new wave of development initiatives (mostly based on PRSPs) does not appear to hold much promise of ushering in real economic transformation in Africa because, like the SAPs before them, the initiatives remain focused on macroeconomic growth, 'thus missing the boat in terms of the fundamentals' (Dante, 2003: 43) and essential ingredients for achieving sustainable homegrown economic development (Obwona and Guloba, 2009). Moreover, it is suggested that these programmes lack genuine national ownership as purported by the World Bank and other international development institutions, and rather continue to be implemented under terms that are heavily dictated by donor institutions (Lazarus, 2008; Muganda, 2004; Whitfield, 2009). The indication is that, at least for Africa, the concept of national ownership and the declaration of a policy of homegrown economic development by African leaders and their funding patterns remains an illusion.

Given the foregoing, an analysis of the emergent development initiatives in Africa to ascertain their qualitative content as well as their prospects and limits as the means of achieving the sustainable economic transformation of Africa is both a practical and theoretical priority. This is the task to which this book is devoted.

Method and cases

In our task of analysing the 'new wave' development initiatives in Africa to determine their indigeneity and effectiveness we draw from different methodological tools including political economy, historical intuitionalism, discourse and content analysis. Methodological eclecticism was informed by the conviction that a deep understanding of common trends and issues in African HGD requires attention to a range of factors including structural, human agency, political and social forces operating across different scales – from the local through to international. Our key interest is in exploring how specific configurations of political and economic factors determine the content, success and failure of these initiatives. Empirically we relied on case studies of four African countries: Ghana, Nigeria, Kenya and South Africa. We conducted as analytical critique of the key policy initiates in these countries covering their content, design, implementation and outcome. In doing so we took time to set out a clear conceptual framework in the book which provides a basis for the individual and comparative analysis of the development strategies.

Although our focus is on the four countries named above, we make copious references to a number of different African nations. Choosing some cases to represent 54 countries of Africa was always going to be difficult given the diversity within the continent. While there are important limitations, we nonetheless believe that the four countries chosen offer a rich variety which allows us to draw common conclusions.

Ghana was the first sub-Saharan African country to gain independence from colonial rule in 1957. With a population of just over 16 million, it has been characterized as 'the beacon on the African continent' (World Bank, 1993 cited in Aryeetey and Harrigan, 2000: 5) and the 'black star' of Africa. Several studies suggest that Ghana was one of the most successful adjusters in Africa, especially in the 1980s (Gyimah-Boadi, 2008; Kirk-Greene, 1990). Ghana has enjoyed a high level of post-independence peace, stability and cultural homogeneity relative to most other countries in Africa.

Nigeria is the most populous country and a clear regional power. It is immensely diverse with well over 250 ethnic groupings. Nigeria survived a three-year, bloody civil war that threatened to divide the country just six years after independence in 1960. Although it is very rich in natural and human resources, Nigeria had been adjudged, by a World Bank publication, one of the worst performing in terms of economic reforms in the SAP era (Devarajan *et al.*, 2001). Following a return to democratic rule in 1999 and the engagement of a team of technocrats including a former Vice President of the World Bank in its economic team, there were widespread expectations that the country would make rapid progress towards socio-economic development.

Kenya is the most influential country in East Africa and was the first to undertake a structural adjustment programme in Africa in the late 1970s (Melamed, 1996). With a population of about 43 million, it is the seventh most populous country in Africa. Like Ghana, Kenya has enjoyed relative post-independence stability and as a result acts as the hub for international and multilateral agencies in Africa. Kenya's performance in SAP-related reform is adjudged medium or mixed (Devarajan *et al.*, 2001).

South Africa is distinctively different from the rest of the group because of its long history of apartheid which is peculiar to the country. It is the most developed economy in Africa. Under apartheid, it operated two economy systems, one for the prosperous white community and the other for an impoverished black community. It is relevant to analyse the progress of South Africa since the end of apartheid rule. In particular it offers the opportunity for comparison with the other countries given the significant development in its institutions and infrastructure. Despite important differences, the four countries, like the rest of sub-Saharan Africa, are united by extreme income inequality and widespread poverty.

Overview and plan

The rest of the book contains eight chapters. In Chapter 2, we provide a potted history of the African development trajectory after independence focusing on key attempts made to engender HGD in the continent. We

10   *African homegrown development*

attempt to provide insight on the complex challenges faced by African leaders and the merits and flaws of these 'first wave' development efforts. In providing this narrative, we make links to the role of key development ideas and theories, from modernization through Keynesianism to post-structuralism. Finally we map the resurgence of HGD impulses in Africa identifying the key proponents of this idea. The chapter underscores the role of ideas and ideational forces in shaping how development was understood and approached in various periods in history.

In Chapter 3 we attempt a rigorous definition and conceptualization of HGD. We noted that while HGD might first seem like a straightforward concept, it actually lends itself to different interpretations. In fact so widely varying are the meaning and usage that some would appear directly contradictory. Given that the different communities clamouring for HGD in Africa might actually have different things in mind, a clear definition and conceptualization, we argue, is a priority before undertaking any qualitative analysis of HGD strategies in Africa. The conceptual development undertaken in Chapter 3 provides the basis for the subsequent empirical analysis in the book.

Chapter 4 begins the empirical analysis. The first case discussed is Ghana, with a focus on its Vision 2020 and Ghana Poverty Reduction Strategy Papers. In Chapter 5 we examine Nigeria's integrated socio-economic strategy, known as the National Economic Empowerment Development Strategy (NEEDS), introduced in 2004 during Obasanjo's second term in office. Chapter 6 focuses on Kenya and the programmes analysed are Kenya Vision 2030 and the Economic Recovery Strategy for Employment and Wealth Creation. The last case, examined in Chapter 7 is South Africa. The South African case covers the Reconstruction and Development Programme (RDP), the Black Economic Empowerment Programme (BEEP) and the Growth, Employment and Redistribution Programme (GEAR). All programmes were introduced in post-apartheid South Africa. Although the four countries discussed in this book passed through colonialism, South Africa's social, political and economic configuration is peculiar due to its history of apartheid which has shaped the present development programme in South Africa.

In Chapter 8 we draw out common lessons and trends based on the conceptual framework and the empirical analysis undertaken in the preceding chapters. In addition we identify various tensions, challenges and patterns implicated in the search for HGD, not just in the four case studies but also in Africa as a whole. Also in this chapter we present a model that shows the various degrees of HGD that can be found in different African (and other developing) countries. These range from outright policy imposition through a hybrid of policy adoption and modification to genuine ownership. This is followed by a short concluding section.

Our analysis suggests that while African countries are taking notable steps to reclaim ownership of their development agenda and define their national priorities, far too much of the existing strategies are still externally dictated

African homegrown development   11

and therefore cannot be reasonably described as HGD strategies. We found that of all the countries studied, only South Africa, with strong policy ownership and quality broad stakeholder participation operates a semblance of HGD. The other three countries – Ghana, Nigeria and Kenya – have made attempts at more leadership but remain too much influenced by external development templates, notably the World Bank's and IMF's PRSP framework.

2 Homegrown development in Africa
Historical and current perspectives

On 5 March 1957, Ghana became the third African country to gain independence with Kwame Nkrumah as its first president. In his Independence Day speech, Nkrumah dedicated his victory to the entire African continent declaring that Ghana's independence 'is meaningless unless it is linked up with total liberation of Africa'. Continuing in his speech he said:

> We must realize that from now on we are no longer a colonial but free and independent people ... that also entails hard work ... That new Africa is ready to fight his own battles and show that after all the black man is capable of managing his own affairs. We are going to demonstrate to the world, to the other nations, that we are prepared to lay our foundation.
>
> (Nkrumah, 1957a)

Three years later, in 1960, 16 other African countries achieved independence thereby making that year one of the most significant in African political history. With the formal independence of Eritrea from Ethiopia in 1993 the end of apartheid in South Africa in 1994, and independence of South Sudan in 2012, the whole of Africa now comprises 54 independent countries.

The view has been occasionally expressed that the African development process did not take off mainly because the nationalist leaders that fought for independence were not interested in development but solely in consolidating political power (Ake, 1996; Mbaku, 2004; Kohli, 2004). This claim however is wholly inaccurate. Although much of the effort and rhetoric in the pre-independence years were focused on the quest for political freedom, African leaders clearly had economic development and prosperity of the continent very much within their purview in their fight for colonial freedom. This point is very easily attested to by countless collections of pre- and post-independence speeches and publications which reveal a rich and stimulating set of debates about the nature of economic policy that independent Africa should pursue and the rationale for such choices (Mutiso and Rohio, 1975).

Historical and current perspectives 13

In a large gathering of party faithful in Lusaka, Zambia in 1962, the would-be President, Kenneth Kaunda, declared that 'Political independence without matching economic independence is meaningless ... It is economic independence that brings in its wake social, cultural and scientific progress of man'. Felix Houphouet-Boigny of Côte d'Ivoire was equally eloquent: 'It is not the shell of independence which counts; it is the context; the economic contents, the social contents, and the human contents' (cited in Meredith, 2011: 69). Even Nkrumah's battle cry to Africans: 'seek first the political kingdom and all else will be added unto you' (Nkrumah, 1957c: 164) communicates the message that political freedom from the West was not an end in itself but a vehicle for economic emancipation. In short, the consensus was the quest for an African renaissance marked by social, cultural and economic rejuvenation. Adedeji (1981: 21) expressed this consensus aptly when he noted that the 'struggle for independence had carried with it promise of a better and more abundant life for all, of a just and egalitarian society, and of a bright future full of opportunities'.

A quick search reveals that by far the dominant approach was for a brand of mixed economy rooted in African socio-economic philosophy. This is viewed in some quarters as 'African socialism' (Arrighi and Saul, 1968; Meredith, 2005; Mutiso and Rohio, 1975). Within this broad vision, there were a number of competing ideas about approaches and policies with at least three traditions discernible. The first, favoured by Nkrumah of Ghana, was rapid modernization anchored in the so-called 'big push' infrastructural development. The second tradition of thought, supported by the likes of Jomo Kenyatta and Tom Mboya of Kenya, favoured a delicate combination of self-reliant economic development and the importation of factor input such as capacity and equipment from abroad. The third economic development philosophy, championed by Julius Nyerere of Tanzania, was a 'pure' and more radical brand of socialism with strong emphasis on self-sufficient agriculture and local cooperative societies.

Despite these differences, the emergent ruling classes were united in their appreciation of the need to completely own their economic development programme and be the sole deciders of the economic destinies of their countries. In essence, the goal was to advance the type of development that promoted self-reliance, indigenous enterprise and equal opportunity for all citizens. As they saw it, a relationship with the rest of the world – where such was necessary to promote economic growth – was to be based on an equal partnership between sovereign nations rather than on conditionality stipulations. The prevailing view expressed repeatedly in rallies and campaign speeches was that the continent possessed the vast resources and capacity to achieve an African brand of development that would bring prosperity for the local population and propel the continent to levels on a par with the rest of the world in terms of living conditions and wellbeing.

At the time, African leaders were generally cautious of foreign aid even though the extent of caution varied among leaders. Some like Mboya of

14 *Historical and current perspectives*

Kenya and Nkrumah of Ghana recognized the danger in external aid but nonetheless expressed the view that financial assistance could be accepted in a manner that would not undermine their independence. Nyerere for his own part was not only cautious, but outright suspicious. He maintained that external aid was a trap that could easily undermine a country's freedom to choose a path to development. One can begin to understand just how much African leaders craved a homegrown development (HGD) approach based on a set of nationally determined priorities and self-reliant effort by noting the vehemence with which President Julius Nyerere in his famous Arusha Declaration denounced ideas about externally oriented growth in Africa as 'stupid'. In the speech he made clear that HGD was not just one of the many ways, but in fact, the only way to ensure sustainable economic prosperity and political freedom for the newly independent Africa. He argued:

> Even if there was a nation, or nations, prepared to give us all the money we need for our development, it would be improper for us to accept such assistance without asking ourselves how this would affect our independence and our very survival as a nation. Gifts which increase, or act as a catalyst, to our own efforts are valuable. Gifts which could have the effect of weakening or distorting our own efforts should not be accepted until we have asked ourselves a number of questions.
>
> (Nyerere, 1967)

Nyerere's tone may have been among the more forceful or revolutionary among the African leaders. However, as noted, a homegrown approach with an emphasis on human development, social services and economic growth through self-reliance was common to African development initiatives at the time of independence in the 1960s (Fraser, 2005). And this much is evidenced by the suite of bold, if ill-fated policies pursued by many leaders across Africa soon after independence.

African homegrown development approach at independence

Following independence, African governments embarked on strategic development of varying degrees, the primary purpose of which was to accelerate the pace of socio-economic development (Adedeji, 1981; Arrighi and Saul, 1968; Meredith, 2005). Ghana under Nkrumah introduced the Seven Year Economic Development Plan; Nigeria under Tafawa Balewa commenced a National Development Plan in 1960; Kenya, under Kenyatta, started the Five Year Development Plan; and President Abdul Nasser of Egypt introduced his first comprehensive five year plan in 1960. All of these post-independence development plans, and many others like them, contained bold attempts by the governments of the day to take full control of their countries' socio-economic development path. Even when external experts were invited, their role was merely as advisors. The ultimate decisions regarding what was

Historical and current perspectives 15

included were made by the local stakeholders. This was expressly played out in the case of Ghana where external economists led by the Nobel laureate Arthur Lewis served as advisors to the Nkrumah led government during the drafting of a first independence development plan in 1960 but made no attempt to dictate to the young government which specific steps it should take.

In order to ensure that locals were actively engaged in driving the economic development of their respective countries, many governments moved to indigenize their economies immediately after political independence in the early 1960s. Africanization which entailed the replacement of most expatriates with local officials was primarily designed to ensure that critical economic and related administrative decisions in the newly independent states were made by Africans and in the interest of Africa. Administrative and political powers have always co-existed with economic powers. To this extent, Africanization was as much an economic as it was a political programme.

They also made notable efforts to diversify their industrial base and develop local manufacturing capabilities. Throughout Africa, many newly independent states, contrary to popular belief, made far reaching efforts to develop self-reliance and build local capacity in many sectors. Nigeria invested in developing the capacity to refine palm oil in Eastern Nigeria. Ghana invested in the development of sugar refining and tomato canning capability. In Sudan, governments established vegetable oil refining mills with considerable success. In Côte d'Ivoire, cotton mills using a significant part of local resources were built. Nigeria experimented with limited success in establishing a local assembly of (Peugeot) automobiles. In Tanzania, the government established village-based self-help co-operative programmes. These were co-community development programmes geared towards encouraging individual enterprise, self-reliance and used locally available resources and skills as far as possible. These programmes helped in the building of schools, dispensaries and personal houses. Self-help was particularly successful in the field of urban housing.

Although some of the specific policies implemented under Africanization and indigenization have been criticised, it is beyond doubt that these programmes had far-reaching developmental implications. Clearly they served the purpose of boosting national pride, instigating a sense of self belief and ensuring that Africans had full control of their socio-economic destinies to the greatest extent possible. They also served to help correct the imbalance in the old order, and compensate locals for their electoral support. However, there were also notable economic benefits. Ezeife (1981) reports that indigenization helped economic performance in Nigeria. According to him, gross national product (GNP) increased to 97.4 and 98.9 from 1974/5 and 1975/6 respectively above the forecast figures of 93.8 and 95.5. Kim (1986: 7) noted that the Tanzanian manufacturing sector grew at an average of 7.8 per cent and its contribution to the GDP increased from 6.6 per cent in 1964 to 11.5 per cent in 1973. In Kenya, the new government put in place policies that resulted in average value of product per hectare rising from KSh 160 in 1964/5 to KSh 247 in 1965/6 and still higher to KSh 299 in 1966/7.

16   *Historical and current perspectives*

As individual independent countries were pushing for indigenous self-reliant development at the national level, there were also concerted collective efforts to promote African-owned development philosophies and initiatives at the sub-continental and continental levels. Notable sub-continental initiatives include the Economic and Customs Union of Central Africa (UDEAC—Union Douanière et Économique de l'Afrique Centrale) (1964), the Custom Union of West African States (UDEAO—Union Douanière des États de l'Afrique de l'Ouest) (1966), and the East African Community (EAC) created in 1967. At the continental level, the second conference of independent African States, which was held in June 1960 in Addis Ababa, recommended the establishment of an African development bank and an African commercial bank to help stimulate and harmonize socio-economic development in Africa. In 1963 the Organization of African Unity (OAU) was created. Although the OAU Charter was essentially political, it 'gave pride of place to economic co-operation' (Economic Commission for Africa 1991: 6). Once in operation, the OAU spawned a number of different frameworks for African cooperation and economic development keeping as its main focus the need for an approach that drew from and reflected African social and cultural characteristics unique to the continent.

Some of the notable ones include the Africa's Strategy for Development introduced in 1970 and the Addis Ababa Declaration leading to the adoption of the Revised Framework of Principles for the Implementation of the New International Economic Order in Africa. Perhaps the best known is the 1980 bold if still-born 'Comprehensive Lagos Action Plan'. The Monrovia Declaration and the Lagos Action Plan were partly in response to the World Bank sponsored Berg Report which intriguingly emphasized increase in agricultural export at a time that the continent was suffering from food shortage. Anchored on a different understanding of priorities, the Lagos Action Plan set out to provide an alternative development pathway for Africa. It suggested strategies such as the establishment of self-sustaining industrial parks, development of regional trading blocs and investment in human capacity building.

The clear notable feature of African development processes in the early 1960s and 1970s was that although external ideas were borrowed, development plans were envisioned, initiated and owned by African leaders and their people. This is not to deny external influences, for quite clearly, they were impacted by the industrialized countries and in particular the Cold War ideology contestations (Fraser, 2005). However, despite different ideological influences, the inclination and frequently expressed desire were very much for a HGD policy that was distinctively African and suited to the needs and priorities of specific individual countries. Nkrumah expressed this sentiment well when he said, that in search for its socio-economic development Africa 'will face neither East nor West, but forward' (Nkrumah, 1957c: 173).

It is widely acknowledged that following heavy investment in human capacity development – mostly education and health – much of Africa witnessed a quick burst in social economic improvement immediately after independence

Historical and current perspectives   17

(UNCTAD, 1969; 1970). For example average life expectancy across Africa increased from 39 years to 47 years between 1960 and 1970 and primary school enrolment increased by about 75 per cent within the same time period in many African countries (Roemer, 1982: 8). In terms of economic growth, several analyses indicate that during the period 1960–73, African economies grew more rapidly than during the first half of the century (UNCTAD, 1973). Furthermore, during the same period, the economic outlook of Africa was very similar, and in some cases even better than Asia. In fact, the general sense as Collier and Gunning (1999: 3) put it was that 'political self-determination in Africa and economic growth seemed to be proceeding hand-in-hand'.

We know that this euphoria did not last. Despite determined effort by the leaders to prove their capabilities in piloting African socio-economic development, Africa began to fall apart as soon as it seemingly started to come together (Guest, 2013). During the 1970s, the economic performance of Africa faltered and sharply declined. By the beginning of 1980 the economy of many African countries was in a state of regression, with aggregate per capita GDP in sub-Saharan Africa declining at almost 1.2 per cent per annum (Collier and Gunning, 1999). By the middle of that decade several nations in the continent were recording negative economic growth. The decline had been so widespread that 32 countries were poorer in 1989 than they were in 1980 (ibid.). In the mid-1990s some countries made some progress but Africa has never really recovered from this decline. Poverty remains widespread and many African countries remain the most backward in the world today.

Explaining the socio-economic decline and onset of poverty

Scholars have postulated various reasons for the regressive pattern of African countries almost a decade after independence. It has been argued that things started falling apart as power struggles and ethnic conflicts became rampant on the continent (Bates, 2008; Easterly and Levine, 1997). Others point at the geography and over dependence on natural resources (Bloom *et al.*, 1998; Collier and Gunning, 1999). Some argue that the main cause was the allure and subsequent enslavement to foreign aid (Ake, 1981, 1982; Hayter, 1971). Many still point to the enormous challenges inherited at independence including the colonial legacy of weak states and divided societies and the lack of human capital and manpower (Englebert, 2002; Gibbon, 1993). It is also well known that the global economic crisis of the 1970s had a major negative impact on the already declining fragile economies of African countries (van de Walle, 2001).

Although we recognize the importance of these factors – and the new trend towards multiple factor casual exploration – our postulation here is that of the various reasons African economic experiment failed, by far the most potent was that African leaders, despite abundant rhetoric, were not after all totally committed to HGD. Rather in most cases, they were trying to do HGD while *at the same time* adopting Western prescriptions and models of

18 *Historical and current perspectives*

development shaped mostly by the modernization theory (Ake, 1982; Amin, 1972; Nnoli, 1981). We hold that the ineluctable tension between the pursuit of endogenous development (often quasi socialist in inclination) and the quest for rapid industrialization (often based on the Western economic model) is fundamental in explaining the economic decline and eventual economic debacle witnessed between 1975 and 2000. It is important to stress here that this state of 'schizophrenia' which saw most African leaders *attempting* to combine a self-reliant, HGD approach with the externally oriented Western prescription, can only be explained by a careful reading of both the national and international political economy that prevailed at the time of independence.

The international political economy context

It is common knowledge that almost all newly independent African countries inherited national economies that had external orientation as their most distinct profile (Amin, 1972; Amjadi and Yeats, 1995). Their main pattern consisted on the one hand, of the exploitation and production of raw materials and primary commodities that were exported to the West, and on the other hand, the importation of factor inputs and manufactured goods from abroad. For example in 1962, African exports accounted for 91 per cent in world trade of palm nuts and kernel, 83 per cent in groundnuts, 53 per cent in palm kernel oil, 51 per cent in palm oil and 15 per cent of fixed vegetable oils (Ng and Yeats, 2002). Quite clearly, Africa's role in the world economy at that time was essentially to supply raw materials to sustain the rapidly developing manufacturing base in the world's industrialized countries. This role was so pronounced to the extent that across many African countries a single product often accounted for 70–90 per cent of total export value (Amjadi *et al.*, 1996). Hence, African economies were anchored in international commodity trade, the price of which is controlled by the West, hence making countries' economies vulnerable to external shock and influences.

In their incursion into Africa, European colonizers had one overriding objective: to exploit and appropriate Africa's natural resources for the benefit of the market and people of Europe. Since the focus was not on broad-based socio-economic development, the revenue generated through the exploitation and export of raw materials was not invested back into the colonies except to the measure that was considered necessary to establish the social and economic infrastructure to enhance the exploitation and export of products, as well as for the collection of taxes. In addition to the aggressive and egoistic search for raw materials, Europe was at the same time looking for markets for its increasingly mass-produced and cheap industrial goods. Utilizing the same trade routes through which the exploitation and export of raw materials occur, it was able to flood African cities and interiors with plenty of foreign goods (sometimes in exchange for raw materials).

The import of cheap foreign goods and the export of various raw materials created, in the mind of the emergent African ruling class and the local population, a sense that real economic development and growth were taking place. The situation was however very deceptive. First, it masked the fact that vast sections of the population were still living in small rural settlements and dependent on subsistence agriculture. Second, it hid from common view the complete absence of local human capacity and the absolute dominance of expatriates in the commercial, economic and administrative activities of the colonized states. From the Mediterranean coasts of Algeria and Tunisia, through the low lying plateau in the central Congo to the highlands of eastern and southern Africa, the colonial administrators had through a combination of anti-protectionist laws, policy incentives (e.g. tax concession and subsidies) and the use of brute force, eliminated competition from indigenous farmers and entrepreneurs, and enthroned white settlers and merchants as the main beneficiary of agricultural production and economic growth (Guest, 2013; Meredith, 2005).

The situation was not any different in the countries where the mainstay of economic activity was mining. In fact, it was worse. The technical nature of the mining activity meant that the West had to import almost all of the key workers and the heavy duty equipment needed to undertake mining operations. With no technology diffusion, training of local manpower, skill transfer or integration with other sectors of the economy through linkages, indigenous Africans were firmly relegated to petty traders, artisanal and menial workers with little or no capacity to govern or gain experience in business management. The most important economic players were foreign companies and expatriates, and key decisions about commodity prices – for food, raw materials and industrial equipment needed for production – were almost exclusively made abroad in colonial metropolises.

Another key feature of the economic profile of newly independent African states, worthy of mention here is the absolute dominance of the West as central trading partners with Africa compared with the Eastern communist bloc. According to Ake (1981) the Western share of the total value of African export in 1965 was 78 per cent while the share of import was 71 per cent. By contrast, the share of export and import from the communist bloc in 1965 was a mere seven per cent and six per cent respectively. This lop-sidedness also applied to technical and financial partnership.

The implication of Western influence as the immediate past colonial master, the main producer and consumer of African primary products and the sole supplier of technology, grants and loans should be clear: New African leaders were seriously dependent on international capital and had very limited capacity for autonomous decisions or economic manoeuvres that were contrary to Western interests. With several carrots and sticks at their disposal – loans and grants, price setting power, boycotts, supply or withdrawal of technical assistance, etc. – the West had, and frequently used, its immense power to dictate the economic policies pursued by the new African political elite. So immense was Western desire to retain command and influence that it was prepared to deny aid and even help topple leaders considered too independent minded

20   *Historical and current perspectives*

and resistant to external control. Kwame Nkrumah of Ghana, Thomas Sankara of Burkina Faso, Julius Nyerere of Tanzania and Patrice Lumumba of Congo represent a few notable examples.

The domestic political economy context

If new African leaders had little room for manoeuvre in their economic policies relative to Western dictates and interests, their domestic political position could at best be described as precarious. On the one hand, the politics of forced unification and the divide and rule tactics deployed by the colonial masters had ensured that many of these leaders inherited for a nation a bunch of heterogeneous societies deeply divided along ethnic and religious lines. The result was the absence of a deep sense of common identity or national unity which was sorely needed for the task of long-term development and nation building. On the other hand, the fight for independence had carried with it a certain nationalistic fervour, with local politicians stressing the indignity of colonial rule and preaching justice and equal opportunity as key benefits for self-rule. Hence, the domestic context was one in which the new ruling elite felt an urgent need to rapidly accumulate economic surplus in order to be able to consolidate their power and prevent the demise of their electoral fortune. At the same time, however, the situation pressed upon them an equally urgent and almost contradictory need to deliver quick economic gains and political reforms to satisfy the revolutionary and egalitarian impulses that underpinned the anticolonial struggle.

Ake (1981) described this situation very well. He suggested that the new African leaders had 'two main competitors', namely the African masses who demanded economic decolonization through endogenous or indigenization policies and international capitalism, who wanted to entrench dependence through the maintenance of capitalist and exploitative relations of production:

> Given the nature of the interest of these three groups, it would appear that we would expect a pattern of political alignments that will pit the African ruling class and the African masses against international capitalism in a struggle for economic decolonization For if, indeed, such an alliance were to emerge, the prospects of economic decolonization would be good. However the possibility of this alliance is more apparent than real ... If the African ruling class does not maintain existing relations of production, it ceases to be a ruling class. And if it makes serious effort to fight for economic independence while maintaining existing relations of production, it endangers its hegemony more than it would be putting up with the political and economic liabilities of economic dependence.
>
> (Ake, 1981: 35–6)

The import of these conflicting pressures on the new African leaders can hardly be over emphasized. It was this set of systemic conditions that

Historical and current perspectives 21

provided the context for the economic policies pursued immediately after independence. The context, as Allen (1995) argues, also goes a long way in explaining the prevalence of neo-patrimonial politics in Africa (cf. Ake, 1981). A mixture of homegrown economic development initiatives and populist policies was necessary for the ruling class to rebalance the externally oriented economic profile they inherited and assert their independence from colonial dictates. Self-reliant development was also necessary to gain political legitimacy and bolster their bargaining power in their dealings with the metropolis and international capitalist structures. However, the need to achieve fast economic growth in keeping with outlandish electoral promises, as well as the need to consolidate power over local political rivals provided a countervailing impetus which pushed the new ruling class back towards the West and whatever money and quick-fix idea they (the West) could offer for rapid economic industrialization. And for the most part the prescription offered by the West was the modernization model of development.

Modernization theory and African development trajectories

In the early 1960s, shortly after most African nations gained independence, western countries popularized the modernization theory (Rostow, 1960) as the ultimate guide for the development of newly independent African states (Almond and Coleman, 1960; Almond and Powell, 1966; Pye, 1966). The thrust of this philosophy was that the most assured course for Africa, if it wished to develop, was to follow at least broadly the same procedure already adopted by the West. To simplify, this involves massive investment in a limited number of sectors in order to boost production and capital accumulation (Rostow, 1960). This so-called linear growth model was based on the analysis of post Second World War development in Europe.

There has been debate about how much of Western recommendation of modernization theory was based on a belief in its efficacy and how much of it was propelled by the West's political and economic calculations and interests. Another line of debate to which we have alluded has focused on whether or not this economic philosophy was imposed on or voluntarily adopted by African states. What is beyond argument, however, is that modernization theory was tremendously influential in defining the trajectory of economic policies in newly independent Africa. While many African governments were making positive gestures towards the pursuit of HGD, they simultaneously pursued policies that were based on a religious adoption of the modernization model of development. Driven by their need to consolidate their political and economic freedom through development, they did not break away from, but in many cases deepened some of the economic policies inherited at independence with emphasis on industrialization and import substitution.

The problem, however, was that newly independent African countries lacked the human and technical capital, basic infrastructure, and requisite institutions to follow through the modernization prescription of development.

22 *Historical and current perspectives*

Beyond this, the validity of modernization as a development theory is arguable since it appears to be based on two questionable assumptions: that countries are homogenous and that the model is universally applicable. Critically, with its emphasis on linear economic growth and advancement, modernization theory as packaged by the West was strictly tied with capitalist ideology, and unorthodox economic policies, including those that privileged self-reliant growth, were viewed as a threat to the western capitalist hegemony. Hence propelled by the need to maintain its ideological hegemony, influence in Africa, and its strategic economic interests, the West pushed Africa hard towards aggressive deregulation and liberalization offering in the process aid, in loans, grants, technical and human resource assistance.

The failure of political leadership

We have already established that in the context of the urgent need to provide economic dividend from independence, the West's promise of friendship, loans, and markets for produce proved extremely tempting for the new leaders. In any case, there was very little room for dissidence as those who proved to be implacable were chastised and severely undermined with a mixture of damaging media propaganda and economic isolation. Moreover, it did not help that African leaders lacked commitment to carry out their own development agenda or genuine political reform that could threaten their own hegemony (Adedeji, 2001; Ake, 1981). Virtually all African leaders at an intellectual level had an understanding that the best way to achieve sustainable economic development for their respective countries was through self-reliant homegrown development, but in practice none was really able to make a clean break from the colonial economic policies they inherited. Rather, in many cases they entrenched it through the wholesale adoption of modernization polices leading to more dependence.

Adedjei (1981) has provided a succinct account of the two key ways in which colonial policies and the post-independence polices in Africa undermined indigenous self-reliance and HGD. First, he says, the continuous import and distribution of cheap commodities across Africa through the colonial transport networks suffocated and eventually choked up local manufacturing industries. He noted that many indigenous industries especially those relating to metal, cloths and salt, which were thriving before the onset of colonialism 'were severely restricted or swiftly collapsed at the face of the influx' (ibid.: 18). Second, and perhaps most critically, he argues that colonial policies led to the loss of self-sufficiency in food production as land and labour were reallocated for export-oriented production. This lack of self-sufficiency in food production, he argues, remains even today one of the gravest African economic problems.

As already indicated the foregoing is not of course to absolve African leaders of blame. In fact as Rugumamu (1987) excellently argued, while systemic conditions may have created constraints that severely limited the options of

Historical and current perspectives 23

new African governments and pushed states to act in certain ways, the room for manoeuvre was never completely closed. It is, he says, 'the task of creative, far sighted and ingenious political leadership to find ways around such constraints' (ibid.: 264). It is precisely in ignoring the agency of states and the available, if limited room for manoeuvre, that dependency theories of African underdevelopment fall short. It is difficult to sustain the argument (Ake, 1982; Amin, 1972; Frank, 1966, 1969, 1974) that Africans are poor because of their relationship with Europe, or conversely, that development in Africa was only possible with a radical break from the international capitalist system (Ake, 1982: 7) because at the very least different African countries recorded different degrees of success in the post-independence period. The fact is that while the conditions may have been harsh, African leaders also lacked an appreciation of the depth of the economic challenges they faced at independence and the experience required to navigate the complex terrain in which they found themselves. Nyereye of Tanzania captured this situation well when he admitted, in his famous 1974 article 'From Uhuru to Ujamaa':

> It was not that we were satisfied with the structure we had inherited; we knew very well the alienation of the colonial government from the people. But we were under the impression that this could be corrected by quite small changes. We believed that to transform the situation we had only to replace expatriate administrators and policy-makers with local people ... In other words, we thought to energize the system we knew, and to reverse certain policies to which we had always been opposed.
>
> (Nyerere 1974: 4)

Several detailed analyses of pre-independence economic policies have shown that these never really had any tangible chance of ensuring sustainable economic growth for Africa. Africanization was rushed for political expediency and then created massive inefficiency in the system. Nationalization was not well thought through and created capital flight which harmed the economy. In some cases nationalization was introduced for populist reasons and power consolidation. For example, evidence from Ghana strongly suggested that nationalization was promoted by Nkrumah because he was afraid of the growth of local business people challenging him. Other times, nationalization consisted in merely replacing European with African elites and government control of means of capital. Despite some attempts at economic diversification, much of the effort concentrated on import substituting industrialization rather than building local indigenous growth. Despite abundant rhetoric, local industries were not given the time and adequate incentive to grow and mature. Nigeria for instance had very promising local industries in textiles, foot wear, plastic and cables, some of which were among the best in the world. However, all of these were eventually destroyed through liberalization, cheap importation and import substitution policies. In far too many countries there was a lot of emphasis on high tech industrialization as a means to

24 *Historical and current perspectives*

development without building commensurate manpower and basic infrastructure. Countries also neglected mid industrialization and intermediate sectors (Roemer, 1982) and areas where they had greater economic strength and advantage. Agricultural sectors that employed about 70 per cent of the population were not developed nor did countries make enough attempts to diversify their economies. Nigeria for example neglected its agricultural sector such as palm kernel, ground nut and cocoa which were its main cash crops. Overall, indigenization and broader economic policies were very ad hoc, piece meal and lacking in internal consistency. Of course in a few cases there were attempts at long-term planning followed with policies, but in far too many cases government first implemented sporadic and politically motivated actions and then afterwards attempted to put justifying policies in place.

The consequence was that the development of state institutions which influence and interact with other institutions created rent-seeking, cronyism and neo-patrimonialism in most African states. These subsequently encouraged a type of governance where the ruling elites monopolized power to allocate resources and enrich themselves while neglecting the general population, consequently creating an unprecedented poor population in the continent (Mbaku, 2004: 9).

Total collapse, the grand rescue and the deepening dependence

By the early to mid-1970s, growth had stagnated and the economy of most nations was in decline. Desiring to stem the tide of decline, African countries, regional organizations and the international donor community started conjuring a complex mix of ideas and remedies resulting in what Ake (1996) has aptly described as an era of 'confusion of agenda'. The Organization for African Unity (OAU) introduced the Lagos Plan to push economic growth and development through self-reliance in Africa. The G77 and China pushed for a New International Economic World Order (NIECO) emphasizing the need for increase in volume of non-traditional export. The Brandt Report called for a large transfer of resources from developed to developing countries and the World Bank introduced 'Accelerated Development in Sub-Sahara Africa: An Agenda for Action' which marked the beginning of increased Bretton Woods involvement in economic policies in Africa. The height of this involvement was the introduction of punitive Structural Adjustment Programmes (SAPs) starting from the 1980s.

Adjustment lending was intended to compel loan-seeking developing countries to, on the one hand, pursue fiscal discipline through public spending cuts and, on the other hand, increase income generation through structural reforms and economic liberalization. The lending was justified on the basis of the manufactured argument that economic predicaments of poor, aid-seeking African countries were caused by a combination of state intervention and protectionist policies. By reducing the role of states in service delivery and allowing markets to function more freely, it was hoped that the economic performance

Historical and current perspectives 25

of these countries would improve quickly (Williamson, 1989). However, while SAPs helped a few countries achieve a temporary measure of macroeconomic stability, they did not improve economic growth and instead unleashed aching poverty on a vast proportion of the populations and wreaked havoc on the economies of many borrowing nations (Melamed, 1996; Rodrik, 2006).

In effect, SAPs turned what was already a serious economic predicament into a full blown development crisis (Melamed, 1996). In addition to large-scale unemployment, a sharp decline in social services, roof-top inflation and average annual GDP growth in Africa fell by nearly half from 4.2 per cent between 1970 and 1979 to 2.3 per cent over the period 1980 to 1999.

Furthermore, this 20 year period saw many African countries experience recurring years of zero and even negative growth. Indeed, rather than result in an improvement in the economic situation of the continent, successive strategies made it stagnate even more, making it susceptible to accepting more cut-throat loans from the international donor agencies.

The new impetus for homegrown African development

Although SAPs had been criticised from the outset as being too intrusive, neo-colonial and ultimately incapable of producing lasting economic transformation in Africa, it was not until the mid-1990s that a broad consensus emerged that the programme had in fact been a big disaster in economic engineering by Washington (Cheru, 1999; Stiglitz, 1998). Having been forced to admit failure, the IMF and the World Bank launched a number of different initiatives to reform the aid system and set out new approaches that sought to remedy the fundamental mistakes inherent in SAPs. These included the Economic and Social Action Programme (ESAP), designed to incorporate poverty alleviation and social dimensions into adjustment lending; and the Sector Wide Approaches (SWAP) intended to broaden policy dialogue and achieve greater coordination in developing single sector policies and programmes. Finally, following a conviction that an entirely new agenda and a corresponding scheme was needed, the IMF and World Bank scrapped SAPs altogether in September 1999 and replaced them with the Poverty Reduction Strategy Papers (PRSPs) and the Comprehensive Development Framework. The PRSP have since emerged as the main guiding framework for providing aid to poor countries by the International Financial Institutions (IFI). They are also the main tool, the IMF claims, for providing 'the crucial link between national public actions, donor support, and the development outcomes needed to meet the United Nations' Millennium Development Goals (MDGs), which are centred on halving poverty between 1990 and 2015' (IMF, 2013).

In theory, the PSRPs are anchored on national ownership through broad-based participation of civil society as one, and indeed the first, of their five core principles. The other four are: (i) a concentration on poverty reduction, (ii) an emphasis on comprehensiveness of strategy in terms of recognizing the multidimensional nature of poverty, (iii) involving coordinated participation

26 Historical and current perspectives

of development partners, and (iv) encompassing a long-term perspective for poverty reduction. According to the IMF, 110 full PRSPs and 57 preliminary or interim PRSPs have been circulated to the Fund's Executive Board as of the end of February 2012 (ibid.). In practice, the emphasis remains, like in the SAP framework, the promotion of macroeconomic stabilization, market liberalization and prudent fiscal policy.

At the same time that the SAP was undergoing a terminal review at the Bretton Woods Institutions, and especially at the turn of the new millennium, African leaders were increasingly asserting the need for 'Africa to restore ownership of its development agenda, policy and programs' (Wangwe, 2002: 28). This desire was expressed among others in terms of a 'new [and] enhanced partnership for African development' premised on 'African ownership of aid-related programmes and policies' (UNECA, 2001: 3). Notable champions of this call include former President Thabo Mbeki of South Africa, former President Olusegun Obasanjo of Nigeria, former President Abdoulaye Wade of Senegal and President Abdelaziz Bouteflika of Algeria. In a vision document entitled *The Millennium Partnership for the African Recovery Programme*, Mbeki, Obasanjo and Bouteflika outlined the hope of an African renaissance based:

> on a common vision and a firm and shared conviction, that they have a pressing duty to eradicate poverty and to place their countries, both individually and collectively, on a path of sustainable growth and development and at the same time to participate actively in the world economy and body politic.
>
> (Millennium Partnership for African Recovery Programme, 2001: 3)

Central to this endeavour, according to the leaders, was a transformation in the aid relationship which entrenches dependency, and a breakaway from the system that fosters marginal concessions to, or outright exclusion of, 'African nations in decisions fundamental to their developmental future' (ibid.: 9). In essence, it was time, they thought, for Africa to take greater responsibility and full ownership in planning and implementing its development programmes. Mbeki expressed the vision forcefully saying:

> What we have said so far is that both our ancient and modern history as well as our own practical and conscious deeds convey the same message: that genuine liberation, in the context of the modern world, is what drives the Africans of today as they seek to confront the problems which for them constitute a daily challenge.
>
> (Mbeki, 2002: 32)

At about the same time in a document grandiosely titled *OMEGA Plan for Africa*, President Bouteflika, for his own part, declared that in order to lift itself from decades of aching poverty, Africa must 'pursue a new strategic development vision based on a comprehensive and realistic programme which clearly sets out the priorities and the resources to be mobilized for strong and sustainable growth which benefits all strata of its population' (Wade, 2001: 4). He stated that the thrust of such plans must be 'principles of self-sustaining' development initiatives and 'new theories of more African-friendly growth' initiatives.

The United Nations Economic Commission for Africa (UNECA) devoted a great deal of effort to provide 'flesh' to what was essentially a set of high-level political declarations by these presidents. The Commission published a rich and comprehensive document, *Compact for African Recovery* (2001), which elaborates on this vision, documenting and sketching out the key features and steps for a new African partnership with their international partners. The *Compact* envisaged transformational change in aid relationship away from conditionality and top-down intrusion towards a mature relationship characterized by mutual trust, accountability and responsibility. Under such an arrangement, Africa would take full ownership of its policies and programmes while adhering 'to agreed principles of governance and to meet criteria for sound public finance management'. The Commission were emphatic that:

> The effectiveness of any social or economic programme or reform is closely associated with the degree to which it is researched, initiated, debated and implemented by institutions and individuals in the countries concerned. The best development programmes and projects are those that are most fully owned by the leaders of the country.
>
> (UNECA, 2001: 14)

African leaders enthusiastically discussed these documents in an extra-ordinary meeting held in Sirte, Libya, in March 2001 and agreed to merge the two separate vision documents from the presidents with the technical paper by UNECA. The amalgamation of these visions gave rise to the New Partnership for African Development Programme (NEPAD) which was presented to, and well received by, the leaders of the world's most industrialized countries in June 2002.

Hence, through a combination of admission of failure by the West and a new expression of the will and determination of African leaders to take the economic destinies of the continent into their own hands, a new development era, marked by an emphasis on homegrown and comprehensive poverty reduction strategies, began for Africa at the dawn of the new millennium. The question now is whether this new wave of determination and initiative translates to anything really new or whether it is yet another illusion. Before embarking on the empirical analysis in an attempt to answer this question, we will first take a close look at the concept of HGD in various African countries.

Summary

The quest for HGD in Africa is not new. It was a desire that was evident in the struggle for independence and in the first wave of development policies implemented after political independence. African leaders had a very clear understanding that sustainable economic development could not possibly be secured by depending on their former colonial masters. But regardless the gusto, it is evident that many of these leaders did not fully appreciate the complexity and immensity of both the internal and external challenges facing them. Moreover there were problems related to insincerity, personal aggrandizement and power consolidation which saw the leaders align with the Western powers against the masses in order to maintain their hegemony. The result of these pressures was that African leaders did not fully break from the externally oriented economic policies that they inherited at independence but instead entrenched them leading to deepening dependence. There is now a renewed impetus for HGD in Africa with some implying this is the time for the African renaissance. It remains unclear the extent to which this new wave of determination and the programmes it engenders can truly be regarded as a self-reliant economic development effort.

3 Conceptualizing homegrown development

So far in this book, we have used the term homegrown development (HGD) quite casually without attempting to define what exactly it means. However, before we can begin to explore answers to the question about to what extent the new wave, post-structural adjustment programme (SAP) developmental initiatives in Africa can truly be described as homegrown, we need to first clearly define what is meant by HGD. It is to this task that this chapter is devoted.

The term homegrown has been previously used in development discourse but very sparsely (Boeckelman, 1996). At the turn of the millennium it was brought into mainstream development discourse by the New Partnership for Africa's Development (NEPAD) and the Bretton Woods Institutions. A 2001 conference paper published by the IMF and authored by Mohsin Khan and Sunil Sharma used the term copiously (Khan and Sharma, 2001). Another conference paper, this time published by the World Bank and authored by Anna Muganda, also makes frequent use of this term (Muganda, 2004). Besides these two conference papers, there is no indication that the concept eventually acquired much popularity within the IMF or World Bank where 'country ownership' and 'national ownership' now appear to be the preferred terminologies.

William Easterly (2006a, 2006b, 2009) is by far the most prominent scholar to consistently adopt the term 'homegrown development' in his publications. In fact, most of the other few appearances of this term in the literature are in the context of the review of, or critical engagement with, Easterly's works. In several of his writings he criticizes the World Bank's 'one-size fits all' approach for delivering aid to poor countries and extensively argues that HGD is the only self-sustaining development strategy that could lift countries from poverty in the long run. Citing the four 'Asian Tigers' (Hong Kong, Singapore, South Korea, Taiwan), he argues with several detailed examples that their successes were based on HGD approaches (Easterly, 2006a). However, in none of his writings does Easterly attempt to coherently define what is meant by HGD initiatives. He nevertheless amply suggests that it has to do with 'self-reliant exploratory efforts and the borrowing of ideas, institutions and technology from the West when it suits the Rest to do so' (Easterly,

30 Conceptualizing homegrown development

2006a: 363). Perhaps his most direct definition was in a media interview in March 2009 where he explained that:

> [Homegrown] does not mean that countries operate in a vacuum and cannot use knowledge gained from other countries; what I mean by homegrown is for the local people in charge to figure out how to imitate and borrow institutions and technologies from other countries in a way that is compatible to local culture and political traditions and situations.
>
> (Easterly, 2009)

Ironically, while Easterly clearly makes the point in several places that there is no automatic formula or 'blueprint for imitation', he nonetheless suggests the centrality of the market and limited role of government. 'Only homegrown development based on the dynamism of individuals and firms in free markets', he says, 'can achieve the end of poverty' (Easterly, 2006a: 368). Kalinowski (2011) agrees with Easterly that only HGD, rooted in self-sustained effort, can enable countries to reduce poverty in the long run, but he criticises Easterly for strongly linking successful HGD with restricted state intervention and free market capitalism. For Kalinowski, all that is required for successful HGD is autonomy in decision making and a capacity for institutional learning.

In their paper, 'Homegrown Responses to Economic Uncertainty in Rural America', Morgan, Lambe and Freyer (2009) explain how rural America is embracing a homegrown strategy in dealing with the global economic crisis that has hit various local rural economies in the USA. They define homegrown as alternatives to industrial recruitment, suggesting that homegrown approaches to economic development seek to leverage local assets rather than focusing primarily on attracting external investment. Growing from within provides the needed foundation of local assets on which to build (Morgan *et al.*, 2009). On a macro level, the Organization for Economic Co-operation and Development (OECD) Policy Insight perspective opines that 'homegrown solutions can only be produced from knowledge and policies that are locally generated and context specific' (Datta and Young, 2011: 35). In both cases, as in many other instances, the authors do not attempt to offer a qualitative description of HGD let alone provide a conceptual analysis of the term.

Joseph Stiglitz, the Nobel laureate and one time Senior Vice President and Chief Economist of the World Bank is another notable figure who has championed HGD as the solution to the African economic predicament although he consistently uses 'country ownership' in his speeches and publications. Again, he does not define his terms carefully but leaves the impression that his vision of ownership has strongly to do with high levels of participation by borrowing countries. In many of his now famous anti-SAP public lectures, Stiglitz argues that the Washington Consensus failed primarily because it conceptualized development in narrow terms (GDP growth) and was characterized by universal technical solutions handed down to

Conceptualizing homegrown development   31

developing countries by elites in the international development agencies. His alternative, what he calls 'a new paradigm for development' (Stiglitz, 1998: 4) or a new 'post-Washington consensus' (ibid.: 4) is an inclusive economic development where greater emphasis is given to broader participation:

> Thus, key ingredients in a successful development strategy are ownership and participation. We have seen again and again that ownership is essential for successful transformation: policies that are imposed from outside may be grudgingly accepted on a superficial basis, but will rarely be implemented as intended. But to achieve the desired ownership and transformation, the process that leads to that strategy must be participatory.
>
> (Stiglitz, 1998: 21)

Recently, in a critical analysis of Poverty Reduction Strategy Papers (PRSPs) in Bangladesh, Mohammad Mizanur Rahman made a very good attempt of providing a working definition. He suggested that:

> Homegrown development strategy is the incarnation of the people's own analysis of development. It gets legitimacy and is strengthened through the direct involvement of the parliament as the major democratic institution that involves the needs of the different constituencies together to make policies context specific. It is devoid of any sort of donor intrusion as loan conditionality at any level.
>
> (Rahman, 2012: 86)

It should already be evident from the foregoing that HGD might mean different things to different people. In Morgan's definition, for example, one sees an emphasis on leveraging local assets complemented with investment from external sources. The Detta and Young (2011) definition, on the other hand, emphasises local generation of knowledge and development policy and not necessarily the source of assets used. For Stiglitz, the thrust of HGD is its inclusivity and participatory nature. Furthermore, while Easterly appears to emphasize a mix of 'self-reliant exploratory efforts' (Easterly, 2006: 363) and adaptation of Western ideas, institutions and technology from the local entrepreneurs, Rahman's definition stresses the role of national parliaments and the absence of loan conditionality from international lending agencies.

We propose to define HGD as an approach to development that emphasises seeking answers from within. We also propose to place heavy emphasis on who controls the ideas and development processes. Combining these we define a HGD framework as one that is initiated, crafted and implemented by a country with attention to unique local imperatives, such as, socio-economic structures, histories and characteristics.

Notably, it is contextual and does not, by its nature, presuppose commitment to any ideology, procedure or policy prescription. It implies the absence of external conditionality in any form, but the freedom to borrow, accept, or reject

32 *Conceptualizing homegrown development*

inputs from external sources. This means, for us, that HGD can be market based (Easterly, 2006a, 2006b) or involve significant state direction and intervention (Kalinowski, 2011). It can involve broad participation from stakeholders including civil societies (Stiglitz, 1998) or be much more rooted in the parliament as the major democratic institution (Rahman, 2012). In terms of technology, emphasis can be based on local knowledge or know-how (Zimmerman, 2008) or the importation of technology and factor input from abroad.

For us the overriding factor, therefore, is that the development initiative is controlled by the country in question, with attention to local imperatives. Hence, such an initiative might borrow ideas from successful foreign models, but without external conditionality and with regard to the home country's differences and structures. In doing this, countries take what works and drop what is deemed irrelevant or inapplicable. Hence, HGD does not necessarily imply that every idea must come from within; rather, it can be an eclectic set of ideas. Fundamentally, it must be initiated, developed, owned and implemented by local stakeholders.

Towards a conceptual understanding of homegrown development

In order to more effectively conceptualize HGD, we propose two operational moves. The first is to distinguish between the *essence* and the *features* of HGD. As implied in our definition of HGD in the previous section, we propose that the *essence* of HGD is not so much self-reliance as Easterly suggests, though this is critical. Rather, the essence is total independence, and absolute autonomy over the development process by the country involved. The key *features,* though, would include attention to local imperatives and comparative advantages, building effective institutions and the enhancement of local capacity to build self-reliance (see Figure 3.1).

The second move in conceptualizing HGD is to dissect the concept along three lines comprising: (a) *who* (agencies or actors) are dictating the development process, (b) *what* is to be done to achieve the desired outcome (object of change), and (c) *how* the change or purpose is to be accomplished (process and procedure). It is the 'who' part that defines the essence, while the 'what' and 'how' questions invite a description of the features of HGD (see Figure 3.2).

The utility of combining these two operational moves is that together they help unpick the key aspects, characteristics and dimensions of HGD. Critically, they provide a clear basis for better description, comparison and empirical assessment of different HGD initiatives. Second and relatedly, unlike the previous attempts in literature, our approach does not put emphasis on normative and ideological content. It becomes, therefore, unnecessary to assume a particular universal role for the state or market, civil society or parliament or even to assume *a priori* that HGD is bound to succeed since a lot depends on the context and processes adopted. This further implies the futility of universal or one-size prescription since what works for country 'A' might not work for country 'B'.

Conceptualizing homegrown development 33

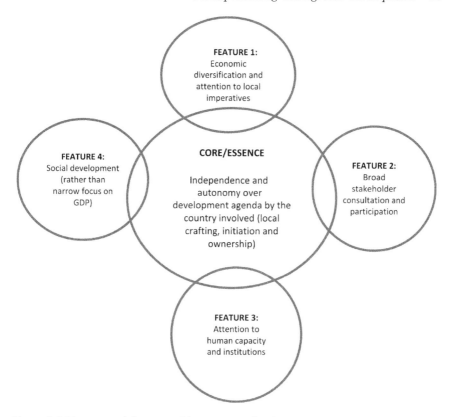

Figure 3.1 Essence and features of homegrown development

Figure 3.2 Dimensions of homegrown development

Before we proceed to discuss the various components of the above proposed conceptual model, it is necessary to clarify another important terminological point. This concerns the relationship between HGD and country ownership. Currently, the dominant tendency in scholarship is to use the terms homegrown development and country ownership interchangeably (Kalinowski, 2011; Khan and Sharma, 2001; Muganda, 2004). However, while these two terms are related, we think that some clear and important distinction can be made. Ownership is mostly used in the context of loan and aid discourse to refer to greater (not total or absolute) commitment of

34 *Conceptualizing homegrown development*

borrowing countries to implement polices agreed with or even mandated by donor agencies usually in keeping with the loan conditionality. Whitfield and Fraser (2009: 3) describe it as the 'degree of commitment shown by recipient governments to implementing the reforms that donors encourage them to adopt' while Johnson (2005) depicts it as commitment to implement policies or obligation to accept responsibility for implementing them however the policies were arrived at. Homegrown development, however, as has been demonstrated above, applies *sensu stricto*, as an alternative to externally driven development efforts. Embracing this distinction allows one to see more clearly that:

- It is possible for a country to have ownership (in the mainstream aid discourse sense) without undertaking HGD. This may come in the form of commitment to drive through a reform prescribed by the donors or what has sometimes been described as 'forced ownership'.
- A highly indebted poor country could still undertake HGD provided it has strong enough leadership to drive a hard bargain with donors and impose control over its own development direction and pace. A good example here would be Rwanda, which although heavily dependent on international aid, has managed to retain reasonable control over its development programmes and policies (see Hayman, 2009).
- HGD is not necessarily anti-aid but is antithetical to surrendering control or leadership of developmental initiatives to donors. As is commonly known, many countries borrow and still maintain sovereignty over their development process.

Although developing countries and donor agencies have different emphases and meanings when they talk of 'ownership', what is much clearer is that neither sees or understands this in terms of total independence or autonomy of borrowing countries over their development policies and programmes. A few extracts from the United Nations Commission for Africa on the one hand and World Bank publications on the other, demonstrate this. UNECA (2001: 30) starts by stating: 'Ownership entails leadership and capacity to define and implement strategies that ensure the economic and social wellbeing of the country's citizens. National identification of development priorities and strategies is the first and most essential step.' But then it goes on to envisage:

> an evolving set of relationships between Africa and its international partners in which each will hold the other accountable for overall performance towards mutually-agreed development outcomes. African governments will commit to adhere to agreed principles of governance and to *meet criteria* for sound public finance management, while international partners will undertake to respect priorities, strategies and policies laid down by African governments and reduce the transaction costs by harmonising and improving their aid modalities and practices.
>
> (UNECA, 2001: 31; emphasis ours)

The IMF publication openly admits that ownership can in fact be one of many conditionality stipulations for obtaining aid. It says:

> The IMF could require or put more pressure on the member country to produce its own homegrown program. In some cases, this may be seen as "forcing ownership," but the design of the program can be worked out cooperatively between the country and the IMF.
>
> (Khan and Sharma, 2001: 17)

Ideally, true ownership (in the ordinary sense of the word) would preclude conditionality and leverage by donor agencies – and a few scholars in the aid discourse are actually trying to reclaim this definition of ownership (e.g. Whitfield and Fraser, 2009). However, we have chosen to stick with homegrown development as our preferred term since our analysis goes beyond the politics of aid relationship and covers the nature and quality of local and national level strategies by countries to define their own development agenda as well as the outcomes of development programmes implemented.

The core or essence of homegrown development

As mentioned, we consider that the main essence of the HGD approach is that a country is fully in control in deciding the content, focus, process and the overall strategy for its development. The importance of local ownership as a core component of a HGD strategy is highlighted in nearly every relevant scholarship (Easterly, 2006a; 2006b; 2009; Khan and Sharma, 2001; Morgan *et al.*, 2009; Rahman, 2012; Zimmerman, 2008). HGD obtains when local stakeholders are fully responsible for decisions to design and introduce a given development agenda or set of policy initiatives. We have established that this responsibility does not preclude borrowing money, ideas, expertise and technology from other countries. However, development can only be described as truly homegrown when the implementing country reserves the prerogative to decide which particular idea to borrow and how best it wishes to integrate and utilize an idea.

The notion of a country borrowing developmental ideas and models is not by any means new. While it is now common to talk about Western models of development, it is worth remembering that Western countries' developmental models mostly consist of an amalgam of eclectic ideas derived from both internal and external sources (Dolowitz and Marsh, 1996, 2000; Floyd, 2009; Hall, 1993; Hu, 2009; Walsh, 2000). For example, even though the modern industrial revolution first started in Great Britain and took hold in Europe, economic historians have demonstrated that Great Britain borrowed bits and pieces of ideas and expertise from India to make its textile technology more efficient (Morris, 1963; Temin, 1988; Ward, 1994). When Japan at the end of the Second World War decided to advance its car industry, it proceeded by borrowing car technology from the USA while modelling its broader

36 *Conceptualizing homegrown development*

technological culture on Germany (Cole, 1980; Morishima, 1982). China, although politically 'communist', decided to transform its economy beginning in 1978 and, in doing so, integrated a number of capitalist economic ideals into its communist political system. The outcome of this unique economic and political experiment is what is known today variously as 'Hybrid Capitalism', the 'Chinese model', 'State Capitalism', 'Parallel Development' and 'Bamboo Capitalism' (Cheow, 2005; Crawford, 2000; Yeung, 2003).

In Africa, Botswana offers a striking example of how a country can combine a suite of local and externally borrowed ideas into a coherent HGD strategy. A very poor and landlocked country, with only 100 secondary graduates at independence in 1966 (Acemoglu, Johnson and Robinson, 2002), Botswana managed to transform itself into one of the very few economic success stories in Africa through a mixture of state interventionism and market deregulation (Hjort, 2010; Mogalakwe, 2003). When diamonds were discovered in the country, Botswana initiated its developmental goal with input from invited external technical experts in advisory roles, but the final decision over the content and direction of its development strategy remained in the hands of local stakeholders (Beaulier, 2003). One striking pattern that exists in these countries is that they succeeded in borrowing and adapting external ideas to local reality. Today, one commonly hears of German technology, Japanese cars, and the Chinese developmental model when in fact these are all incarnations of a mixture of developmental ideas adapted from various sources. To repeat then, what is crucial for a developmental effort to be described as homegrown is not that all ideas must emanate from local sources. Rather, the litmus test is that the country in question has full autonomy in initiating and deciding its preferred development path and pace.

It is worth reiterating that HGD and borrowing are not mutually exclusive. It is in fact notable that the top 20 debtor countries, led by the EU and the USA, are also the richest and most developed, but none of these countries go through the external policy imposition found in most developing countries (Cline, 2005). Specifically, Japan and China are America's biggest creditors. However, they do not meddle in American policy. There is therefore scope to question whether imposing ownership conditionality is more important for achieving sustainable development or whether other levers such as reducing interest rates on debt is far more important. After all, many scholars have suggested that high interest rates are one of the major contributing factors to heavy debt and socio-economic crises of most developing countries (Collier, 2000; Deaton, 1999; Easterly, 2002).

Essential features of homegrown development strategies

While the essence of HGD is total control and ownership, experience suggests that the chances of attaining self-reliant sustainable homegrown development are higher when certain features are integrated. Based on extensive literature survey and practical observation, we have identified four features which are

Conceptualizing homegrown development   37

not only essential features but appear germane for achieving self-reliant sustainable development. These include: (i) economic diversification and sensitivity to local imperatives; (ii) broad stakeholder consultation and participation; (iii) building local capacity and institutions; and (iv) attention to broad-based social and human development rather than narrow focus on GDP. In the following sections, we will examine these features in closer detail.

Economic diversification and sensitivity to local imperatives

The first important feature of HGD, as we see it, is that such a model recognizes and takes into serious consideration local imperatives. By local imperatives we mean, economic advantages, demography, historical and other cultural realities that could stimulate or obstruct development. Local imperatives could be broadly divided into advantages and disadvantages. The advantages might include local knowledge and culture, various natural and human resources that need to be enhanced for the socio-economic progress of a society (Mosse, 2005; Porter, 2000).

Since the situation of each country is different, it ought to be common knowledge that an understanding of the nation's unique circumstances and comparative advantages is key to devising an expedient and successful pathway to development (Hall and Soskice, 2001; Porter, 2000; 2011). And, conversely, that implementing borrowed ideas without fully considering how they fit with or enhance local advantages will result in suboptimal if not outright negative outcomes (Booth, 2012; Evans, 2004; Grindle, 2007). Evidence abounds from countries that implemented SAPs in the 1980s that imposing policies without due consideration of local socio-economic situations is wasteful and harmful. More positively, one can see that the countries that have made good progress economically are the ones that have not only identified their comparative advantages but devised sensible polices to leverage their competitiveness. A good recent example is Brazil which has become the economic power-house of South America by investing in better natural resources management, consolidating its position as a regional power, and addressing the challenge of racial inequality with the introduction of affirmative action policies (Htun, 2004; Martins, Medeiros and Nascimento, 2004).

When a country starts from where it has economic advantage and capability, it is easier to leverage specific skills and assets. The dividend gained from expanding such a sector can subsequently be invested in other sectors to encourage a balanced growth with simultaneous consolidation in a number of sectors (Chenery, 1961: 21; Minondo, 2011; Ray, 1988; Rosenstein, 1943). The need for diversification does not of course mean that a country should try to do or be good at everything. However, examples from successfully developed countries, including newly developed and emerging countries, suggest that priority should be given to developing local economic resources, especially in the areas where they have some advantage, in order to sustain growth as a means to development (Stiglitz, 1998).

38 *Conceptualizing homegrown development*

For most countries in Africa, whose development process is still at a rudimentary level, it would be difficult, especially with the lack of technical know-how, to start competing in high-technology goods and industrialization. A far more sensible option would be to identify and target those areas where they have 'dynamic comparative advantage' (Stiglitz 1998: 18). Specifically, given their richness in agriculture and natural resources, obvious areas of emphasis can include mechanization of agriculture and manufacturing of agricultural intermediary goods (Okereke, 2011; Okereke and Yusuf, 2013).

Recognition of, and sensitivity to local imperatives does not in any way suggest ignoring global structures and trends. In fact the opposite is the case. As Porter (2011), Hall and Soskice (2001), and many others exhaustively show, optimum performance is achieved when external and internal conditions are complementary (cf. Sachs *et al.*, 1995). That said, there is a need here to stress the usefulness of understanding and embracing local imperatives. Because local cultures and structures were seen as obsolete and barbaric systems that must be replaced, many African societies are constantly in conflict, attempting to completely rid themselves of their traditions and fully assimilate the Western development paradigm (Ake, 1996; Battersby, 2004; Easterly, 2006a). The vacuum and chaos this strategy creates is arguably one of the main reasons why African development attempts have failed so abysmally (Collier, 1995; Evans, 2004; Mkandawire and Soludo, 1998; Stiglitz, 1998). So far, the new industrialized and emerging economies of Asia and Latin America have not developed by eliminating their own cultures, but by integrating some Western development models into their own plans (Easterly, 2006a). It is ultimately important that African leaders have the confidence and the full support of donor communities to seriously consider local environment and culture, and how they might best take advantage of these in framing their development strategies.

Broad stakeholder consultation and participation

The second important feature of HGD is broad stakeholder consultation and participation. The concept of stakeholder involvement has been a prominent feature in development discourse. Although the conceptualization of the term varies, the underlying message is broadly the same. According to Carroll (1996: 74) a stakeholder may be thought of as 'any individual or group who can affect or is affected by the actions, decisions, policies, practices, or goals of the organization'. Stakeholders in this context, therefore, are those who have a stake in, and could be affected by potential development policies.

Literatures suggest that broad stakeholder consultation and participation can provide at least four benefits in the pursuit of HGD in particular and economic development agendas in general (Baiocchi,Heller and Silva, 2011; Hickey and Mohan, 2004; Irvin and Stansbury, 2004; McFarlane, 2000; Ostrom, 1990; Stiglitz, 2002). First, a broad participation helps policy makers to better understand local realities and imperatives. Hence, in order to fully

Conceptualizing homegrown development 39

understand the diverse local imperatives and integrate them in the framing of a policy, there is the need for broad stakeholder consultation (Evans, 2004; Stiglitz, 1998).

Second, a broad-based and meaningful consultation process provides an opportunity for various and often conflicting interest groups to effectively resolve their differences (Stiglitz, 1998; Ostrom, 1996). In general, there are conflicting interests involved in any development process and the ability to resolve them plays an important role in the success of a programme's implementation and its impact (Sabatier, 2006). A broad consultation process is especially critical in diverse societies as seen in African countries. For example, after 2008 post-election conflict, Kenya carried out a broad consultative process that led to a referendum and change of the constitution. Although this was a laborious exercise, the dividend could be seen in the peaceful and fair elections of 2013.

The third benefit of broad-based consultation is that by eliciting ideas from a wide range of stakeholders, there is an increased chance that the policy developed will be more dynamic and effective (Varavasouzsky and Brugha, 2000). Input from diverse stakeholders can help to refine, hone or sharpen ideas. It can help to detect and avoid hidden errors that could hamper implementation. Finally, broad-based consultation and participation create a sense of ownership in the public and help in consensus building, which in turn helps to ensure the success of programmes in the long run (Baiocchi *et al.*, 2011; Stiglitz, 2002).

While the virtue in consultation is undeniable, notes of warning have been sounded about the need to avoid 'the tyranny of participation' (Cooke and Kothari, 2001) or 'the illusion of participation' (Few *et al.*, 2007) where it is erroneously assumed that participation must take a particular pattern in all countries and societies. Rather, policy makers and analysts alike need to recognize that both the makeup and participation of stakeholders depend on a country's political structure and policy process. For example, in a democratic setting, a wide range of stakeholders might include lobbyists, various interest groups, the public, expert groups, and legislative bodies. Conversely, in less democratic systems such as China, it could be just government functionaries and a cadre of political elites. The temptation for universal prescription must therefore be resisted.

Building local capacity and institutions

The third main feature of HGD is that it gives attention to local capacity building and institutional learning (Easterly, 2006a; 2006b; Kalinowski, 2011; Porter, 2011). No country yet has been able to develop without investing in its human capital through education and organizing its core institutions to promote efficiency, entrepreneurship and technological innovation (Acemoglu *et al.*, 2012; Coase, 1960; North, 1990; Rodrik, Subraminian and Trebbi, 2002; Williamson, 1975). Hence, it is critically important for any country's take-off

40 *Conceptualizing homegrown development*

that the HGD programme must include investing in local human capacity building through high quality education, science and technology, developing indigenous ingenuity, entrepreneurship and innovation.

South Korea, Singapore, Israel, India and China are a few of the recent examples of countries that owe their success to building human capital through investment in education broadly and science and technology in particular. It is instructive that most European and American brands of goods are currently made in China and that India exports IT labour to Europe and North America (Arora and Gambardella, 2006). It is also noteworthy that India is now one of the fastest growing medical tourism destinations across the world (Crooks *et al.*, 2011). In their famous book, *The Start-up Nation* (2011), Dan Senor and Saul Singer, paint a vivid and compelling picture of how Israel's passion for self-reliance coupled with an almost obsessive investment in technological innovation have helped to create 'an economic miracle' for the young country. Although De Soto (2003) and a few others have placed heavy weight on the role of capital accumulation in Chinese growth, it is often ignored that an equally crucial part was the country's investment in science and education and a determination to transform their institutions to incentivize innovation.

We suggest as many scholars before us (Evans, 2005; Ostrom, 1990, 2008; Stiglitz, 1998), that effective and inclusive institutions are crucial for the success of not just HGD but virtually all models of national economic development. People who advocate HGD strategies are not necessarily trying to advocate a return to traditional medieval institutions. Rather, the argument is for modern structures that infuse local values, needs and challenges. For example, entrepreneurs in all countries irrespective of institutional formats want legal frameworks governing transactions to be efficient and signed contracts to be enforceable. Regardless of cultural differences, people in all countries want effective public services, a just legal system and those in public office to be accountable. It must be emphasised that stressing the fundamental importance of institutions in development, does not translate to advocacy for a particular template for institutional development. We are quite simply saying that institutional capacity and efficiency at every level are crucial for the successful implementation of development programmes. It does not require one to take sides in the heated debate over political systems to accept that accountability, clarity of rules and procedure, good incentives to work and invest, the rule of law, efficient administration and judicious use of resources will enhance a nation's competitive advantage while the opposites will create a drag on growth. Evans (1996, 2004) was right when he argued that contemporary development strategies that focus attention on the macroeconomic result without close attention to the micro institutional foundation on which they depend are doomed to fail.

Social and human development

One of the major criticisms levelled against SAPs and similar foreign imposed development programmes in Africa is that they concentrate far too much on

Conceptualizing homegrown development 41

macroeconomic stabilization while ignoring socio-political and human aspects of development (Chossudovsky, 1996; Loewenson, 1993). For critics, the narrow conceptualization of development, mostly in terms of an increase in GNI and GDP – results in situations where many borrowing countries are forced to bear the pain of adjustment without reaping the fruits of development. Defenders of mainstream economic planning are, however, always quick to point out that social development requires economic growth which can only come from tight fiscal policies and monetary discipline (Herbst, 1990; Mkandawire, and Soludo, 2003; Williamson, 2000).

In our view much needleless energy has been expended on this argument. Clearly, economic growth is important for development. It is obvious that without stable financial resources, it will be almost impossible to provide good roads, clean water, good education and adequate medical care for the population. However, it is also fairly common sense, or at least so we think, that growth is not an end in itself but only a means to an end, which is improved human wellbeing. At the same time, economic growth depends not only on natural resources but also on wellbeing, good education, effective institutions, good governance and the human ability to stimulate innovation (Okereke, 2011). One can easily see from a dispassionate lens that economic growth and social development are mutually reinforcing and accordingly ought to be given equal emphasis in any national development strategy

Sadly though, this has not been the case. African countries are prime examples of where development intervention by the donor community has been focused on achieving macroeconomic stability while less attention is paid to social and human development (Adedeji, 1999; Adekanye, 1995). The consequence is that far too many times, growth has not spurred development, but has in some instances rather contributed to unemployment, poverty, poor wellbeing and the weakening of existing political systems. Other associated negative impacts include poor resource management, social inequality and loss of local identity and values.

Wealth correlates with quality of life when it is well utilized, if not then wealth can undermine quality of life (especially when it is controlled by a small percentage of the population) and consequently development. The fact that economic interventions in most African countries have not led to social, human and environment development is one main reason growth cannot be sustained (Okereke, 2006, 2008). The 1996 Human Development Report was notable for helping to mediate between the growth versus human development debate by showing, based on records from 1960 to 1992 that countries which did not succeed in mutual economic growth and development ended up in a vicious circle of underdevelopment and declining economic growth.

We therefore strongly subscribe to the notion that HGD must consist not only of achieving increase in GDP but also of providing access to basic human necessities – food, clothing, shelter, sanitation, clean water, quality education, healthcare, and promoting general wellbeing. Furthermore, it would also include creating a viable environment that helps individuals to develop capabilities to create their means of livelihood and encourage

42 *Conceptualizing homegrown development*

innovation. In other words, development, here, also includes political freedom, civil rights and security. As Sen (1999: 18) famously argues, freedom is linked not just to development but also to the ability for individuals, groups and a country to take control of their own development process.

Homegrown as a tested development strategy: the example of China

The homegrown approach to development is not just a theoretical framework but one that is supported by empirical evidence. Before concluding this chapter we provide a short case study of HGD focusing on China. We indicate very briefly how the Chinese model engages with the essence and features of HGD discussed in the previous sections.

The quest for development in China began in the 1950s, but failed after the Cultural Revolution. With the death of Mao and change of leadership in 1977, the country broke away from heavy Soviet influence, and took a different path in 1978 under the leadership of Deng Xiaoping who is known as the architect of Chinese development today. Deng Xiaoping's assertion was that for China to develop there must be social and economic institutional change. Even though China borrowed money and has continued to borrow from the World Bank to support its development process, the country resisted any external interference in its development agenda. China's shift from a closed economy to an open one was purely the decision of its leaders and this was carried out at the pace they thought suitable to their local imperative.

Notable leaders like Deng Xiaoping have consistently insisted that developmental policies must be realistically based, systematic and staged, and must take Chinese conditions into account (cf. Tisdal, 2009). Following this conviction, Xiaoping was able to persuade the Communist China Party leadership to endorse a systematic social and economic reform in a staged manner. China began with human capacity building through investment in education, science and technology. The first major reform was education. They changed the university entrance system, which was previously based on connection to be merit based. The educational system was also relaxed and broadened from the compartment model of the former Soviet Union to a more open approach. However, it was the reform of the agricultural system that became the first economic reform. Prior to 1978, China was a predominantly agricultural country with about 90 per cent of its population living in rural farming areas while employing 71 per cent of the total labour force (Qian and Xu, 1993).

The economic reform took several components, starting with the agricultural system where they had an advantage, and progressing to the gradual reform of state-owned enterprises and the legal system to attract foreign investment. They also consistently promoted investment in infrastructure. The transformation process did not do away completely with the traditional system, but rather changed what did not work and built on what did work. The Chinese communist system integrated political, social, and economic institutions which were then divided into national provincial, municipal and

Conceptualizing homegrown development 43

country authorities. The approach gradually transformed the agricultural system into a more open and competitive one.

Despite retaining most of its political system, the socio-economic reform also focused on enhancing institutional effectiveness all through the political levels of authority. The leadership of Xiaoping in the transformation of the agricultural system retained the decentralized system, but changed the communal peasantry system to a relatively free market competition. This gave farmers the opportunity to produce on their own and allowed markets to dictate the price of many agricultural goods as well as increase the state procurement price to raise income of farmers. The land ownership system was also changed to a lease system while retaining the collective ownership. This transformation increased grain production to about 30 per cent and doubled the production of cotton, sugarcane, tobacco, and fruit (Qi Cheng, 2012). With the success of the agricultural system reform, the state embarked on a systematic restructuring of other sectors.

The legal system was reformed and infrastructure was built especially in the economic zones to attract foreign investors. Foreign Direct Investment (FDI) in China took three different dimensions – jointly financed enterprises, cooperative ventures, and entirely foreign owned enterprises. Following the reform, China turned from a country with almost zero FDI prior to 1978 to an annual FDI of 30 billion dollars in 1998 and 105 billion dollars in 2010 (Bloomberg, 2011; Chew, 1994). Notably, Chinese economic reform did not concentrate solely on the economy, but was running concurrently with social reform. The country went on an aggressive infrastructural development, building roads and world class railway systems, among others. Other social sectors such as health, the welfare system, and education were restructured with special focus on education and promotion of science and technology. China graduated from basic export production to high technology. In the 1990s, China made higher education its main priority increasing the share of higher education graduates from 50 per cent in 1995 to 75 per cent in 2006 and gross enrolment to tertiary education from 6 per cent in 1999 to 30 per cent in 2006 (Waldman, 2008). Due to continuous emphasis matched with investment in the development of science and technology, by 2006, 36 per cent of Chinese undergraduate degrees were in engineering (ibid.).

Even though China's success was driven by the opening of its socio-economic system including State-Owned Enterprises (SOE) to market competition, China did not embark on an aggressive establishment of market economy as seen in most African countries. Despite abundant research on China's economic development model and using it as an example for most developing countries (as has been done in this book), China does not have a development blueprint. The socio-economic progress made in China was mostly by a decision of its leaders and commitment to move the country ahead through a systematic restructure of its institutions and trial and error which Deng Xiaoping likened to 'a person walking across the river by feeling the stones in each step' (cited in Tisdell, 2009: 140).

44 *Conceptualizing homegrown development*

Chinese policies were mainly an experimentation process that looked for what works and discarded what did not work. China capitalized on its greatest comparative advantage and invested in building up areas where it had less advantage. It adapted external ideas to local knowledge and resources instead of discarding local values and character. The Chinese model could therefore be explained by its slogan 'Chinese to build an economic system with Chinese characteristic' (Breslin, 2004; Zhao Ziyang, 1987). We are well aware that it is not all good news with China. Even today, there are growing rates of inequality, human rights abuses and large scale environmental pollution among other peculiar developmental challenges. However few will dispute that China has invested effort to explore what works for it in a pragmatic way and recorded impressive success in the process. Their leader has often be quoted as saying, 'it does not matter whether a cat is black or white, as long as it caught mice' (Deng Xiaoping cited in Gucheng Li, 1995: 13).

Today, African leaders are turning to Asian countries such as South Korea, China, Singapore and Malaysia in search of ideas. Clearly studying the Chinese development model with a view to adopting it wholesale by Africa is out of question, since China is different in many ways and has its own characteristics. Notwithstanding, there are many areas in which the Chinese success story could be beneficial to countries of Africa wanting to pursue development. Perhaps of the greatest importance, say Ohno and Ohno (2012: 221), is the focus on 'the *methodology* by which individually unique, but equally effective, policies were designed and implemented' (emphasis in the original). Equally crucial, in our view is the importance of a determination to embark on structural institutional reform with serious considerations of local characteristic, values, and economic advantage. Implicitly it is not about ideology, but what works and the commitment to take the country forward based on local characteristics.

Summary

We have attempted to conceptualize HGD in this chapter. The term may be new in the development discourse, but the practice, as highlighted above, is not. Ownership understood in terms of total control over development policies and programmes is the main essence of HGD. A homegrown approach to development does not, however, end with local ownership, but also entails other features such as considering local characteristics, building local capacity, and establishing effective institutional arrangement in ways that would sustain the development process. Contrary to the perception that African governments failed due to their socialist ideals, evidence from the Chinese model suggests the main problem might be lack of commitment by African leaders. Equally critical was intrusion by donor agencies that saw African social and political culture as obsolete and an obstacle to development (see James Scott, 1999).

Conceptualizing homegrown development   45

African countries have gone through conflicts and struggles, and stability has returned in many countries. African economies have been growing since 1999 and growth is predicted to continue. Human capital and technical knowledge have increased and there is a renewed call by Africans to go back to the drawing table and renegotiate their development approach. International donors like the Bretton Wood Institutions have admitted that external meddling in policy and institutional reform in Africa has failed to produce economic growth that could jumpstart development in Africa. Importantly, evidence abounds from the emerging economies in South Asia and Latin America that a homegrown approach that takes into account local imperatives can bring about a sustained development process. Having armed ourselves with a conceptual discussion that explores the essence and features of HGD, we are now in a position to systematically investigate whether, and to what degree African countries are embracing HGD in a manner that could lead the continent to the path of sustainable development. This is the task to which we turn in the set of empirical chapters that follow.

4 Ghana
Vision 2020 and Poverty Reduction Strategy Papers

We start our empirical analysis with Ghana, the first sub-Saharan African country to gain independence, and a nation that has been variously characterized as the 'light bearer', 'trailblazer', and 'beacon of the African continent' (Gyimah-Boadi, 2008). With one of the most advanced and stable institutional infrastructures in colonial Africa, Ghana was deemed as having a very high chance of flourishing post-independence (Kirk-Greene, 1991; Meng, 2004). Ghana's developmental prospects looked particularly bright given the quality and vision of its founding fathers. In particular, Kwame Nkrumah, the first President of Ghana and champion of African freedom, was known for his firm belief in and advocacy for the doctrine of *African solutions to African problems.*

Our analysis suggests that although there were some inconsistencies in execution, Nkrumah instigated and implemented some bold and admirable policies to steer Ghana towards the path of homegrown development (HGD). However, in the decades after the end of his presidency, Ghana gradually gravitated towards external political and economic dependency. Today, Ghana has started taking steps towards HGD but remains tethered to external donors' priorities due to a high and unsustainable debt burden.

In keeping with our focus on development policies post 1990, this chapter will analyse two main development initiatives in Ghana. The first is Ghana's Vision 2020 introduced in 1995 under the elected government of President Jerry Rawlings and his National Democratic Congress (NDC) party. The other is the Poverty Reduction Strategy Papers (PRSP), an initiative which was introduced by President John Kufuor in 2003 under the Word Bank/IMF mandatory strategic reform developed as a condition for the Highly Indebted Poor Countries (HIPC). Before analysing these initiatives, we first provide a short history of HGD efforts in Ghana.

A brief history of Ghana's homegrown development effort

Although the economic policy in colonial Ghana, as with other African countries, was inevitably extractive and externally oriented (see Chapter 2), Ghana actually had the good fortune of a relatively benign leadership that also invested in infrastructure, social services and human capital development. As the Governor of the then Gold Coast in 1919, Sir Gordon Guggisberg introduced a ten-year development programme with two major goals: first, training Ghanaians and recruiting them in half of the country's technical positions; and second, embarking on infrastructural development that emphasized transportation development, water supply and drainage and education (Agyei-Mensa and de-Graft Aikins, 2010; Ofosu-Mensa, 2011; Scott, 1956). Kirk-Greene (1990: 30) has pointed out that Ghana, at independence, had more 'health services per capita and better road system than any other British Territory in Africa'. In addition to a relatively good number of educated public administrators and strong institutions, Ghana also entered independence with a decent economy and significant amount of foreign reserves. Kirk-Greene estimated the country had an average savings of about 18 per cent of GDP and up to 200 million pounds foreign exchange reserves at independence.

We have noted that Kwame Nkrumah was a firm believer in HGD for Africa. In 1961, four years after independence, Nkrumah's government embarked on a project to craft a large scale comprehensive development programme – the Seven Year Development Plan – which was eventually introduced in 1964. In his *National Development Plan* address to the parliament introducing the programme in 1964, Nkrumah proudly declared that the ultimate aim of the initiative was 'to determine and direct the forms and conditions of foreign investment, in order to safeguard our socialist policy and national independence'. He went on to acknowledge the need for close attention to unique local imperatives and histories, saying, 'naturally, we must develop in each part of the country the type of economic activity to which it is best suited by reason of natural resources and geographical location' (Nkrumah, 1964).

It is easy to see from the extracts that Nkrumah wanted to continue to attract foreign capital and investment to Ghana while at the same time maintaining full control of the pace and direction of development. The goal was to steer Ghana on the path of socio-economic development through an African brand of economic socialism or what Nkrumah liked to call 'scientific socialism' (Nkrumah, 1966). In fact, the ambitious plan was so emphatically rooted in socialist ideals and local imperatives that Killick (2010) described it as the boldest step that marked Nkrumah's total break away from the inherited colonial policies.

In his determination to ensure success and avoid external interference, Nkrumah established a Planning Commission manned by his close associates and protégés. These were mostly young Ghanaian graduates of economics led by Joseph Henry Mensah. The Seven Year Development Plan known as the 'big push' emphasized industrialization and capacity building. Nkrumah's aim was to consolidate and expand the socio-economic infrastructure inherited from the colonial masters while increasing growth and social services. The Plan identified three major areas of priority – education, agriculture and

48 *Ghana*

industry – and argued that for Ghana to increase its capital and productive capacity there would have to be massive investment in construction, industries and science and technology (White, 2003: 106). Clearly, Nkrumah's vision was for an industrial Ghana with increased standard of living for a majority of the populace. For Nkrumah, scientific socialism implied essentially approaching development through the modernization model while incorporating strong elements of social welfare and self-sufficiency (Nkrumah, 1966).

While making clear their intention to ensure that the ultimate decision about the direction of the big push remained in the hands of locals, Nkrumah and his associates had no qualms about entertaining contributions from foreign economists. For example, in 1963, a conference was held to discuss the draft with several foreign economists led by the renowned Nobel Laureate, Arthur Lewis. It turned out, however, that the young Ghanaian graduates responsible for crafting the initiative had done such a thorough job that the foreign experts did not make substantial criticism apart from noting that the Plan was ambitious and could be more specific (Grischow, 2011; Killick, 2010). The consensus was that the plan was largely in consonance with the prevailing modernization model of development while retaining virtues of local control and sensitivity (Killick, 2010).

Nkrumah's government was toppled in a coup in February 1966 and the new military regime promptly abandoned the seven year economic programme. Despite its short lifespan, however, much was achieved in the form of HGD. During the time of the Plan, cocoa output increased and contributed 60 per cent of export earning as government invested heavily in mechanized farming (Kirk-Green, 1990). New roads were constructed resulting in wide improvement in the road network. School enrolment as well as education standard increased (Leith, 1996). Furthermore, there were also significant improvements in the health system with increases in hospital, clinics and health personnel (Baah, 2003). Ghana also witnessed expansion in housing and the building of the Volta Dam, a reservoir covering 8,500 square kilometres (Goldsmith and Hildyard, 1984).

This is not, of course, to suggest that the 'big push' was a comprehensive success in all its ramifications. In fact, it is widely known that the strategy suffered from plenty of problems related to poor project conception and implementation, misplaced priorities (due to largely political calculations), inefficiency and outright corruption (Ayelazuno, 2012; Grischow, 2011; Killick, 2010). For example a mango-processing plant was built in an area where there were no mango trees, and even if mango trees had been planted they would have taken years to mature so that they could be harvested. Thayer Watkins (n.d.) noted that a leather plant was situated in the South – a far distance from the cattle industry in the North. A major problem was Nkrumah's quest for massive high scale industrialization against the stage by stage strategy advocated in the Plan (Grischow, 2011; Killick, 2010). Moreover, the implementation process did not take into account Ghana's economic advantages and capabilities as outlined in the Plan (Anamuah-Mensah and Towse, 1995).

For example, there were expensive investments in areas where the country had no advantage. A notable instance was the decision to build a Bauxite production plant, when the presence of sufficient quantity of bauxite was not proven. It was not at all surprising that production never took off.

Critically, most of the projects in the big push were funded from Western loans either bilaterally or multilaterally through the World Bank (e.g. the US $100 million external loan from the World Bank and other Western creditors for the Volta River Project) which escalated Ghana's external debt. Nkrumah was clearly trying to be smart by collecting large sums of money from Europe and America to fund his Western inspired industrial projects while at the same championing his vision of African socialism, a big part of which was motivated by his relationship with the East. Leaving aside for a moment the ideological tension which Nkrumah embodied, the 'economic reality', as Biney (2011: 111) points out, was that 'the government's failure to adhere to local conditions as captured in the Plan inevitably resulted in massive indebtedness'. One hypothesis was that Nkrumah was embarrassed at Ghana's size and, preferring to see Africa as his stage, he pushed things much further and faster than was economically logical. Scott Thompson aptly observed that 'his fatal flaw was undoubtedly his lack of sense of proportion' (Thompson, 1969: 385). This is not far from Killick's (1978) argument that Nkrumah impatiently and excessively accelerated the industrialization process that was phased over a 20 year period.

Significantly, the so called strong economy left by the colonial government which was supposed to provide the foundation of the ambitious industrialization project turned out to be not as strong as trumpeted. Whilst the British managed cocoa production in Ghana, during the colonial period, they set the international price at a very high level thereby generating good revenue. After independence, however and with competition from new cocoa producing countries in Latin America there was market volatility and a drastic fall in cocoa prices. This proved fatal for Ghana which had based its grand economic projections on the hope of abundant and continuous inflow of revenue from cocoa. Furthermore, it did not help that the so called surplus which was to be managed by the British Crown following Ghana's independence was not well invested (Biney, 2011). This situation provided the context for Killick's (1998) argument that neither the Western powers nor the new African political leaders fully grasped the scale of the challenges against nation building faced by Africa at time of independence.

Still, it is also probably fair to say that Nkrumah's economic decisions were mostly affected by his ideological overdrive that sometimes blinded him from reality (Biney, 2011: 103). For example, he was reported to have declared: 'we would be hampering our advance to socialism if we were to encourage the growth of [the] private sector' (Killick, 1978: 142). In addition, Nkrumah assumed the position of a demi god and refused to listen to close associates and advisers. He thought it wise to deviate from the plan as and when he deemed fit, thereby introducing inconsistencies between the original vision

50 Ghana

and the actions on the ground. For example, when Nkrumah was told that one of his decisions was contrary to the plan, he retorted: 'Who decides, Mensah or me?' (Biney, 2011: 110).

John Esseks provides evidence to show that significant parts of what passed for HGD under Nkrumah were in fact state-run and state-dominated economies (Esseks, 1971). He notes that by 1965:

> the state importing enterprise handled 35 per cent of the country's total commercial imports; the state insurance corporation transacted about 50 per cent of all insurance business; and the government's commercial bank accounted for over 60 per cent of total deposits most of which in turn were state-owned.
>
> (Esseks, 1971: 63)

Paradoxically, the inevitable result of such a level of state monopoly of the economy was that local enterprises were not developed, leaving the remaining private sector to external control through foreign firms. Despite the many shortcomings in implementing the programme as noted above, it is probably fair to say that it was during this time that Ghana made the biggest attempt to develop, especially in terms of social and human development.

There is evidence that Western governments were involved in the overthrow of President Nkrumah, their main reason being the disenchantment with Nkrumah's socialist orientation and his anti-Western radicalism (Gebe, 2008). It is very instructive, for example, that one of the first things the military junta did after the overthrow of Nkrumah was to abandon the Seven Year Development Plan and invite the World Bank/IMF to offer expert advice on Ghana's economic policies (Hettne, 1980: 180). What is beyond speculation was that a few months before the coup, the American government had withdrawn US $35 million in aid earmarked for Ghana citing the need for more accountability (Botchwey, 2010). Similarly, it is common knowledge that several lending agencies, angered by Nkrumah's scathing critique of colonial and post-colonial exploitation in his 1965 book, *Neo-colonialism*, sought to introduce harsh lending conditions. In fact it has been argued that Nkrumah's rejection of a proposal demanding greater Western interference as a condition for debt relief heavily contributed to the toppling of his regime with the help of the USA Central Intelligence Agency (CIA) (Hutchful, 1979: 36).

Following the overthrow of Nkrumah in 1966, Ghana entered a long period of political crisis marked by coups, counter coups and periods of democratic interregnum (Awoonor, 1990; Gocking, 2005). During this period, Ghana's economic policy landscape changed frequently and assumed many different orientations although in reality many of these governments had little time to formulate and implement any coherent economic policy. The consequence was an economic downturn that 'took Ghana from an economy growing rapidly at the time of its independence in 1957 to an economy declining precipitously in the 1960s and beyond' (Ayelazuno, 2012: 132).

Ghana 51

Gyimah-Boadi (2008) describes the situation even more graphically, saying that in a space of three decades Ghana went 'from being Africa's "Black Star" to become the poster child of a failing African state, cursed with incompetent, corrupt and repressive governments presiding over political instability, stagnant economy, broken down infrastructure and decaying society' (cited in Awal, 2012: 98).

On 31 December 1981, Lt Colonel Rawlings led a coup (his second in less than two years) and eventually stayed in office till 2001, bringing in his wake a measure of political stability. Rawlings had a declared mission to sanitize governance, address the persistent economic woes that had befallen the county and transform the weak institutions that had dilapidated since Nkrumah was removed from office. He proposed a new social contract between the state and the citizens where government's power was based on 'nothing more than … the consent and authority of the people' (Shillington, 1992; cf. Adedeji, 2001: 3). The new government formed a Provisional National Defence Council (PNDC) that comprised both military and civilians. It introduced governing coalitions as a strategy for maintaining a government of national unity and rolled out some distributional economic polices, ostensibly to gain the support of the low income class. However, without any money with which to execute the populist policies, the government was compelled to turn to the World Bank for monetary assistance with the conditionality of introducing structural adjustment (KonaduAgyemang, 2000). This marked the beginning of a new turn in the relationship between Ghana and the Breton Wood Institutions, characterized mainly by a departure from Nkrumah's ideals that eschewed external influences.

In 1981 Ghana introduced a four-year Economic Recovery Programme (ERP) that was aimed at stabilizing the economy. The introduction of the ERP was in fact the final step to full-blown economic liberalization in Ghana. Interestingly, a major goal of the programme was to attract increased foreign capital to redress the limitation the country had suffered in this area due to Nkrumah's statist policies (Boafo-Arthur, 1999; Konadu-Agyemang, 2000; Weissman, 1990). With its manifest zeal to implement externally recommended reforms, Ghana became a favourite of the IMF and World Bank, both of which showered the country with loans while working closely with the government to help shape its economic liberalization policies (Konadu-Agyemang, 2000; Weissman, 1990). On the flip side, however, financial support led to increasing reliance on foreign aid while driving the country's debt from US \$1.117 billion in 1983 to US \$4.88 billion (Economist Intelligence Unit (EIU), 1998; Boafo-Arthur, 1999: 52).

Ghana development policies since the 1990s

In 1992, Rawlings resigned from the Armed Forces, initiated a transition to democracy and subsequently went on to become an elected president in 1993. While Rawlings did manage to stabilize the economy in the early to mid-1980s,

52 *Ghana*

the period between 1987 and 1990 witnessed major slippages, reversals in economic growth, increasing domestic indebtedness and the reduction of the much needed donor support (Awal, 2012; Hutchful, 2002; Sandbrook and Oelbaum, 1999). Hence, the return to democratic rule had carried with it a widely felt impetus for change in economic policy. The transition to democracy, as Awal (2012: 97) puts it 'marked a struggle to consolidate a democratic political framework that [would] deepen democratic governance as the basis for enhancing sustainable economic growth and human development'. The attempt to keep faith with this ambition saw the introduction of a suite of broad as well as *ad hoc* development policies starting from 1993.

Our analysis here, however, will focus on two main policies since many of the others were too transient to warrant any significant analysis. The first is the Ghana Vision 2020 – a grand but short-lived plan – introduced soon after the return to democratic rule in 1992. The other and more important for the work here is the Ghana Poverty Reduction Strategy Papers (GPRSPs) introduced in 2003 by the John Kufour-led New Patriotic Party (NPP). Since 2010, Ghana has introduced a new development programme known as Ghana Shared Growth and Development Agenda (GSGDA). This has been viewed as a corrective to the GPRSP with the intention of exerting greater local control over national economic policy. We do not analyse the GSGDA in detail because regardless of positive noises, much of Ghana's development projects continue to occur in the context of the PRSP framework.

Ghana Vision 2020

One of the key constitutional changes made following the return to democracy by Ghana in 1993 was the introduction of a law that required every government to put forward a comprehensive and coordinated developmental programme within two years in office (Article 36, clause 5, 1992). In pursuit of this constitutional requirement, the Rawlings' led government mandated the National Development Planning Commission (NDPC) to craft a long-term coordinated programme for the country. In 1995, following a broad consultation process, Ghana Vision 2020 was introduced to the parliament as required by law. The plan was divided into two parts. The long-term vision known as the National Development Policy Framework (NDPF) had the goal of making Ghana a medium income country by the year 2020. Specifically, the aim was that 'by the year 2020, Ghana will have achieved a balanced economy and a middle-income country status and standard of living, with a level of development close to the present level in Singapore' (NDPC, 1995: 1).

The second part of the document was an immediate medium-term plan branded the Co-ordinated Programme of Economic and Social Development Policies (CPESDP). According to the Vision 2020 document, the objectives of the CPESDP in the medium term (1996–2000) were to secure improved human development and poverty reduction through rapid expansion of

Ghana 53

opportunities, employment creation and strengthening social infrastructure and services. The specific target of the CPESDP was to achieve up to eight per cent growth and more than US $5,000 of income per head by the year 2000. Other objectives included rural and urban development, creating an enabling environment for business investments and re-structuring public institutions.

Vision 2020 contains several references to the effect that the ideas and plans were formulated by Ghanaians and for Ghana without external influence. It boasts, for example that 'This co-ordinated programme is the first of its kind in that it is human-centred, comprehensive and based on the co-ordinated endeavours of government agencies – national, sectoral, regional and district – as well as the private sector, including NGOs' (NDPC, 1995: iv).

As stated, the planning process and the development policy framework had been spearheaded by the National Development Planning Commission acting on behalf of the whole country. The NDPC was made up of four cross-sectoral planning groups that comprised academics, consultants and professionals from both public and private sectors (NDPC, 1995: i). The NDPC coordinated and monitored district consultative committees through the Regional Coordinating Council (RCC). Committees held several workshops where inputs from various regions and sectors were collated and analysed.

Overall, the political climate was in favour of extensive consultation and national ownership of the plan. With the restructuring of the political system that ushered in democracy, there had been a decentralization of Ghana's public administrative system to the district level with a commitment to allow districts to take responsibility of their development process. Moreover, the new constitution had specifically stressed the need to enhance parliament's power and citizen's participation in governance (Article 365). Therefore, to a large extent, Vision 2020 was both an opportunity to prove, as well as the ultimate evidence, that Ghanaians had taken back their economic destinies into their own hands after many years of foreign induced adjustment policies. It was for many a counterpoint to the top-down SAP which had been in operation over the previous ten years. So palpable was the notion of the dawn of a new era with emphasis on public participation in governance that Vision 2020 spoke of an intention to monitor the implementation stage of the plan through the same consultative process used in its design 'in order to ensure that all programmes and projects are mutually supportive and compatible with the approved national development objectives' (NDPC, 1995: viii).

In presenting Vision 2020 to the parliament, President Rawlings sought to identify with the mood of the nation. He expressed his disappointment with the outcome of over ten years of World Bank imposed SAPs, many of which, ironically, had been implemented under his watch as the military Head of State, declaring: 'I should be the first to admit that the economic recovery program launched in 1983 and since acclaimed internationally as a success, especially in the corridors of the World Bank has not provided all the answers to our national problems' (cf. Boafo-Arthur, 1999). He made it clear that he strongly shared the view that the time had come to try a different approach

54 *Ghana*

that was more citizen-led and sensitive to local economic imperatives. The expressed hope was that the new Vision 2020 plan would provide that much needed alternative to foreign led economic programmes.

Despite the wide acclaim and pomp that greeted this programme, it failed almost as soon as it started (Whitfield and Jones, 2008). Its implementation, to the extent there was any, was sporadic and mired in one controversy after another. Internal coordination was chaotic with the Ministry of Finance, which outlined activities and expenditures for all ministries and agencies, choosing to operate on the basis of a competing three year Medium-Term Expenditure Framework (MTEF) (Whitfield, 2009). It also did not help that donors did not support the programme and that the NDPC lacked a plan and the authority to effectively communicate and promote Vision 2020.

Crucially, the publicity and consultation which had marked the drafting of the policy became a source of vulnerability for the government as many of the citizens felt emboldened to voice passionate opinions for and against key elements of the policy (Awal, 2012; Hearn, 2001). Nationwide demonstrations against the introduction of Value Added Tax (VAT), a cardinal element in Vision 2020, resulted in the death of five protesters and subsequently the resignation of the long standing minister of finance (Harem, 2001). Sensing imminent economic decline, the World Bank used the opportunity to intervene and issued a warning of the need to sustain the economic restructuring of the past decade by accelerating 'the implementation of a large unfinished agenda of adjustment' (Armstrong, 1996: 1). Ghanaians however were not impressed by the argument of the World Bank; rather they continued to agitate not only for minimal relief from the pressure caused by the structural adjustment programme but also for much more expansive welfare related economic benefits which they envisioned as 'dividends' of the new democratic dispensation. Meanwhile, caught in the conflict between stabilization and poverty reduction, the economy stagnated and Ghana once again found itself 'in the throes of a fiscal crisis' (Hutchful, 2001: 1).

Commentaries on the reasons why Ghana's Vision 2020 was short-lived (some will even say still born) are divergent. Awal (2012: 100) identifies lack of commitment by government and 'considerable laxity in selectively implementing reform programmes'. Ninsin (2007) and Sandbrook (2000) pinpoint the problem to hesitations and policy reversals while Booth *et al.* (2002) conclude the key reason for failure was the return of unbridled corruption and neo-patrimonial politics. However, it is not very helpful to speak of conflicting demands without providing insight into the political and economic conditions that necessitated those contradictions and policy reversals. Insightful analyses from Abugre (2001), Hearn (2001), and Hutchful (2002) have shown that in addition to undue pressure from the World Bank, by far the most important reasons for the demise of Vision 2020 lay in the difficulty in achieving broad-based inclusive economic growth in the context of a newly liberalized political framework, on the one hand, and a very constrained macroeconomic framework, on the other hand.

Seeking to achieve the objectives of widespread poverty eradication and employment creation in line with the new democratic aspirations, while at the same time shouldering the financial burden associated with the newly expanded democratic structures of the state, the government soon experienced the return of rapid deterioration of balance of payments resulting in massive inflation. Runaway inflation and huge deficits in the balance of payments quickly led to acceleration in the decline of foreign exchange value of the Ghanaian currency and consequently the need for even more borrowing. It seemed then that the only way out was to abandon Vision 2020 with its home-grown development approach and turn back again to the World Bank for money under the condition of fiscal prudence and stronger macroeconomic stabilizing measures.

Ghana Poverty Reduction Strategy

Given the state of the economy in 2000 and the controversy that had surrounded Vision 2020, it was no surprise that the opposition party (the National Patriotic Party – NPP) – which defeated the incumbent government in the 2001 election promptly discarded Vision 2020 in favour of the Word Bank's stipulated Interim Poverty Reduction Paper (IPRP) in 2002. This measure was later replaced with a full blown Ghana Poverty Reduction Strategy designed to comply with the conditions for borrowing under the World Bank's Highly Indebted Poor Countries (HIPC) initiative. This was despite arguments that the initiative provided little additional financing for development (Martin, 2004) and that the so called debt relief was severely hampered by the macroeconomic conditions set by the World Bank for the implementation of debt relief (Dijkstra, 2004).

The GPRS was formulated as a two part programme: (GPRS I) ran from 2003 to 2005 and GPRS II from 2006 to 2009. The overarching objective was to quickly transform the nature of the economy to achieve growth, accelerated poverty reduction and the protection of the vulnerable (Government of Ghana, 2003). In reality, the immediate need, as the government widely acknowledged then, was to restore macroeconomic stability and the confidence of major development partners (Government of Ghana, 2007).

Looking further ahead, the government set out an ambitious goal to make Ghana a medium income country by doubling the national income within a decade. Key targets included increasing the GDP steadily from between four and five per cent to seven and ten per cent in the medium term and between 11 and 15 per cent in the long term. In the same vein, it also set out to reduce poverty from 39 per cent of the population in 2000 to 32 per cent in 2005, as well as to decrease the mortality rate from 110/1000 to 95/1000 over the same period (Government of Ghana, 2003). Other goals included increasing investment in social services such as education, health and sanitation and private sector development within a stable macroeconomic environment and good governance. According to key documents these goals and targets were to

56 *Ghana*

be achieved in the medium term period through rapid infrastructural development and the modernization of agriculture to create employment. Equally important was the improvement of the business environment to enhance the growth of the private sector as well as wider institutional reforms to promote good governance.

The following sections will now look at the GPRS to examine the extent of its *indigeneity* as well as its outcome based on the conceptual framework established in Chapter 3. We will explore the quality of stakeholder consultation, extent of economic diversification, investment in institutions and capacity building, and attention to social development. We will then examine the implementation and performance of the programme.

Broad stakeholder consultation and participation

The new government made some effort to model the consultative process for the GPRS after Vision 2020 but with very limited success. The NDPC which had been so active in mobilizing citizen participation with regards to the Vision 2020 programme attempted to leverage previously built stakeholder platforms. This time, however, a significant aspect of the consultative process was managed by Core Teams (CTs) of mostly technical experts. Interestingly, some of the CTs have representatives from donor organizations as members which raises questions about the ownership and *indigeneity* of the process. The CTs organized consultative meetings with local stakeholders through various nationwide public forums. The stakeholder meetings were organized according to major thematic areas derived from the two foci of the policy – poverty reduction and economic growth. Hence, superficially the impression is given of an attempt to unite macroeconomic growth with social development and poverty reduction. Key documents suggest that consultation was in three stages. The first involved 36 communities and involved dissemination of information on the PRSP process and obtaining views of different perspectives on poverty. Representatives included men, women, youth and traditional authorities. The second involved 'wrap up sessions' (Government of Ghana, 2003: 6) with CTs and District Assembly personnel. The third stage was regional workshops involving civil society organizations (CSOs). Some use was also made of the media through a one day seminar and talk show involving various civil society groups. Consultations were also held with Ghanaians abroad – notably in Berlin, Germany; London, UK; Washington DC, USA; and Pretoria, South Africa.

The government drew attention to the quality of participatory democracy within which the GPRS was developed stating that 'one of the key principles adopted in the preparation of the PRSP was the participation of Ghanaians to ensure national ownership' by all stakeholders (Government of Ghana, 2003: 5). Independent commentaries, however, indicate that the exercise was shambolic and 'riddled with contractions' (McGee, Levene and Hughes, 2002: 35). While the government attempted to put on a bold face, there were ample indications that the consultation was less an attempt at participation and more of a box ticking gesture designed to satisfy the demands of lending International Financial Institutions (IFIs) (Killick and Abugre, 2001; McGee *et al.*, 2002; Whitfield, 2005; 2009). Whitfield (2005) suggests that the GPRS did not generate much interest from the government ministries and department due to fatigue of the Bretton Wood process. She observed that high ranking officials participated in the process only when the World Bank country director was in attendance. McGee *et al.* (2002) note that the NDPC was severely under resourced and poorly integrated with other ministries and the broader civil service. Accordingly there was no commitment or sense of ownership of the policy across the government departments.

Given the serve lack of resources, much of the participatory process was shallow and very limited. It did not involve as broad an audience as the Vision 2020 process. The government was wary of CSOs and handpicked those that participated (McGee, 2002: 36). Even for the ones selected to attend, information from government was not detailed and the few documents provided were distributed in the last minute leaving little or no room for quality engagement (Godfrey and Sheehey, 2001). The media workshop referred to by the government was a single slot event involving over 200 participants so that quality was severely compromised. While the donor representatives of the CTs were pushing for more openness and consultation, the government officials showed no appetite for in-depth participation and wanted to keep the process as short as possible. This generated much tension within the teams and affected the quality of the process. It is suggested that some of the donors resorted to 'overly active behind the scene' (McGee, 2002: 35) activities including discretely distributing documents to civil society organizations. At the same time Whitfield (2005: 650) suggests that donors almost actively took over the writing process and refused to incorporate some of the President's priority programmes in the document.

Interestingly, governments recognized that the extent of public consultation that took place before crafting Vision 2020 was not replicated with regards to the GPRS. They however sought to put a positive spin on this, explaining that 'the results of past participatory studies were also included as inputs into the formulation of the GPRS to reduce the pressure and costs of undertaking fresh participatory studies'(Government of Ghana 2003: 5). It is not clear how true or reasonable this was. In the first place, the two programmes had such different emphases that it would have been difficult to graft public views from one to the other. In fact the overriding sense expressed by Ghanaians was that the restrictive macroeconomic adjustment conditionalities of the GPRS implied that the consultation was ultimately perfunctory. According to McGee (2002), there are no reasons to believe that the contributions from civil society or analyses from the district level assessment were synthesized and incorporated into the paper. It is also noteworthy that the plan was not tabled for debate in the house of parliament as some sections of the constitution would appear to demand. The document, however mentions that

58 *Ghana*

parliament did review the priorities and consider them as part of its agenda in a two day parliamentary retreat (which was not open to the public). It continues that a Ministerial Committee on Monitoring and Implementation was set up 'following a statement by the Minister for Economic Planning and Regional Co-operation in the parliament on the GPRS' (Government of Ghana, 2003: 9).

We have suggested in Chapter 2 that participation is a crucial feature of HGD. However, evidence from Ghana, as presented above, indicates that the impact of stakeholder participation in the GPRS was dubious. Although participation, no matter how limited in nature, is bound to exert some positive impact at least in terms of broadening awareness, the signal is that participation can actually undermine ownership if it becomes a source of tension between donor and recipient countries. Moreover, even in the absence of such a tension, serious questions remain about the quality of the participation as it was practiced in Ghana's PRS to improve the quality of the policies under discussion.

Economic diversification and local imperatives

Like most African countries, Ghana's economy is not diversified. Agriculture is the mainstay of Ghana's economy. The country is known to be very rich in agricultural land and produces some of the finest cocoa on earth. Accounting for about 51 per cent, agriculture is the largest contributor to Ghana's gross domestic product. It also provides 45 per cent of all export earnings. A large part of Ghana's export earning agricultural activity is centred on cocoa. West Africa accounts for 70 per cent of the world's cocoa output and Ghana is the second highest producer, after the Côte d'Ivoire. Ghana is also known to be rich in mineral resources with much mining focused on gold. It has a huge potential for tourism due to its rich culture and history. More recently, oil and gas exploration have also started in Ghana. Despite all of this, the country's economy remains at a rudimentary level with a very weak manufacturing sector. The country has suffered persistent deficit in development financing leading to heavy borrowing and massive debt overhang, with an external debt to GDP ratio of 120 per cent – the highest in Africa.

The GPRS noted that Ghana's mono-cultural economy had been the key impediment to growth and poverty reduction in the country. It stressed that 'one of the fundamental problems that have faced the country is the persistent reliance on the export of a few primary products with little or no added value' (Government of Ghana, 2003: i). The situation, as the document noted, makes the country vulnerable to internal shocks and 'price fluctuations dictated by buyers in the developed economies' (ibid.: i). Interestingly, the document stated that Ghana's development predicament had been caused by the external looking economic profile and priorities laid by the colonial masters and the inability of subsequent indigenous governments to reverse the trend by adopting endogenous or homegrown approaches to development:

Ghana 59

> Ghana's early development within the world economy was accompanied by a high level of geographical polarization and an interruption of the development of indigenous political, economic, and spatial structures and systems. Colonial penetration consolidated a process informed largely by external circumstance and priorities. This situation led to a condition commonly referred to as the *producing what is not consumed and consuming what is not produced syndrome.* This characteristic still obtains today.
>
> (Government of Ghana, 2003: 30; emphasis in the original)

Underlining the urgent need to diversify the economy, the document identified agriculture as the country's area of primary economic advantage and the sector on which effort should be concentrated. Following the observation that the vast majority of the population is involved in one form of subsistence agriculture or another, the GPRS identified expanding the agricultural sector as a key link to achieving poverty reduction and food security. The GPRS then set out plans to restructure the economy by developing the agro-based industries, diversifying export and stimulating private sector participation. Specific strategies for expanding the sector included providing support for wide-scale development of irrigation systems, introducing more varieties of crop for export and improving access to relevant technologies (Government of Ghana, 2003).

In addition to agriculture the government also said it would promote small and medium scale industries that can capitalize on Ghana's rich cultural heritage and natural resources, with the textile sector singled out for attention. Other sectors identified as needing urgent investment were tourism and information and communications technology.

Another major blight in the country's economy, which the document attributed to colonial legacy, was a wide regional disparity in development. The government stressed that an indigenous approach to growth could not permit a system where some regions made progress while others were left behind. For example, the government noted that while the country was suffering from a generally high rate of unemployment (40 per cent of population), the situation, it said, was particularly acute in the three northern savannah regions (the Upper East, Upper West and Northern regions) where poverty ranged from 69 per cent to 88 per cent (Government of Ghana, 2003: 15). Other forms of disparities noted include urban versus rural, occupational, and gender inequalities. The government vowed to correct these inequities through broad-based affirmative programmes, stressing that the overarching goal of the GPRS was 'to ensure *sustainable equitable growth, accelerated poverty reduction and the protection of the vulnerable and the excluded with a decentralized, democratic environment*' (Government of Ghana, 2003: 30; emphasis in the original).

Despite correctly identifying agriculture as an area of comparative advantage, the GPRS did not devote enough space to elaborating specific steps to transform the sector. Moreover, the main focus remained on expanding

60 *Ghana*

primary commodity goods while little attention was paid to how to boost intermediate manufacturing sectors such as the production industries. The continued neglect of the manufacturing sector in Ghana is worrying. Evidence from developed countries and more recently the Asian Tigers suggests that manufacturing is critical for real economy take off and sustainable economic development. Yet, diversifying the economy through manufacturing has been a major economic challenge for Ghana.

According to Sutton and Kpentey (2012), manufacturing is the slowest growing sector of the economy. Ghana does not have a history of facilitating indigenous entrepreneurs. The GPRS recognized this but only made mention of the need to strengthen the National Board for Small-Scale Industries (NBSSI) (Government of Ghana, 2003). Kwabena Frimpong-Boateng associated the challenge of stimulating manufacturing sector growth in Ghana with the low priority given to science and technology in the GPRS and previous development plans. 'No wonder', he said, 'we are still stuck with hoe and cutlass, importation of fertilizer and massive post-harvest losses of almost everything our farmers break their backs to produce' (Frimpong-Boateng, 2011).

The fact is that even though the GPRS I and II identified some of the key economic challenges that are linked to the widespread poverty and lack of investment in social development programmes, the emphases of both frameworks remained debt servicing and macroeconomic stabilization. Despite dedicating both documents to the goal of accelerated wealth creation and 'overall disappearance of poverty by 2020' (Government of Ghana, 2003: 35), the clear impression conveyed in the subtext was that poverty reduction was conditional to the achievement of macroeconomic goals as set by the international financial institutions.

Social development

Both historically, and more recently following the global economic crisis, one can see that even in the developed economies, there is always an abiding tension between fiscal prudence and social development which tends to come to the fore during periods of austerity. We have suggested in Chapter 2 that one of the key features of HGD models is that the concern over macroeconomic growth, which is often the emphasis of external donors, is never allowed to result in the relegation of social development even in periods of austerity. Insofar as the end goal of development is the promotion of human wellbeing rather than economic growth for its own sake, one would expect that any government that is not shackled by rigid loan conditionalities would take a more long-term, pragmatic and 'human-faced' approach in balancing its budget deficits. Hence, to the degree that Africans are exerting more control over their economic policies, one should expect to see more attention given to social development while not neglecting the need for debt servicing and macroeconomic stability.

We have noted that the attempt to balance these two objectives was, at least in theory, a major emphasis of the World Bank and the IMF in formulating the GPRS.

Ghana's poverty reduction strategy was heavily focused on poverty reduction with great emphasis on social development and the provision of basic services. Although GPRS recognized the importance of macroeconomic stability, it also underscored the point that macroeconomic stability is not 'a sufficient condition for poverty reduction [but] fosters a positive environment for growth' (Government of Ghana, 2003: 50). It goes on to say that, 'to the extent that strategy for growth is pro-poor, growth will lead to significant reductions in poverty' (ibid.: 50). One of the unique features of GPRS I was actually the Participatory Poverty Analysis (PPA) survey which was administered in 36 sample communities from 14 districts in six regions of the country. The government claimed that PPA gave it a deep and comprehensive understanding of the various dimensions of poverty and insight into how best this problem might be tackled. GPRS I identified three clusters of issues which needed urgent attention to comprehensively address poverty in Ghana. These included (i) providing basic services especially health, education and sanitation; (ii) providing gainful employment to the population; and (iii) eliminating the many dimensions of inequalities in the economy and providing special programmes in support of the excluded. GPRS II continued along the same lines but with even greater emphasis on human development through education.

The government recognized that poverty was unacceptably high in Ghana. It was noted that government's expenditure had historically been biased in favour of recurrent expenditure while 'spending on social programs for poverty reduction such as health and education has been low' (Government of Ghana, 2003: 42). GRSP I went on to note that expenditure on health and education stood at 2.0 per cent and 2.8 per cent of GDP respectively putting Ghana at a level that is much lower that even African averages. The document stated that the government was determined to reverse the trend by investing heavily to enhance the delivery of social services. Specific targets included changing the educational system to ensure uninterrupted education for all Ghanaians from pre-school to age 17 and developing model senior secondary schools and health centres in every district in the country. The GPRS I stressed increasing access to primary education, while the GPRS II went further by making school attendance compulsory for all children for 11 years starting from two years of kindergarten to three years in Junior High School. Other areas identified by the programmes are improvement of social and living conditions through housing projects, enhancing the National Health Insurance Scheme, providing access to clean water and sanitation, and rehousing street children. The programme recognized the challenges of access to clean water and sanitary environment and set out three strategies for improvement: to accelerate provision of safe water in rural and urban areas; to accelerate the provision of adequate sanitation; and to improve environmental sanitation in urban and rural areas.

62 *Ghana*

GPRS I indicated the main reason Ghanaians were poor was that the vast majority of citizens engaged in what was described as self-subsistence food crop farming. According to the document, 'smallholder farms dominate the sector accounting for about 80 % of total agricultural production' (Government of Ghana, 2003: 69). Average farm size was estimated at 1.2 hectares, fertilizers and hired labour are rarely used and there is a wide gap between actual and potential yield. Government indicated that the core intervention required was four fold: (i) reforming land acquisition laws to ensure easier access and more efficient title process; (ii) providing incentives such as affordable credits and extension services to help increase the involvement of poor people in agriculture; (iii) encouraging the production of cash crops to boost export; and (iv) supporting the private sector to process or add value to traditional crops such as cocoa.

Thirdly, the document observed that Ghana's development had been characterized by a strong regional disparity and other dimensions on inequalities. The GPRS 1 recognized the historical contingents that led to the regional dichotomy in Ghana and the need to address it. It was noted that early development within the world economy was accompanied by a high level of geographical polarization and that subsequent development patterns have exacerbated these disparities. A significant portion of the GPRS I was devoted to an analysis of other dimensions of disparities in the country including economy, gender, age and location. Attention was also devoted to the analysis of disparities caused by disability. Furthermore:

> The GPRS will focus on providing the enabling environment that will empower *all* Ghanaians to participate in wealth creation and to partake in the wealth created. It will ensure that all Ghanaian irrespective of their socio-economic status or where they reside have access to basics social services such as health care, quality education, potable drinking water, decent housing security from crime and violence and the ability to participate in decisions that affect their own lives.
>
> (Government of Ghana, 2003: I, emphasis in the original)

It is fair to say that on paper the GPRS did a fair job in identifying key areas of some challenges facing the country. However, as the two documents duly recognize, the real challenge lies in how to mobilize sufficient finance to meet the ambitious goals. Moreover, given that bilateral and multilateral donors still accounted for a significant proportion of development expenditure in Ghana, the real test relates to what will happen if donors' priorities or loan conditionality conflict with those of national leaders.

To solve the problem of development costs while meeting the fiscal target, the government depends on external funding for some projects. With the commercial oil exploration in 2010, the government is now hopeful that a large chunk of social development will be funded with petro dollars. To this end Annual Budget Funding Amount (ABFA) has been earmarked for social

Ghana 63

expenditure. However, as experience from other oil rich African countries abundantly shows, oil money does not automatically translate to efficient social development. Another main challenge that faced Ghana was how to ensure the effective implementation of plans in the context of low human and technical capacity.

Building local capacity and institutions

Although Ghana is well ahead of some of its neighbours in terms of having effective institutions, much remains to be done by the country in this area. Similarly, although the literacy level in Ghana is relatively high compared to the rest of sub-Saharan Africa, it still lacks the quality and quantity of human and technical capacity needed to spur self-reliant sustainable development. In both GPRS I and GPRS II, ample space is devoted to the assessment of the local capacity and institutional needs of the country with some remedies proposed. This quote from GPRS I provided a picture of the challenge as it was perceived:

> Plans to reform the public services in the 1980s by improving institutional structures and creating more clearly defined roles had very limited success. There appeared to be a lack of political commitment to the programmes. Few of the reforms including decentralization and the decomposition of power, were implemented. The capacity of the public service remains limited despite available talents and skills. This situation would appear to have been caused by a number of interactive factors including a dysfunctional relationship between political and official decision makers, politicisation of public service posts, patronage lack of discipline, endemic corruption and unacceptably poor conditions of service.
> (Government of Ghana, 2003: 34)

GPRS I identified strengthening good governance as one of the core areas of emphasis. Under this rubric, at least five sub themes were identified as priorities. Firstly the government recognized that the civil service was heavily bloated with salaries accounting for nearly 30 per cent of government's recurrent expenditure. It also lamented that despite being oversized service delivery was poor and inefficient. A two pronged solution was proposed. It committed, on the one hand, to restructure the civil service to ensure greater efficiency and effectiveness, and on the other hand, to improve conditions of work in order to motivate workers and attract high skilled talents. The second area of priority was strengthening public policy management by enhancing transparency, accountability and public participation in governance. Thirdly, there was commitment to improve the rule of law and checks and balances within the system. Despite limited reforms in the 1980s, there was recognition that power remained overly concentrated at the centre and within the executive arm of government. Effective implementation of the decentralization

64   *Ghana*

reform was seen as crucial for enhancing government. To this effect, several targets were set including defining and rationalizing the role of regional and district departments, the review and strengthening of the Local Government Service Bill, increasing the allocation of District Assembly Common Fund (DACF) allocation, and the completion of a legal review on the legislation related to decentralization. Finally, it was recommended to strengthen the parliamentary and judiciary arms of government so they could enhance democratic checks and balances and effectively play their roles in promoting good governance.

If GPRS I emphasized effective institutions and good governance as the means of achieving poverty alleviation, the unmistakable battle cry of GPRS II was the need for human resource development through quality education and technical training. It boldly announced its intent to focus on human development by stating that 'the educational sector reform policy of government most sharply illustrates the intended change in strategic focus between GPRS I and GPRS II'. GPRS II goes on to state unequivocally that, for Ghana, by far 'the most important lesson of contemporary economic history' was that 'the single most crucial key to the attainment of economic success is the educational quality of a nation's work force' (Government of Ghana, 2007: vi). Accordingly government reeled out a number of interventions intended to create and nurture a workforce which is equipped to support an economy which can realistically aim to achieve rapid progress by absorbing modern high-productivity and high income technology.

The plan outlined in GPRS II for human capacity development in Ghana is four-fold. First, school attendance was to be made obligatory but also free for all children for 11 years – from age four to 15. This included two years of Kindergarten, and three years of Junior High School. Second, the intellectual and physical content of school was to be improved. This involved revising schools' curricula to raise standards and increase graduate's employability, training and retraining of teachers, upgrading all teacher training schools to diploma awarding institutions, and on the physical side, proving schools with modern facilities including buildings, laboratories and computers. The third dimension involved investing in technical and vocational training to prepare more youth for the world of work. Here, one key policy was to establish a structured system of apprenticeship to cater for those that do not go into higher education. The fourth leg was massive investment in tertiary education. Noting that 'the absorption and application of a great deal more science and technology than is presently deployed is a critical ingredient for successful growth in the third world' (Government of Ghana, 2007: vii) the government committed to promote the development of science and technology research in all relevant tertiary institutions in the country.

However having outlined these policy measures, GPRS II raised some notes of caution. It warned that the strategy would be 'very expensive to execute' and the implementation process 'bound to be very painful, costly and turbulent' (Government of Ghana, 2007: vii). Interestingly, although it expressed the hope that the development partners would buy into the vision, it also offered a veiled defence against the possibility of the plan being undermined by donors by declaring that in so far as donors request clarity of focus, '*the development of Ghana's human resources* should unambiguously settle the issue of priorities in the nation's development plans for the next four years' (Government of Ghana, 2007: vii, emphasis in the original).

Country ownership of development agenda

There is evidence that in moving away from Vision 2020 to the GPRS, Ghana surrendered significant control over its development plan to foreign lenders. The GPRS, like the SAP came with conditionality that allowed significant external influence in setting the country's development priorities and programmes. By far the most significant problem for Ghana was structural weakness of its economy expressed mainly in high spending to revenue ratio, a rudimentary monocultural economy and unsustainable public debt overhang. This combination of factors keeps Ghana mostly focused on satisfying donors' demands in order to guarantee the release of the next tranche of aid. The government has recently sought to increase its ownership of development policies by diversifying the sources from which it borrows but this has only served to expand the sources of external influences beyond the Bretton Wood Institutions to include other development agencies such as the African Development Bank, the European Union, Germany, Canada, Denmark, Netherlands, Switzerland and the United Kingdom.

It is true that Ghana continued to encourage wider stakeholder participation as a prelude to the adoption of GPRSP I and GPRSP II in keeping with the tradition set by Vision 2020. In reality however, the quality of participation has been weaker than what was experienced in the run up to Vision 2020. Although the Bretton Wood Institutions have urged public participation and ownership upon Ghana in the context of the PRSPs, they have continued to maintain a very high level of direct involvement in the decision making of the programmes in ways that in fact limit or even undermine real ownership for Ghana. Moreover, it has been fairly clear that no matter the level of public consultation or participation the policies outlined would have to adhere to the World Bank PRSPs framework to stand any chance of being approved. Hence, while there may be a few areas where the government and citizens are allowed some latitude, the scope for choice remains severely restricted. As one of the key actors in the policy process put it, 'we had to do what we had to do to satisfy the international donors and ensure that the loan conditionalities were fulfilled' (Anonymous government source). The sense of helplessness is so far-reaching that in the context of GPRS I, the President felt there was nothing he could do when his priority initiative was edited out in the last stages of the document preparation by donor officials.

Killick and Abugre (2001), Tsikata (2001), Whitfield (2005) and Whitfield and Jones (2008) have provided interesting commentaries on the ownership of

66 Ghana

GPRS with all concluding that local control was (and remained) very limited. There is a wide acknowledgment that the development process in Ghana continues to suffer from the intrusion of donor organizations. Killick and Abugre (2001) have specifically noted the irony in submitting what is supposed to be a country-owned programme to the World Bank for final approval. In service to the same argument, Whitfield (2005) notes how the parliament was severely undermined by the World Bank's timelines which necessitated the programme being sent for approval before the parliament was ready to make any contribution. Whitfield and Jones (2008) conclude that the '*default programme*' has emerged as the key way of managing aid in Ghana over the course of the 1990s. They describe this as a situation where:

> Governments and civil servants negotiate as far as they think they can on a particular loan or grant, but accept the aid package in the end even if the policy and programmes attached to it do not adhere to a ministry's priorities or are seen by the government negotiators as not particularly useful.
>
> (Whitfield and Jones, 2008: 188)

As Hutchful (2002) observes there is a huge mismatch between the national development priorities of Ghana and what donors emphasise. He goes further by arguing that the PRS inspired agenda seemed more designed to meet specific IMF conditionalities in exchange for aid and loan than as an earnest attempt at national development. This he says includes even the poverty reduction aspects of the programme, insofar as these are directly tied to the conditions set by the IMF and the World Bank. Whitfield (2005) describes in detail how the content and direction of policies are closely monitored by the World Bank and the IMF through numerous avenues such as yearly and quarterly consultative meetings as well as various other so-called 'donors' dialogue' which provide avenues for micromanagement.

All of this clearly exposes the dilemma and the contradiction in the relationship between donor institutions and the government as concerns programme and policy ownership. In particular, even though in some countries like Ghana, existing constitutional requirements ensure active public participation, in practice, policy autonomy and true ownership are restricted by the conditionalities stipulated by the donors.

Implementation and general outcomes

Both GPRS I and GPRS II emphasize the importance of effective implementation to realize the objectives spelt out in the documents. Furthermore there was a commitment that the implementation process would be participatory and decentralized in nature. The National Development Planning Commission was given the mandate to monitor implementation both directly and through regional consultative workshops. The monitoring of specific aspects of the programme was assigned to groups according to areas of interest and expertise with GPRS I emphasizing the need for active involvement of civil society organizations.

Regarding outcome, it is obvious that the GPRS was a recorded success in terms of macroeconomic stabilization. By the end of the second phase of the GPRS Ghana's economy, which was on the precipice of collapse before the multi-party elections in 2000, had relatively stabilized. The GDP increased from 3.7 per cent in 2000 to 7.3 per cent in 2008, although it declined in 2009 due to the world economic crisis. There was a significant growth in its three main economic sectors. Agriculture grew by 5.7 per cent, manufacturing rose by 6.5 per cent, and the service industry recorded a 7.3 per cent rise (IMF, 2012: 28). The local currency appreciated remarkably and stabilized against the dollar. Inflation also declined radically from 40.5 per cent in 2000 to 10.6 per cent in 2006. The monetary policy also helped to raise the country's external reserves. With strong growth performance, an increase in remittance from overseas, and debt relief, the country managed to record a huge surplus of US $178.8 million in balance of payments by 2007 (ibid.: xiv).

While the economy saw significant improvement compared to the 1990s many commentators have observed that there is yet to be a structural change that would make for a long-term, self-reliant and sustainable economy (Awal, 2012; Whitfield and Jones, 2008). The country still remains a predominantly primary commodity economy whose growth rate is dependent on international trade, especially the price of cocoa, mining to some extent and more recently oil. Even though the industrial sector improved slightly, manufacturing later declined.

Generally, the economic growth has been positive since 2001, but like many African countries that have recorded two decades of steady growth, Ghana's economy has failed to make visible impact in terms of translating this to poverty reduction especially among the most vulnerable sections of the society. This is most visible in the three northern regions of the country where unemployment and poverty rates remain very high. Managing the fiscal deficit continues to pose a challenge to the government. In fact the deficit rose from 8.4 per cent in 2000 to 14.5 per cent in 2008, a timeframe which corresponds to the period of the implementation of GPRS I and GPRS II (Government of Ghana, 2010). This high deficit is also exacerbated by the rise in external debt to over 60 per cent of the GDP (IMF, 2012: 18) in spite of having taken advantage of the HIPC debt relief. This reaffirms Martin's (2004) argument that the HIPC is not sustainable and does little in relieving a country from its debt burden.

The report card of the programmes look even grimmer when one considers performance in areas of the social services delivery. The state of key infrastructure remains very poor and grossly inadequate for supporting growth. Roads account for 95 per cent of the total transportation system in Ghana but vast portions of the country do not enjoy good connections. The railway network has not been developed beyond colonial days, while sea and air

68   *Ghana*

sectors operate at a fraction of potential capacity due to poor maintenance. In human development, the progress has also been slow. There has been a slight improvement in gross enrolment at all levels. Primary school enrolment increased from 93.7 per cent in 2006 to 95.2 per cent in 2008 while junior high school enrolment progressed from 77.4 per cent to 78.8 per cent in the same period. However, when using a net enrolment for assessment, the percentage drops to 83.7 per cent for primary and 53 per cent for junior high schools suggesting that many children are still finding it hard to stay in school. Moreover even though enrolment at all levels as well as the percentage of trained teachers has increased, there are still serious concerns over the quality of education.

The programmes pitched employment generation as being at the centre of growth and poverty reduction strategies. However, unemployment and poverty are still very high and both the urban rural and the south north dichotomy which the programmes vowed to tackle persist. The consistent growth experienced in the country has not been able to yield comparable job creation. Hence employment generation that would reduce poverty remains one of the major challenges of the country. This could be linked to the continuous low investment in agricultural and manufacturing sectors despite much positive rhetoric. Similarly, despite some progress the public service remains bloated and inefficient. As a result, Ghana's system continues to retain political patronage which usually peaks during election time. Ghana's public service has received mixed scores internationally; the Mo Ibrahim Foundation ranked Ghana's public service as one of the weakest in the region, but the World Governance Indicators ranked the country eighth in Africa. Meanwhile, there has been a progressive procedural institutional reform in Ghana since 1993 which is expected to affect attitudinal changes and become more substantive over time if the process continues.

Summary

Despite the relative social and civil stability, Ghana is plagued with severe economic structural weakness which hampers its attempt to take bold steps towards taking full control of its own development agenda. A large proportion of the development expenditure is still funded through bilateral and multilateral development assistance. Even though there has been a modest oil-boom which has cushioned pressure, economic growth remains far outpaced by the government's debt obligations to banks, global lenders and national governments in the West. With a total public debt stock of about US $24 million at the end of December 2013, Ghana external debt to GDP ratio is one of the highest in Africa. Saddled with huge foreign debt and limited sources of income, Ghana has found it difficult to break out of aid and take control of its own development agenda.

Within the limited policy space, Ghana has made some effort to outline a set of national development priorities which place emphasis on poverty alleviation and human resource development. It aims to achieve a middle income status by the year 2020, which is very ambitious. In the context of poverty alleviation Ghana envisages that the key opportunity lies in modernizing agriculture to yield more foreign exchange and absorb the country's rapidly growing workforce. Economic diversification, especially stimulating growth in agro-allied industries, is also high in the agenda of government. There is also a desire to create and nurture a workforce that is equipped to absorb modern high-productivity and high income technology and realistically support sustainable self-reliant growth. However, due to emphasis on meeting the PRS requirements and the conditionalities attached to it, the country has not been able to take enough action to firmly set itself on the path of meeting these goals.

Ghana suffers from a condition akin to a split personality syndrome. On the one hand, the country glorifies its 'tradition of high expectations' (Government of Ghana, 2007) as epitomized in the grand vision of its founding leader, Dr Kwame Nkrumah. Standing on this platform, present leaders envision a Ghana that can attain a middle income status by 2020 and contribute to the overall development of the continent. On the other hand, there is a recognition that one of the key reasons for Ghana's economic stagnation and susceptibility to crises has been that the state has often 'attempted to accomplish more than it is able to given the limited resources it can command' (Government of Ghana, 2003: 31). The challenge is how to keep the high hopes alive while retaining focus on immediate and mid-term steps that can be taken to regain control over the country's development trajectory and destiny.

5 Nigeria
National Economic Empowerment and Development Strategy

Next in our case studies we turn to Nigeria, the most populous country in Africa by population and currently also the largest economy on the continent. Like Ghana, Nigeria also showed good prospects for development immediately after independence in 1960 and was in fact numbered among the rising stars (Guest, 2013; Meredith, 2005). However, even though Nigeria entered independence with good potential in terms of its natural resource base, it lacked a strong foundation, with gaping cracks already visible before the country sounded its first national anthem as an independent country. Six years after independence, things finally fell apart following a military coup which subsequently led into a brutal and bloody civil war (1966–1970). Since then, Nigeria has been plagued by recurring ethno-religious crises and military interventions which have hampered political stability and socio-economic development.

In 1999 the country returned to democracy with great pomp and enthusiasm. The collective aspiration was that things might turn again in the right direction after decades of military rule characterized by mismanagement and underdevelopment. Soon after its inauguration, the new democratic government introduced the National Economic Direction (NED) with the primary objective of achieving economic diversification. In 2003, following re-election the government replaced NED with a purported homegrown integrated socio-economic strategy known as the National Economic Empowerment and Development Strategy (NEEDS). The stated aims of NEEDS, widely touted as a transformational agenda, were wealth creation, employment generation, poverty eradication and value reorientation. This chapter examines the policy process and document of NEEDS as well as the implementation to explore the extent of its *indigeneity* and its impact in shaping the socio-economic development in the country.

In 2010, a long term development plan known as Vision 2020 was introduced by late President Musa Yar'adua and later inherited by President Goodluck Jonathan. We do not analyse Vision 2020 here since its first mid-term report would not be ready until the end of 2014. We begin however, with a brief historical narrative to aid the understanding of the country's current socio-economic institutional foundation for development.

Homegrown development effort in Nigeria: a synopsis

Colonial legacy

In 1914, Nigeria became the country as it is known today when the British colonial administration amalgamated the formally independently administered Northern, Southern and Lagos protectorates. A stated policy objective of the British colonial rule in Nigeria, as in other African countries, was to secure political stability and resource extraction from conquered states with as little British presence on the ground as possible (Meredith, 2005). The 1914 amalgamation of vastly different and in some cases incompatible groups into one big country was clearly underpinned by this objective.

At the end of the Second World War there was a rise in vocal indigenous criticism of the colonial administration's policies and especially the lack of integration of the locals in the political and public administrative system. The colonial administration responded with the introduction of the first economic plan in 1946, known as the Ten Year Plan of Development and Welfare for Nigeria. In theory, the goal was to reallocate resources with the aim of improving the wellbeing of citizens. In practice, however, the plan was nothing more than an expenditure plan by the British Empire's government for the allocation of welfare funds with emphasis on developing transport and communication channels to intensify resource extraction and export from the colony for the interest and benefit of the Empire (Adamolekun, 1983; Helleiner, 1966; Ikeanyibe, 2007). There was, for example, little or no attention given to the productive sector or human capacity development.

With an increase in local representatives in the parliament, neglect of indigenous enterprise was identified as a key weakness in the development programme and there were calls for the plan to be revised (Obikeze and Obi, 2004). This resulted in an initiative to amend the plan which began in 1953 with the World Bank being invited for an 'economic mission' to Nigeria as part of international input (Ojo, 2012). With the recommendation of the Bank's report a new mid-term Plan (1955–1960) was introduced by the colonial government. This time, the Plan was modified to include more attention to industrial and agricultural development (ibid.).

However, despite wide acclaim, this document was not implemented. With a concentration on resource extraction and import substitution, the colonial government showed little interest in diversifying the economy beyond commodity export. Little investment was made to develop the agricultural and mining sectors with only 6.4 per cent of the Ten Years Plan allocated to these two sectors, which were the main export earning areas. Despite the interest in the growth of cash crops, the agricultural sector was not advanced and food crop production through mechanization was discouraged (Oluwasanmi, 1966). Instead, cheap labour and local farmers were utilized (Usoro, 1977). Manufacturing was completely neglected (Adamolekun, 1983; Ayo, 1988) and indigenous enterprise was supressed.

72 *Nigeria*

Efforts to introduce foreign investment did little to help the economy, as the policy in place was only beneficial to the foreign investors without any structured plan to benefit the country through capital inflow. Technology transfers were not encouraged, as foreign companies did not integrate local entrepreneurs. Instead they were given free income tax and allowed to repatriate their profit and capital (Adamolekun, 1983; Ayoade, 1983). It would appear in fact that the introduction of the Plan in the first place was merely to quash the rising nationalist agitation at the time (Lambo, 1989; O'Connell, 1971).

Homegrown development in post-colonial Nigeria

Nigerian independence was obtained by an elite group divided along ethnic lines. Owing to this division the independence fighters lacked common and coherent ideas for nation-building. The inability of Nigerian leaders to unite with a sense of nationalism resulted in acrimonious regional politics and eventually constitutional decentralization (Coleman, 1958; Sklar, 1963). This helped in regional political mobilization but was not conducive for socio-economic development or national cohesion.

Despite inheriting a fractured polity steeped in ethnic cleavages and strife, the newly independent government showed intent to embark on the expansion of the economy through industrialization. The first main step to this end was the formulation of the First National Development Plan of 1962–1968. It was intended to be a six-year development plan but was interrupted by the civil war which broke out in 1966. The Plan's main objectives, drawing from the modernization development model, were economic growth and industrialization. The First National Development Plan to a large extent was a break away from the colonial pattern that was entirely externally driven. The process that led to it started with the establishment of a National Economic Council in 1955 with responsibility for developing a framework for national economic development. The Council, which was made up of representatives of central and regional government, was to coordinate the process in conjunction with a national Joint Planning Commission (JPC) and in consultation with the regional governments, federal ministries and other relevant stakeholders (Ikeanyibe, 2009). The Council was initially headed by the Governor General, but was later headed by the Prime Minister after independence. In addition, other statutory institutions were established to speed up the process of coordinating the various projects (Ekundare, 1973). For the large part, these institutions were managed by local professionals hurriedly trained at the end of colonial rule, with foreign experts invited by the government solely for technical advice. There was however very limited public consultation as originally intended (Ikeanyibe, 2009).

Despite weak policy process, lack of capacity and the volatile social and political environment that eventually resulted in civil war, the government was able to achieve some objectives of the Plan. In terms of infrastructural development, an oil refinery was completed in Port Harcourt and new roads and ports were built. In pursuit of electricity generation two large dams and several thousands of kilometres of transmission lines were constructed. To boost manufacturing, the government built a number of sugar, flour and palm oil processing mills (Nnoli, 1981; Oguntoyinbo, Areola, and Filani, 1983). Significant investments were also made in the education sector with the establishment of five universities. All of these were achieved in part due to a coordinated guideline that monitored the programme, and to a large extent the government commitment to development at independence.

However, while progress was made in some areas there were a lot of lapses and gaps. Many manufacturing plants were poorly constructed or inadequately maintained. More importantly the government did not create an environment for developing local entrepreneurs. In fact the new government was lax in implementing the plan. It paid little attention to local imperatives but rather followed the same narrow economic strategy of the colonial rule (Adedeji, 1981). Accordingly, foreign companies were protected with incentives at the expense of local entrepreneur development (Nnoli, 1981). There were also significant waste and administrative inefficiencies occasioned by corruption and lack of capacity. In fact, at some point the emphasis of the plan was almost completely diverted away from economic planning towards Africanization, which was basically replacing foreign expatriates with poor and hurriedly trained local technocrats. It did not help that the political upheaval that began in 1966 degenerated into a civil war that lasted from 1967–1970 (Adedeji, 1981; Ake, 1981).

At the end of civil war in 1970, a Second Development Plan was introduced by the military government, headed by General Yakubu Gowan. This Second Plan attempted to improve on the first by strengthening the planning mechanism and broadening the consultation process and public participation through a national conference. The process was also more diverse, including representatives of various sectors like the universities, labour unions and the private sector. Additionally, the process was more comprehensive and made a better attempt to integrate various local challenges (Ekundare, 1971).

Given the peculiar post-war challenges, the primary objective of the Second Plan was to rebuild damaged social, political and physical infrastructure. The Second Plan was anchored around the concept of the three Rs: reintegration, rehabilitation, and reconstruction. These were broken down into five guiding principles – (i) united people, (ii) strong nation, (iii) self-reliant nation, (iv) great and dynamic economy, and (v) just and egalitarian society.

Critically, the new Plan made clear that the idea of self-reliance and promoting local enterprise were cardinal in the government's economic development vision. This commitment was later given statutory backing through the promulgation of the indigenization decree in 1972 which went as far as barring foreign private firms from some selected enterprises (Donovan, 1974; Ogbuagu, 1983). The government also embarked on nationalization polices which allowed it to buy 60 per cent in equity shares in the marketing operations of the major oil companies (Ogbuagu, 1983). Other highlights include

74   *Nigeria*

the establishment of more universities and the introduction of the National Youth Service Corps to foster integration.

However, just as before the war, the implementation of the Second Plan was very sporadic and half-hearted. Social development like health services, access to clean water and other services continued to be neglected, economic diversification and indigenization were, at most, partially implemented. With over dependence on oil which contributed over 90 per cent of government revenue, 'prebendalism' (Joseph, 1983) became the order of the day as government polices increasingly concentrated solely on collecting and squaring rents accruing from oil exploration in the southern parts of the country (Okereke, 2006, 2008). In fact things steadily moved from bad to worse with successive governments most of which have been military dictators looting the treasury, increasing the national debt through reckless borrowing and eventually capitulating to the Structural Adjustment Programme (SAP) imposed by lending organizations.

Nigerian development policies since 1999: from NED to NEEDS

In 1999, after 16 years of military rule marked by widespread institutional breakdown, economic decline and rise in poverty, Nigeria once again returned to democracy. Given a history of many aborted democratic transition experiments, Nigerians welcomed the new democratic government with great enthusiasm and high hopes for a bright and prosperous future. It was in the midst of this euphoria that the new democratic government, led by Olusegun Obasanjo, invited key stakeholders to articulate a new development plan that would take the country in a new direction. The outcome of this process was a four-year national economic development plan called the National Economic Direction (NED) (1999–2003).

The NED aimed to broaden the economy and crucially make it more competitive by reforming public institutions to reduce bureaucratic bottlenecks and corruption. In the end, however, very little success was recorded. Public institution reform did not take place, bureaucratic challenges increased, and human development declined with a rise in unemployment and poverty as Obasanjo spent most of his tenure on diplomatic travelling to boost his international image (LaFraniere, 2005). At the same time there was no visible impact in infrastructural development despite the huge amount of resources garnered from the rise in oil price. In fact, Donli (2004) wonders whether NED can be truly regarded as a comprehensive development plan since the programme was merely aimed at the development of a highly competitive private-sector-led economy based on market-oriented philosophy. Ikeanibe (2009) goes even further by saying the model adopted in NED was no different from the SAP. With the total failure of NED and the re-election of Obasanjo in 2003, there was a clear need for rethinking and strategizing a new approach to development. The result was the National Economic Empowerment and Development Strategy (NEEDS).

Nigeria 75

Policy content of NEEDS

Introduced at a time that sentiment for a 'new' and 'enhanced partnership for African development' (UNECA, 2001: 3) was running high, the National Economic Empowerment and Development Strategy (NEEDS) was supposed to be the blue print for homegrown development (HGD) – not only for Nigeria but also for Africa as a whole. After all, President Obasanjo, the man behind the policy had learned a bitter lesson from the poor performance of NED and had also crucially become one of the champions of an African renaissance based on self-reliant growth and new partnerships with the West and aid agencies.

The overarching objective of NEEDS was to achieve a major and sustainable economic turnaround for the country in the shortest possible time. According to the primary document, there were four key goals to be pursued. These included: (i) wealth creation (ii) employment generation (iii) poverty reduction, and (iv) value re-orientation. The document further specified that the stated goals would be pursed through three overarching themes. First, under 'Empowering people' it listed many human and social development objectives such as health, education, employment creation and housing development as priorities. Second, under, 'Promoting private enterprise' the document identified privatization and liberalization of trade enabled by rule of law and infrastructural development as cardinal objectives. And, thirdly, under 'Changing the way the government does its work', the government noted public sector reform, good governance, transparency and efficient service delivery as main priorities.

Notably, the document was clear that the three core themes mentioned above were all subject to the goal of macroeconomic stabilization. Moreover the document was absolutely clear of the government's intention to aggressively drive the stated reform in the context of a neoliberal economic framework. The document was peppered with references to the importance of the free market and the private sector. It asserted that 'the private sector will be the engine of economic growth' under NEEDS (National Planning Commission, 2004: xi; xvii, 55), stressed the 'need to unburden business of the red tape and complex procedures that hinder it from flourishing' (ibid.: xi, 53), and promised to diminish government control through deregulation to 'attract private sector investment' (ibid.: xi).

In terms of specific policies and interventions, the document lists providing improved irrigation machinery and crop varieties to boost the agricultural sector, supporting small and medium enterprises to create jobs and reduce poverty, and creating a functioning public institution devoid of corruption as some of the priorities. There is also emphasis on social institutions and infrastructures such as education and the health system to improve wellbeing. Overall, the goal was to see Nigeria take pride of place as an economic giant in Africa and provide inspiration for other African countries.

76 Nigeria

Stakeholder consultation and participation

The official document explicitly stated that NEEDS was a result of extensive consultation with various stakeholders and the Nigerian public. The claim was that it took three years to develop NEEDS and that the process involved a dedicated team that 'travelled the country, holding meetings and workshops to identify what the Nigerian people want for the future' (National Planning Commission, 2004: viii). It is indicated that the policy process was coordinated by the National Economic Council in conjunction with Council for Development Planning and the Joint Planning Board.

The strategy document was keen to emphasize the extent of consultation that had gone into the preparation of the document claiming this was one the things that distinguished NEEDS from previous strategies. It said, 'people from all walks of life and all parts of Nigeria were consulted' (ibid.: xiii) and that information was gathered from farmers, factory workers, labourers, teachers, university professors, charities and other stakeholders. For this reason it declared '[i]t is really the people's plan for prosperity. Our government wrote it using the information it collected from the Nigerian people'. Continuing, it declared, that 'the plan enjoys widespread commitment from the President to the village chiefs' (ibid.: xii).

Despite these bold assertions it is not quite clear just how much public consultation went into the formulation of NEEDS. It is known that soon after Obasanjo won a second term he initiated a discussion on developing a framework for socio-economic reconstruction which later led to the establishment of an Economic Team, chaired by then Finance Minister and former World Bank Vice President, Ngozi Okonjo-Iweala and presided over by President Obasanjo. The Team was tasked to develop a framework for the economic reform and development in the country. Later the remit was expanded to include public institution reforms, in effect bringing the two initiatives under the economic team.

The Team first drafted a 17 page paper that explored the major economic and social problems and challenges facing the country, and identified debt overhang and a volatile macroeconomic environment as the critical issues. Accordingly, it recommended structural reform, the tackling of debt and solving the problem of huge budget deficit as key priorities (Okonjo-Iweala, 2012:13). It was, therefore, on this basis that the conceptualization of development framework that culminated in NEEDS was adopted.

A draft of the first comprehensive document was sent to various ministers, state governors and local governments for comments and suggestions as well as for adoption into the State Economic Empowerment Development Strategy (SEEDS) and the Local Economic Empowerment Development Strategy (LEEDS) respectively. However, there was no indication of any change made despite criticism that the framework was too neoliberal and western oriented (Ja'afaruBambale, 2011; Okonjo-Iweala, 2012). The point here is that contrary to the claim by the NEEDS document that the initiative was a product of extensive consultative process, the strategy was in fact birthed by a few bureaucrats in Nigeria with assistance from their European colleagues and the World Bank. This point is admitted by Okonjo-Iweala herself who makes it clear that the strategy was developed by an Economic Team and subsequently marketed to different stakeholders, these being the state governors, legislatures, representatives of labour unions, the private sector and international donors (Okonjo-Iweala, 2012).

So then, unlike the consultative process in countries like South Africa, Kenya and Ghana that included an element of grass-roots participation, the NEEDS consultation process was limited to donor agencies and a few elites in Nigeria, contrary to the claim in the NEEDS document. The foregoing is not to suggest that the initiative was misguided or even that the impact of an inclusive and grassroots approach to policy is always positive (see Chapter 3). However, in a society as diverse as Nigeria with a history of war, involving experts and the public alike in a comprehensive civil society consultation could perhaps have gone a long way to help improve integration of local imperatives, a sense of ownership, implementation and accountability.

Economic diversification and local imperatives

The NEEDS document aptly identified that one of the key problems of the Nigerian economy was the over reliance on a single primary product – in this case crude oil (Adelabu, 2012, Idemudia, 2009; Odukoya, 2006). The document noted that over dependence on oil has been mostly responsible for the high volatility of the economy. Crude oil export, as the document observed, accounted for 40 per cent of the GDP, about 95 per cent of foreign exchange earnings and at least 70 per cent of total government revenue. This situation sharply contrasts with what obtained at independence when agriculture contributed up to 70 per cent of the GDP. The document noted that a mono-economy does not provide adequate basis for sustainable development but also renders the country extremely vulnerable in an era of a fast changing global market environment. Consequently, economic diversification was recognized as a prime goal of the strategy.

The strategy document proceeded to outline some of the steps that would be taken to achieve economic diversification and made note of some of the unique local factors and comparative advantages that could be leveraged in the process. Chief of these steps included saving, debt payment, wide scale privatization and liberalization of the economy. The document was absolutely clear in the government's intention to aggressively promote a neoliberal economic framework. In its view, government saving, debt payment, the acceleration of privatization, liberalization and deregulation were key elements to promoting competition and economic diversification.

Second, NEEDS identified agricultural development as another step in achieving economic diversification. As noted, agriculture was the mainstay of the Nigerian economy at independence, accounting for over 90 per cent of foreign

78　*Nigeria*

exchange earnings. The document lamented that subsequent administration since independence had neglected the economic potential of agriculture and pledged to place emphasis on revitalizing this sector. Noting that 'half of Nigeria's poor work in agriculture', the document pledged that government would 'offer farmers improved irrigation, machinery, and crop varieties to help boost productivity' (National Planning Commission, 2004: ix).

Third, the programme recognized the entrepreneurial culture of the country as an advantage that could be harnessed. Hence, in addition to privatizing government owned enterprises, it also pledged to create an enabling environment to stimulate the growth of homegrown small and medium scale industries. It noted that the manufacturing sector had been stagnant and pledged to promote polices that would harness the abundant entrepreneurial spirit of the population to boost diversification through manufacturing. As it puts it:

> The overall strategy is to diversify the productive base of the economy away from oil and to foster market-oriented, private sector-driven economic development with strong local participation. The goal is to develop an indigenous entrepreneurial class capable of competing in a global market in which technology and skills play dominant roles.
>
> (National Planning Commission, 2004: 67)

The document observed in several places that one of the most important barriers to the development of the non-oil productive sector was the binding policy and infrastructural constraints that hinder enterprise. Accordingly, the document expressed the need to invest heavily in infrastructural development, especially building roads and providing electricity.

Social and human development

Despite clearly stating that macroeconomic stabilization was its overriding priority, the programme made copious reference to the importance of social development and the need for this sector to be given prime attention. In fact the document suggested that one of the key ways in which NEEDS was different from previous economic strategies in the country was that it 'relies on a holistic view of social economic challenges facing Nigeria and offers a multi-pronged approach to tackling them' (National Planning Commission, 2004: xiv). It notably entitled the social development pillar of the programme a 'social charter or bargain'. Following this, the document declared that 'every Nigerian has the right to adequate water and sanitation, nutrition, clothing, shelter, basic education and health care as well as physical security and the means of making a living' (ibid.: xv). It proceeded to assert that 'meeting the needs of our people and nation is the primary aim of the plan for prosperity' and made an audacious declaration of a commitment to 'make poverty a thing of the past in Nigeria' (ibid.: ix).

It lamented that despite the abundance of rich natural resources and an increase in oil revenue since independence, the level of poverty in Nigeria had actually increased. As an example, it noted that while an estimated 27 per cent of Nigerians lived in poverty in 1980 just before the advent of the SAP, the number had gone up to a massive 70 per cent by 1990. It also noted that a situation where seven out of every ten Nigerians lived on less than US $1 a day in midst of oil wealth was totally unacceptable.

The document blames the wide incidence of poverty in the country on many causes including poor resource and economic management, lack of basic services, such as clean water, education and health care, unequal economic opportunity, lack of assets such as lands and credit, and discrimination on the basis of gender, age or disability. Noting that only a comprehensive solution will do, the programme offered a pledge to take a multi-pronged approach to tacking poverty.

More specifically, the programme identified a number of areas of priority. These included job creation (a pledge to create 7 million jobs by 2007); providing affordable housing, improving health care services and strengthening the skill base through quality education and appropriate vocational training. Two flagship policies proposed were the creation of a National Health Insurance Scheme and Blood Transfusion Service and the implementation of the newly passed Universal Basic Education law. Interestingly, the document, in the language of the World Bank and apparently reflecting the ancestry of the main authors also talked about an intention to create a set of social safety net programmes to prevent people from becoming poor or poorer. These included saving and insurance schemes for the poor, access to credit, adult education, prevention and control of HIV/AIDS, and providing agricultural extension services. Furthermore, it recognized the need to invest in manpower development crucial to policy implementation and fostering development.

Building local capacity and institutions

Ineffective institutions and bad governance have long been widely seen as the most potent barriers against socio-economic development in Nigeria (Ake, 1995; Fagbadebo, 2007). Preposterous degrees of inefficiency, contract inflation, kickbacks, and diversion of funds, false declarations, ineptitude, favouritism and similar vices are all common characteristics of the Nigerian institution. So pervasive and widely internalized are these vices that the Nigerian government and public service have been variously described as 'a powerful mandarin' (Kew, 2006), a 'predatory monster or a gangster' (Ayittery, 2006; Lewis, 1996), a 'baneful structure' (Fagbadebo, 2007), and as perpetually 'besieged by a multitude of hostility forces' (Ake, 1995). 'Nigerian factor' – a euphemism for corruption and institutional ineptitude – is a well-known phrase in both public and private circles, and by consensus, the most important reason why the country does not work. Even President Obasanjo himself, once, in his address to the parliament, described Nigerian public

80 *Nigeria*

offices as long standing 'show-cases for the combined evils of inefficiency and corruption' (Obasanjo, 2004: iv).

A popular view had been that weak institutions and inefficient service delivery were the main reasons for the failure of the reform implemented by Obasanjo during his first term in office (LaFraniere, 2005). Determined to tackle this head on, the president, soon after his re-election in 2003, dispatched a service delivery research team to the UK to investigate the British approach to service delivery. Subsequently, Obasanjo and by the advice of then UK Prime Minister Tony Blair set up a committee for public sector reform in Nigeria headed by Wendy Thompson, Tony Blair's special adviser on public service reform. Working under the name SERVICOM, Dr Wendy Thomson and her team did a rapid diagnostic of the Nigerian system of service delivery in the public sector and came out with plenty of recommendations for improvement.

The NEEDS document duly recognized the central importance of institutional reform to the success of any socio-economic development agenda in Nigeria. While candidly observing that changing the entrenched culture of inefficiency and corruption 'is a colossal task' (National Planning Commission, 2004: xix, xx), the document noted that the National Orientation Agency and its state-level counterparts would work to 're-instil the virtues of honesty, hard work, selfless service moral rectitude and patriotism' (ibid.: ix) across all cadres of Nigerian institution. It promised to strengthen and modernize the anti-corruption institutions to ensure 'that graft and corruption will be punished' (ibid.: ix). Furthermore, it pledged to encourage organizations to adopt and publish formal codes of ethics that would foster the culture of excellence.

The NEEDS document noted that corruption was 'practically institutionalized' in Nigeria mainly because past governments assumed control of major sources of national income rather than concentrating on delivering essential public services. The result, it said, was that the state soon became mostly a distributor of largesse and a money source to be controlled through do or die politics. The remedy proposed was radical restructuring to achieve a minimal state through deregulation, privatization and liberalization. The aim it said was to make government smaller and stronger and transform it from a 'haven of corruption to an institution that spurs development and serves the people' (ibid.: xi).

Finally, NEEDS stressed the importance of building local human capacity to develop the pool of technical expertise required to drive and sustain the county's development. It recognized a need to reduce current high levels of reliance on expatriates and also the importance of increasing the contribution of the local labour force in foreign investments. The document noted that the limited growth of investment and technological innovation placed a major constraint on both the number of jobs and available skill sets in the manufacturing and service sectors. To make progress, NEEDS committed to revamp the educational system so that it could produce and supply the personnel 'required to propel and sustain the NEEDS initiative'. Key policy thrust to this effect included strengthening the country's technological and

Nigeria 81

scientific base, encouraging technical, vocational, and entrepreneurial education as well as investing in information and communication technologies.

Programme ownership

As noted, the government boasted that NEEDS was a HGD strategy. It was claimed to be the people's own plan for prosperity and one which enjoyed the widest possible commitment – from the top echelon of government to the ordinary man in the village. President Obasanjo clearly believed this. In presenting the NEEDS to Nigerians he placed serious emphasis on how glad he was that the plan was uniquely homegrown, saying:

> I am particularly happy that if there is anything like a home-grown programme, NEEDS is it. For the first time, we embarked on an extensive consultative and participatory process involving major stakeholders in the design of NEEDS. It is this national ownership, together with the results already visible that will ensure the sustainability of the NEEDS beyond 2007.
> (Obasanjo, 2004)

Yet, this claim merits some scrutiny. Given that NEEDS was designed under the World Bank/IMF Poverty Reduction Strategy Papers (PRSPs) and, mostly financed by loans from these institutions (and other International Development Agencies) a close look at the relationship between these institutions and Nigerian stakeholders is necessary to determine the extent of ownership. We know that the initiation of the development framework was by the presidency, even though the direction had some foreign input. We also know that the crafting of the programme was by an economic team of mostly government ministers led by the finance minister Ngozi Okonjo-Iweala. However, it happens that the finance minister was also the World Bank vice-president at the time. This suggests that a definite statement on the true ownership of NEEDS might be questionable. Luckily however, one is not condemned to a state of endless speculation as Okonjo-Iweala provides some insight in her own narration of the programme process in her book *Reforming the Unreformable*. She writes:

> After completing the first draft, I invited comments and inputs from team members ... and the President's review and comment ... I presented the plan first to a joint UK technical team from the Department of International Development and the Treasury, the ministers and the Prime Minister Tony Blair. The Prime Minister Tony Blair also invited the World Bank President Jim Wolfensohn to the meeting to get his view on Nigerian reforms.
> (Okonjo-Iweala, 2012: 13)

This account not only appears to fly in the face of the claim that the NEEDS was a people's plan, it also appears to suggest, in fact, that the Nigerian

82 *Nigeria*

people had little say in deciding the content. Okonjo-Iweala goes on in her account to say that it was after these meetings that the idea of reaching out to other local stakeholder was suggested by a member of the economic team, Charles Soludo, who opined that 'It would be good to reach out to the academic community, the private sector, civil society, government employees and other stakeholders and involve them in the task' (ibid.: 14).

It was obvious that the priority of the team was to obtain the approval of the international stakeholders rather than the local ones. In fact, according to Okonjo-Iweala, it had to be approved and endorsed by the international finance institutions, including the World Bank, IMF and Department of International Development who also monitored NEEDS' implementation. It also appears that in relating with the limited stakeholders involved, the emphasis was on 'marketing' the programme rather than permitting unfettered criticism and input. Even the government controlled National Assembly as it seems merely rubber stamped it while the states and local government were mandated to adopt the programme.

Literature suggests that the degree of external involvement in the policy framework is often dependent on the strength of the government and institution capacity in a country (Awal, 2012; Tsikata, 2001). An analysis of development effectiveness and the relationship between donor agencies and Nigeria by Monye (2010), shows that the existence of weak and ineffective systems in borrowing countries almost compels donors to get more involved in the policy process to strengthen institutional capacity. In the case of Nigeria, it appears, it was the government that was keener on seeking external involvement and affirmation.

From the foregoing, one can strongly suggest that NEEDS was essentially an incarnation of the PRSP. Its main goals were to simultaneously justify and fulfil the requirement for IMF and World Bank loans. It was a document crafted by a few technocrats with a subsequent invitation to other sectors and stakeholder to endorse it (National Planning Commission, 2004: 5; Okonjo-Iweala, 2012). Even though the programme was drafted by Nigerian bureaucrats, it was a World Bank/IMF macroeconomic framework requirement for Highly Indebted Poor Countries (HIPCs). It was adopted by the Nigerian Federal Government on behalf of Nigeria with the watchful eyes and advice of the International Development Agencies. Okonjo-Iweala (2012: 16) argues that 'Nigerian NEEDS was the only framework that was completely accepted by the World Bank/IMF as PRSP framework for the country without any change'. Notwithstanding that Nigeria is one of the least dependent countries in Africa on external loans and aid, Nigerian has internalized policy rent and tended to adopt a Bretton Woods framework rather than looking within to develop a plan that would cater for the country. Hence, despite claims of having crafted an exemplar HGD model, NEEDS struggles to fulfil the key essence of homegrown development approach as conceptualized in Chapter 3.

Implementation and outcomes

Previous development plans in Nigeria have suffered because of poor implementation planning and process (Anger, 2010; Mambula, 2002; Ogwumike, 2002). The problem is so endemic that extant literature has widely discussed what Ikpeze, Soludo, and Elekwa (2004) call the 'implementation failure in Nigeria'. NEEDS acknowledged this problem, confessed that 'Nigeria's experience has been one of formulating good plans, policies, programmes, and projects and then failing to achieve objectives because of ineffective implementation – or no implementation' (National Planning Commission, 2004: 104). Determined to avoid this trap, the document proceeded to set out an elaborate arrangement to ensure effective project implementation.

Institutions listed as closely involved in the NEEDS implementation include the National Planning Commission (NPC), the National Council on Development Planning/Joint Planning Board, Line Ministries and public enterprises, the Ministry of Finance and the Central Bank. Others include an Independent Monitoring Committee, a special Service Delivery Unit, and the National Economic Council. Close coordination among these institutions was envisaged. In addition, the institutional framework also involved close coordination between the federal, state and local government coordinated in part by the NPC and in part by the Independent Monitoring Committee. Furthermore, provision was made for a peer review mechanism involving the private sector, labour, civil society, private–public enterprises, donor community and others. The development plan also looked forward to a set of detailed sectoral plans and strategies coordinated by relevant ministries, the NPC, state government and other stakeholders. In terms of activities and outputs, NEEDS lists a raft – including quarterly reviews and reports, periodic report presentations to the President and the National Assembly, regular postings of updates on the Nigerian Economic Website, regular summary briefings to be widely distributed to ordinary Nigerians through the print and electronic media. The document ends with stating that implementation needs to be rigorous and persistence as '*half measures yield not half results but often failure*' (National Planning Commission, 2004: 103; emphasis in the original).

Nigeria's economy has been growing at an average annual rate of 7.0 per cent since 2000. This represents about one per cent growth higher than the annual target of 6.0 per cent. This growth rate is clearly impressive especially in the context of the damping effect of the global economic recession. A 2007 report from the IMF indicates that Nigeria has experienced growth in almost every sector following the implementation of NEEDS. According to the report, annual average growth in the oil sector between 2004 and 2006 was 0.23 per cent as against the 0.0 per cent projected within the same period. Growth in the non-oil sector has been equally impressive with 8.2 per cent achieved compared to the 8.0 per cent targeted.

Many agree that remarkable progress has been made in achieving the macroeconomic stabilization objectives set out in NEEDS. Through astute

84 *Nigeria*

management and leadership skills, Okonjoo-Iwela and her economic team managed to impose a tight fiscal and monetary regime that yielded positive results on many fronts. Public spending went down from 47.0 per cent in 2001 to 35.4 per cent in 2004. The budget was turned from a deficit of 4.5 per cent of GDP in 2003 to a surplus of 7.7 per cent GDP in 2004. And inflation came down from 18.5 per cent in 2001 to 10.1 per cent in 2005. As a result, the government had enough finance and critically the credibility to arrange a series of favourable debt restructuring and payment plans with its foreign creditors. Between 2003 and 2006 Nigeria paid back about US $12.4 billion and enjoyed a total debt relief of about US $18 billion. This led to a fall from over US $30 billion to just about US$ 5 billion in external debt stock. Similarly, the domestic debt, owed to contractors and civil service pensioners, which constituted about 12 per cent of GDP in 2005 was paid off (IMF, 2008; Okonjo-Iweala and Osafo-Kwaako, 2007).

Another major area of success was the banking sector reform. Here, a set of new rules and standards was enforced resulting in the growth of market capitalization from N 285.8 billion in 1996 to N 2.9 trillion in 2005. This in turn resulted in growth in the confidence of private and foreign investors. Consequently, foreign direct investment (FDI) increased by a huge proportion, rising from US $1.866 billion in 2004 to US $4.8 billion in 2006. Okonjo-Iweala (2007: 7, 19) indicates that 116 government enterprises were privatized from 1999 to 2006. It is also claimed that by far the most impactful was the privatization of the telecommunication industry which has resulted in an increase in the telephone lines from 500,000 landlines in 2001 to currently over 120 million GSM lines.

The government also attempted to implement significant governance and institutional reforms as promised by NEEDS. In recognition of the pervasive and paralyzing impact of corruption in the system, the government set up two institutions to help fight corruption. One is the Independent Corrupt Practices and other Related Offences Commission (ICPC) and the other is the Economic and Financial Crime Commission (EFCC). Both institutions were given a wide mandate to investigate, prosecute and punish offenders regardless of how highly placed they might be. Another major initiative was the creation of a Budget Monitoring and Price Intelligence Unit, which reviews, oversees, and certifies government contracts to ensure value for money. This mechanism which is commonly known as 'due process', has promoted a more open and transparent approach to contract tendering which has helped to stem corruption and waste. According to Ngozi Okonjo-Iweala (2007: 18), the due process mechanism has helped to save the Nigerian government over N200 billion (about US $1.5 billion) since its introduction in 2001. As a means of enhancing transparency in government disbursement, the government started a monthly publication which detailed the shares of Federal account released to all the 36 states and 774 local governments in the country.

However, while the report card of NEEDS shows decent marks in macroeconomic stabilization areas, the record is not impressive with respect to poverty reduction and human and social development. Unemployment has remained high with the annual unemployment rate growing at 16 per cent since 2006 (Fapohunda, 2013: 236). Investment in education and health services has remained low. The consequence of enduring low investment in education is poor quality of education in the country which directly correlates with poverty and a high mortality rate of 94.4 per 1,000 births. Incidentally, the rise in the unemployment rate is attributed to the aforementioned fiscal discipline and the progressive shrinking of the number of public jobs associated with the goal of achieving a leaner government. Poverty also remained at an unacceptably high level. Records show that poverty in Nigeria, as of 2011, is over 70 per cent. In a study of 81 countries on the new poverty and hunger index by Gentilini and Webb (2008), Nigeria was ranked 73rd on both the poverty and hunger scales.

Although the programme articulated well some of the human and social development challenges in the country, it lacked a sense of devotion to concrete strategies and mechanisms for turning them around. For example, in the case of HIV/AIDS, it promised to 'ensure that at least 20 per cent of all local government areas offer home-based care to people living with HIV/AIDS by 2007' without indicating how this would be carried out. This pattern runs through the document. In the same vein despite rhetoric about commitment to wide-scale infrastructural development, the government failed to make its many promised deliveries in this regard. This has led many to assert that instead of ameliorating poverty, NEEDS had actually made matters worse (Ja'afaruBambale, 2011: 20).

Nigeria: the crippled giant

A final verdict on how homegrown NEEDS is and its performance as a national socio-economic policy is somewhat difficult. It is beyond doubt that the new democratic government that came into power in 1999 inherited a comatose economy and a dysfunctional system. It has always been known that transforming the system was going to be a long and difficult task. At the same time, government achievements in reforming the banks, stabilizing the national currency, reducing its budget deficit, paying off its debts, and increasing savings and FDI are not feats that can be scorned at even by the fiercest critics.

However, there are also many who will argue fiercely that as a transformative socio-economic policy designed to transform Nigeria and create prosperity for the Nigerian people, NEEDS has been a colossal failure. For one, it is obvious that while the core ideas may have originated from some external stakeholder and a few learned and well-meaning Nigerians – as opposed to being completely imposed by Western institutions – the plan did not have anywhere as much public input as is claimed by its architects. Hence statements like 'it is your plan: seize it with both hands' (Obasanjo, 2004: iii) and 'it really is the people's plan for prosperity' (National Planning Commission, 2004: xii) are, to say the least, gross exaggerations.

86 *Nigeria*

But perhaps even more important is that the plan failed to deliver on its promise to lift the Nigerian masses out of poverty. Let us recall what the programme claimed as its four main goals: (i) wealth creation, (ii) employment generation, (iii) poverty reduction, and (iv) value re-orientation. However, since the inception of the NEEDS programme, poverty and unemployment rates have been on the rise. A key target of the plan was to increase average per capita consumption by at least 2.0 per cent per year and to create 7 million jobs by 2007. However, despite Nigeria's enviable oil wealth, the human development index (HDI) of the country remains at 0.459 (UNDP, 2010). On the basis of this figure Nigeria ranks 156 out 187 in the world and lower than the Sub-Saharan Africa average. If one judges the programme on the central objectives it set for itself, then it will be hard to escape the conclusion that it was an abysmal failure.

A major policy thrust of the transformational agenda expressed in NEEDS was the determination to diversify the economy away from oil and solid mineral exploration in order to cushion it from a cyclic boom and bust in oil prices. In doing so it was promised that particular attention would be paid to agriculture, industry and local small and medium enterprises. However, to date, the economy remains disproportionately oil-based and effort at diversification has at best been tokenistic. Precious little effort went into revitalizing various cash produces like groundnut, cocoa, palm oil rubber and cotton that disappeared in the 1970s as all eyes turned to oil. Although the entrepreneurial disposition of the population was identified by NEEDS, there were not specific policjes devoted to harness this unique competitive advantage. In fact, local manufacturing continued to suffer due to the harsh environment that increased the cost of doing business and restrained business performance. Obstacles include acute power shortages, multiple taxations, high interest rates, poor infrastructure and inefficient port administration (Amanze-Nwachukwu, 2007). The result was that many local entrepreneurs and some foreign companies (e.g. Dunlop, Michelin and Pirelli) were forced to move their businesses either partially or totally to Ghana with the country witnessing a decline of more than 45 per cent of industrial capacity utilization and the closure of more than 60 per cent of industrial companies (Amanze-Nwachukwu, 2007).

NEEDS noted wide scale infrastructural deficiency as major constraints to business development and the economy in general. It promised to invest heavily in infrastructure especially electricity, transport, and water. There is ample evidence that government followed through with its promise to invest. But sadly, making investment does not necessarily translate into getting results. Despite huge investment in the power sector there has been no improvement in electricity supply in the country. In 2007, a supply of about 4,500 megawatts daily was recorded, but this had decreased to 3,500 megawatts daily by October 2012. To put this into perspective, Nigeria generates 3,500 megawatts for over 150 million people per day, while South Africa generates 45,000 megawatts per day for 45 million people. Nigerian's 2 kilowatts per hour per capita is lower than the 3,000 kilowatts per hour per capita in South Africa and lower than the average of 456 kilowatts per hour per capita for sub-Saharan Africa. It has been stated that for Nigeria to meet its quota for electricity generation, it would need to invest US $3.5 billion annually for the next ten years (Olugbenga, Jumah and Phillips, 2013).

Unfortunately, failure in the rehabilitation of the electricity infrastructure is not an isolated case as similar stories obtain with regards to transportation, water, housing and public institutions. The present government, through Dr Doyin Okupe, the President's spokesman on public affairs, provides a damning verdict on the infrastructural rehabilitation conducted under NEEDS. It says that the current government 'inherited a road transport network that was near total collapse' with virtually all the 'critical economic roads in a state of total or near total disrepair' (Okupe, 2014: 6). It claimed that at the time it took over office from Obasanjo, 'rail transport in Nigeria was … virtually comatose due to a lack of infrastructure and commitment from [previous] government' (ibid.: 5) and moreover that 'none of the 22 federally owned airports in Nigeria had been reformed in any manner for more than thirty years' (ibid.: 6). All of this implies that the heavy investment promised in NEEDS either failed to materialize or happened without producing the expected results. It is understandable that Okupe may be prone to exaggeration to boost the public perception of the government relative to its predecessor but many analysts concur that infrastructural development endeavours, under NEEDS, were a sad tale of woes.

The performance of NEEDS also leaves much to be desired in terms of human and social development. Despite an audacious declaration that at the heart of NEEDS was a 'social charter' to enhance 'the Nigerian people – their health, education, employment, sense of fulfilment, and general well-being' (National Planning Commission, 2004: 28), the government subsequently focused on macroeconomic stabilization while social development was utterly neglected. For instance, despite the country being endowed with abundant water resources, water supply is in critical shortage in many parts of the country and completely depleted in other parts. The problem of water resources is linked to sanitation and proper sewage disposal, which poses serious health concerns, including an increase in water borne diseases such as typhoid. The government introduced a National Water Supply and Sanitation Policy (2000) with the aim of providing access to potable water to at least 60 per cent of the population. However as at 2008, only about 58 per cent of the population had access to water (Akpor and Muchie, 2011: 480); moreover the individual efforts of many who had been frustrated into using their life savings and pensions to dig private boreholes to extract water from underground accounted for a large proportion of this percentage (Demographic and Health Survey (DHS) 2008).

The NEEDS claimed that the government inherited a 'dysfunctional' education system (National Planning Commission, 2004: 10), which is true. However, it also true that the government left the educational system as

88 *Nigeria*

dysfunctional or even more so than they had found it. And this was despite promising a major campaign to revamp the sector by increasing access and quality. According to UNDP (2010), the Nigerian education index is at 0.442, just on par with the African average. While Okinjo-Iweala is proud to draw attention to gross excess crude savings of about US $17.68 billion over the period 2003 to 2006 and a fivefold increase in foreign reserves from US $7.5 billion to about US $38 billion over the same period (Okonjo-Iweala and Kwaako, 2007: 11) investment in education remains far behind the level necessary to promote good quality. Of course, the current government established six new universities, but it provided little resources for the new and old universities, and denied proper autonomy to tertiary education. There has been an increase in private sector involvement in education with several private schools, including universities being established. But the standard of the education system remains very poor and as yet, there is still no mission to reform and create an autonomous body for monitoring the standard and quality of education. The Nigerian education system used to be one of the best in Africa, but now parents who can afford it send their children to Europe and North America to study, while others opt for universities in Ghana. The implication is the reproduction of unproductive and underachieving graduates which is in turn worsening the problem of unemployment.

The programme had a target to increase Nigerian literacy from 57 to 65 per cent by 2007, but this target was not met and Nigeria's literacy rate remained at 57 per cent in 2007, according to the UNDP. This literacy rate also reflects the human developmental divide between the north and south in Nigeria that started during the colonial era. While the literacy rate in the south is above 87 per cent; the north has a literacy rate of about 30 per cent. Evidently, NEEDS did not have an adequate strategy for engaging with religious leaders in the north for reducing illiteracy in the region due to the limited nature of the policy process that lacked consultation. Despite noting a link between technological innovation and economic growth and recognising 'education as the vital transformational tool and a formidable instrument for socioeconomic empowerment' (National Planning Commission, 2004: 35), investment in science and innovation remained poor. Nigeria is not ranked among the top 72 countries in research and development expenditures, meaning that it spends less than US $100 million on research and development. As Otobo rightly points out, it is a piquant irony that a country that aspires to be among the top 20 economies by 2020 was not ranked among the top 72 nations in research and development expenditures in 2010 (Otobo, 2011). In innovation, Nigeria is ranked 88 out of 110 countries.

Since the introduction of SAPs in the 1980s in Nigeria, the emphasis has been on aggressive implementation of fiscal market liberalization and savings. Despite the wide legitimacy this economic management approach enjoys among donor agencies and their ideological demagogues, the practical outcome in improving welfare continues to be highly debatable. It has never translated to economic growth and general development in the country. Although the framework document emphasised reform of every sector as well as improvement in the social charter, the implementation process completely neglected the social charter while focussing on aggressive fiscal and macroeconomic reform.

Finally, in terms of governance and institutional reform – the two main areas long identified as posing the greatest obstacle to development in Nigeria – NEEDS' performance was also miserable. Critical evaluation of NEEDS by many international organizations has shown that by all indicators Nigeria has done little in terms of institutional reform. Corruption still runs rampant in both the public and private sector. Anti-corruption efforts have been at best very selective and at worst a mechanism for hounding and silencing political opposition. For example, after investigating and finding 31 out of the 36 state governors extremely corrupt the EFCC was able to prosecute only one of these officials and then only with the help of the London Metropolitan Police.

The government had suggested that wide scale privatization was the solution to making government leaner and smarter. However, the privatization process lacked transparency and competitive bidding, and the inadequate institutional capacity and regulatory framework have been constantly manipulated by the political leaders. Investigations showed that the political elites, including the former president and vice president, exploited the privatization process to enhance political patronage and enrich their cronies (Adogamhe, 2007; Alechenu and Josiah, 2007; Izibili and Aiya, 2007; Orilade, 2007). The government is yet to account for over two billion US dollars in annual investments since 2000 for the rehabilitation of the power grid even though the electricity problem has become worse in the country. In fact the EFCC estimates that the value of economic and financial crime committed within this period was about 1.2 trillion Nigeria Naira, which is equivalent to about US \$100 billion (Ja'afaruBambale, 2011: 22).

Interestingly, the 'Nigerian factor' or the implementation curse that bedevils the country could already be seen in the elaborate and convoluted implementation framework proposed in NEEDS. With more than nine agencies and government organs listed as responsible for implementation (National Planning Commission, 2004: 105), the process already looked chaotic from the outset, doomed to be trapped in the bureaucratic bottleneck. Such a complicated set up was clearly unnecessary. Duplicating and introducing redundancies was also an irony that flies in the face of the stated goal of improving service and reducing waste. This is also perhaps a clear evidence that the problem is not ignorance of what needs to be done to facilitate development. Rather the major obstacle remains as Ja'afaruBambale (2011: 22) aptly puts it 'at the level of Nigerian leadership where the political will and ethical considerations seems to be lacking'.

Summary

NEEDS claimed to be a homegrown model *par excellence*. This claim turns out to be dubious. Certainly, the country made progress in its macroeconomic

90   *Nigeria*

framework by reforming the banks, stabilizing its currency and reducing its budget deficit. However, these macroeconomic successes did not translate into much positive social development. Economic diversification was not achieved and indigenous enterprise was not promoted. Unemployment is still very high, and efforts to rehabilitate infrastructure have not fared well either. Basic social services such as water, health and education are yet to improve. According to a United Nations Human Development Report (UNDP, 2010), Nigeria is still listed as a low-income country, with no improvement in its HDI. The cost of doing business in Nigeria is astronomically high. This is discouraging not only foreign investors but also local entrepreneurs. According to the International Finance Corporation Doing Business Ranking, Nigeria ranks 133 in the world. This is in comparison to South Africa at 33, Rwanda at 45, Ghana at 64 and Kenya at 121. The OECD (Organisation for Economic Co-operation and Development) analysis of Nigeria's development operational strategies using ten indicators shows that the country scored very poorly in nine out of ten development effectiveness indicators and in its relationship with donor agencies (Monye, 2010). This, to some extent, explains why NEEDS had a very poor outcome, even in those projects supported by donor agencies.

It is clear that while an attempt at public consultation was made, the document remained largely the construction of a few elites heavily influenced by the Washington Consensus ideology. Given the complexity and diversity of the country, lack of widespread consultation was a major flaw. A clear result was that NEEDS failed to recognize local capabilities and strengths. Also, there was no economic strategy for diversification that could lead to more sustainable job generating growth. The implementation of NEEDS was focussed on fiscal prudence, macroeconomic stabilization, privatization, liberalization and deregulation, gaining international approval and acceptance. The social and human development aspect and plight of the poor was hugely neglected, and Nigeria still lacks a comprehensive long term HGD strategy for development. Key to the success of any such strategy will be good leadership and the abundance of political will to tackle the cankerworm of corruption and the dysfunctional public institutions.

6 Kenya
Economic Recovery Strategy and Vision 2030

From Ghana and Nigeria in West Africa we now move to East Africa where we focus on Kenya, a country fondly called 'the pride of Africa and the cradle of mankind' in reference to the largest collection of human related fossils found there. Like most African countries, Kenya made a start at introducing and implementing a homegrown development (HGD) strategy based on the philosophy of African socialism. The country however subsequently went through a period of political and social upheaval that halted its initial development process and deteriorated the socio-economic environment. By 1980 the economy was virtually crippled with high levels of inflation, unemployment and budget deficit. In response, the government, with support from the World Bank and IMF, introduced a structural adjustment programme (SAP) and economic liberalization and reform programmes in the 1980s and 1990s respectively to address the socio-economic structural problems. However, the reforms were of little success due to political instability and lack of sensitivity to socio-economic and historical imperatives. Unemployment and an increase in poverty as well as economic decline were compounded by the spread of HIV/AIDS.

In 2002, for the first time since 1964, Kenya had a multi-party presidential election which resulted in a coalition government headed by Mwai Kibaki. Following this, a new transformation programme – Economic Recovery Strategy for Wealth Creation (ERS) was introduced in 2003 as a four-year blueprint to addressing the social and economic malaise that had been crippling the country over the previous three decades. At the end of the ERS in 2007, and following the re-election of Kibaki as president, Kenya developed a long term framework known as Vision 2030 with the aspiration of transforming Kenya to a middle income economy. The analysis in this chapter focuses on these two programmes – the ERS and Vision 2030. Drawing from the work done in the conceptual chapter we will explore the extent of *indigeneity* of both programmes and how well they have performed in driving the development process in Kenya.

Homegrown development in Kenya at independence

Kenya was colonized by the British in the late nineteenth century and because of its climate and wildlife-rich savannah grassland, attracted some settlers that

92   *Kenya*

subsequently appropriated land from the African population for both arable and pastoral farming. The number of white settlers increased after the Second World War following severe food shortages in Britain in the immediate aftermath of the war. Pressured by the need to produce for the war-ravaged empire and backed by land-discriminatory laws and state force, the settlers engaged in further widespread land appropriation, brutally repressing local populations in the process. This created a situation where the vast proportion of agricultural production, which formed the main basis of the economy, was in the hands of white settlers (Meredith, 2005; Stichter, 1982).

When Kenya gained independence from the British in 1962, it inherited a relatively viable agricultural sector but also a fragile society with deep seated ethnic politics (Meredith, 2005). Ethnic politics had grown deep and fractious in the pre independence days because the colonial administrations were using land allocation as the main resource to gain patronage and political support from various rival ethnic groups (Branch, 2009; Meredith, 2005; Mutua, 2008).

When Jomo Kenyatta became President in 1963, he appointed Tom Mboya as the Minister of Economic Development who set out a vision for HGD built on a unique concept of African egalitarian societal development – 'Harambee'. The core of Harambee philosophy was communal service, self-help, investment in human capability and opportunity creation. The idea created optimism among the people and a kind of synergy between the various groups; but more importantly, it established a social contract that gave many a sense of inclusiveness in the affairs of government. Under Harambee, citizen voice and participation were encouraged especially in areas that pertained to people's immediate welfare. A key aspect of Harambee was the creation of several grass-roots cooperative organizations which helped to encourage development in rural areas.

In the first development plan entitled *African Socialism and its Application to Planning in Kenya*, Tom Mboya set out a vision for how Kenya would achieve sustained and self-reliant economic growth based on the African brand of social egalitarianism. He said:

> We declared that our country would develop on the basis of the concepts and philosophy of Democratic African Socialism. We rejected both Western Capitalism and Eastern Communism and chose for ourselves a policy of positive non-alignment ... Our task remains to try and achieve these two goals without doing harm to the economy itself and within the declared aims of our society ... When all is said and done we must settle down to the job of building the Kenya nation ... Let all the people of our country roll up their sleeves in a spirit of self-help to create the true fruits of *UHURU*. THIS IS WHAT WE MEAN BY *HARAMBEE*.
>
> (Mboya, 1965: 17; emphasis in the original)

It is clear that the founding fathers of Kenyan independence had a vision of development that was based on harnessing local imperatives and building

Kenya 93

local capacity as opposed to importing external models. Tom Mboya, who was tasked with the job of crafting the first development model, explained the thinking behind African socialism and how it translated to the programmes and priorities in the plan, saying there were three key principles: 1) It must draw on the best African traditions. 2) It must be adaptable to new and rapidly changing circumstances. 3) It must not rest for its success on a satellite relationship with any other country or group of countries. Continuing he said:

> When I talk of African Socialism I refer to those proven codes of conduct in the African societies which have, over the ages, conferred dignity on our people and afforded them security regardless of their station in life. I refer to universal charity, which characterised our societies and I refer to the African's thought processes and cosmological ideas, which regard man not as a social means, but as an end and entity in the society.
>
> (Mboya, 1963: 17)

As said, community cooperatives were central in delivering the vision encapsulated in Harambee. However, in addition to the cooperatives, Kenya also carried out nationalization of some sectors of the economy, especially the agricultural sector through land distribution, and at the same time encouraged foreign investment and welcomed foreign corporations (Swainson, 1980). Some agrarian reforms were implemented that included the redistribution of Highlands from colonial settlers to locals, especially the emerging African elites and some landless peasants. The government introduced Import Substitution Industrialization (ISI) policies and facilitated rapid expansion of commercial farming (Holmquist, Weaver and Ford, 1994). These measures helped to increase expansion of commercial farming and created an African middle class. Agrarian reform was further facilitated through the Harambee framework at the local level by extending credit and services to small-holders.

The framework also set its goals to focus on the promotion of universal education, health care and elimination of illiteracy, which advanced health care infrastructure from the 1960s to the 1980s. Furthermore, the government also encouraged economic diversification, investing in manufacturing and value added goods (Branch, 2009; Holmquist, et al., 1994). Kenya attracted tourism and foreign investment more than its neighbours and other African countries, which helped in the economic expansion. The country also benefited hugely from Western foreign aid during the Cold War because the West saw Kenya as anti-communist, whereas its neighbour, Tanzania, was thought to be leaning towards socialism (Dunning, 2004; Whitfield and Fraser, 2009). Overall, Kenya experienced decent social and economic expansion during the first two decades of independence, and seemed to have performed better than most African countries at the time. Average growth rate in the first two decades was about 7 per cent (Jerven, 2011) and the GDP was on a par with or higher than some Asian countries such as Malaysia, Thailand and South Korea.

94 *Kenya*

But it was not all smooth-sailing for the country. First, despite agreement that government would follow the path of African socialism to growth, there were significant differences between two of the top ruling party's elites – Oginga Odinga and Tom Mboya – which created tension and contradictions. Despite both subscribing to African socialism as the guiding principle for Kenyan development the two men had different interpretations of how it should work in practice. Mboya's vision was influenced by the modernization theory of development, that external technical assistance was a necessary complement to social engineering in the effort to stimulate growth and solve Kenya's social problems (Mboya, 1963). Odinga, for his own part, linked political freedom far more strongly with economic self-reliance and therefore favoured a more socialist model which was far more sceptical of external technical and financial assistance (Odinga and Odinga, 1967).

More important in derailing Harambee was the fact that the new political elite sought to consolidate power through the same tactics previously used by the colonial administration to weaken independence agitations. Like the colonial administrations before them, they resorted to the allocation of public land as a means of securing rent, patronage and gaining or retaining political support from various ethnic groups (Branch, 2009; Meredith, 2005). In addition political opponents were also hounded and brutally repressed. As cronyism increased, the aggregate success recorded in economic growth did not spill over to the rural and urban sector that made up the majority of the population. The Harambee-inspired cooperatives, which had proven so popular, were hijacked by local elites that used the cooperatives as a ladder for political and economic power instead of service and promotion of communal support and self-help (Hunt, 1984). Hence, the concept helped in creating African petty bourgeoisies at the local level, with ethnic cleavages that were encouraged by the government due to the ethnic bias of Kenyatta that favoured his own Kukuyu group (Hunt, 1984; Leo, 1984; Livingstone, 1986; Migot-Adholla, 1984).

In fact, it is fair to say that although Kenya sought a HGD approach, it never really cut the umbilical cord that tied it to the colonial political economy nor was it ever consistent in the implementation of the programme. Economically, Kenya was built on commodity agricultural goods with little diversification of the economy, hence the country was at the mercy of the international commodity price and over-dependent on foreign aid. Despite the growth of the manufacturing sector, especially when compared to other sectors, it was not developed enough to contribute to Kenya's exports as the country still depended on commodity exports as a major source of revenue. The Harambee concept that would have bridged the rural urban dichotomy while developing local capital was not well implemented. The result was the stagnation and then steady decline of the economy beginning from the late 1970s. As dissidence grew, the government turned even more authoritarian and resorted to a series of ludicrous constitutional amendments to gain more power. By 1980, the ratio of budget deficit to GDP had risen to US $317 million, and current account debt rose to US $878 million (Morrison, 2007: 125). Economic woes were further worsened by a food shortage that was caused by the 1980s' drought, escalating inflation and poverty, and the general decrease in the living standard and wellbeing.

Kenya's second phase of development was therefore the introduction of Structural Adjustment Programmes (SAPs) in 1980 making it one of the first countries in Africa to implement the World Bank/IMF imposed programmes (O'Brien and Ryan, 2001). Not surprisingly, as with many other countries, SAPs created more problems that they solved in Kenya. With their emphasis on macroeconomic stabilization and growth, while ignoring social and human capital development, poverty, unemployment and hardship all worsened in the time of their implementation. Moreover, the so called financial assistance that came with SAPs were loans that left the country in more debt after 20 years of trying to implement comprehensive SAPs as a condition to obtain loans from these institutions. For example, according to the Central Bureau of Statistics (1999), Kenya's debt grew by 362 per cent (from Kshs36.7 billion at the end of the 1990s to Kshs 169.4 billion by 1998. Official figures indicate that interest rate in debts were sometimes as high as 25 per cent. During the 1997/98 financial year interest payments on domestic debt alone amounted to 15 per cent of the total government expenditure (Central Bureau of Statistics, 1999). It was therefore clear by the time the first coalition government came into power in 2002 that a new direction of economic growth had to be charted.

Post-2002 development policies: the Economic Restructuring Strategy and Vision 2030

In 2002, Kenya transitioned from a one party to a multiparty system and held its first multiparty elections since independence. Since then the country has initiated two main post-SAP economic development frameworks. The first was a midterm development plan entitled Economic Recovery Strategy (ERS) which was anchored on the IMF/World Bank pro-poor growth framework. ERS was introduced and run by Mwai Kibaki during his first term in office as president. The second and more recent plan was Kenya Vision 2030 which was introduced in 2008 to coincide with Kibaki's second term in office. As the name implies, the Vision is intended to run until 2030 with a five-year review inbuilt. Since the approach adopted in the two programmes differ only in very minor details, they will be treated together in the proceeding sections.

The Economic Recovery Strategy for Wealth Creation (ERS) was introduced by the National Rainbow Coalition as a mid-term development blue print in 2003. It was based on the Bretton Woods Institutions' Poverty Reduction Strategy Paper (PRSP). Given Kenya's decades of economic decline it is not surprising that the focus of the ERS was on stimulating economic recovery and achieving growth. The strategy was anchored around four major pillars covering economic, political and social dimensions. The

96 *Kenya*

first pillar was to stabilize the macroeconomic environment with a specific target of increasing revenue to above 21 per cent of the GDP by expanding tax to include the informal sector and restructuring expenditure to be based on achieved growth. In an attempt to stabilize the macroeconomic environment, the government also emphasized deficit financing from non-domestic sources and the introduction of monetary policy that would reduce inflation. The second fundamental pillar was strengthening the institutions of governance through various reforms of the public sector, national security, law and order, building capacity and enhancing efficiency. The reforms were to underscore the centrality of the rule of law as opposed to rule of man in establishing good governance in the country (Government of Kenya, 2003). The third pillar was the rehabilitation and expansion of physical infrastructure with a specific focus on transportation. This would be carried out through the implementation of the so-called Road 2000 programme to improve the rural road network. Rehabilitation also included railway and telecommunications. Another key priority was improving access to energy. The fourth pillar according to the ERS policy document was on human capital development through investment in health and education to enhance productive and economic performance.

Over the course of the programme, Kenya was able to improve the economy as the GDP grew from a low of 0.6 per cent in 2002 to 6.1 per cent in 2006 (Kenya Vision 2030, 2010: 10). As a result, the Vision 2030 introduced in 2008 was built on the foundation of ERS. The Vision is a long term development framework covering the period from 2008 to 2030 but broken down into midterm programmes. The primary long-term goal of Vision 2030 is to create a globally competitive and prosperous nation with high quality of life by 2030. This goal is broken down into three pillars – economic, social and political components and aspirations.

Broad stakeholder consultation and participation

The introduction of the ERS and Vision 2030 were both coordinated by the National Economic Social Council (NESC). The NESC made attempts in both cases to elicit contributions from stakeholders but the consultative process was far broader in the case of Vision 2030 with McKinsey & Company serving as one of the international consultants (Linehan, 2007).

It would appear that the pressure on the NESC to broaden the consultative process came from both above and below. The programme document makes clear that then-president Kibaki strongly advocated for the consultation of ordinary Kenyans and stakeholders so as to obtain an in-depth understanding of the country's development challenges (Kenya Vision 2030, 2010: 3). At the same time pressure for consultation came from growing agitation from NGOs that were demanding more active involvement. The NESC sought to achieve civil society participation through NGO-organized workshops in rural and urban areas. In addition the Kenya Joint Assistance Strategy (KJAS) was introduced in 2007 to increase broader participation of stakeholders and civil society.

After a series of consultations, the National Vision Steering Committee coordinated more workshops for local and international experts from research institutions, private and public sector stakeholders, for the purpose of synthesizing the findings. The process also involved visiting various firms, farmers, informal and formal businesses, and investors, and gathering information from the nine provincial forums. After the first phase of the consultation process, the NESC led the core team made up of selected permanent secretaries and other stakeholders for information dissemination at the district level for the final recommendation.

In addition to the active participation of local stakeholders, the government also made an attempt to engage international development partners and Kenyans in the diaspora. The consultation process also included interviews with key stakeholders and investors, and sector-based problem solving workshops (Thugge, Ndung'u and Otieno, 2011). Recent review of the KJAS acknowledges that while a decent attempt was made there was less involvement of the civil society and the public than could have been achieved (Tomlinson, 2011). Moreover, there is also some doubt that public opinions were taken very seriously given that the major decisions were eventually made by a few government bureaucrats and foreign partners. According to Tomlinson (2011: 64), even parliamentary involvement was limited to rubber-stamping as they were not informed about negotiation of mutually agreed conditions between government and donor officials.

Economic diversification and sensitivity to local imperatives

As noted earlier, the goal of the ERS was mainly economic recovery. This would seem right given the dire state of the economy in 2003 when the coalition government came into office. We also noted that the ERS appeared to have achieved its objective with the GDP rising from 0.6 per cent in 2002 to 6.1 per cent in 2007. Having stabilized the economy with the ERS, at least in a relative sense, the government sketched a far more ambitious plan in the Vision document, which, as said, was to achieve a proper development take-off. One of the immediate targets set in a bid to achieve this goal was to increase the GDP growth to 10 per cent by 2012, through the expansion of six sectors – tourism, agriculture, wholesale and retail trade, manufacturing, ICT and Business Process Outsourcing (BPO), and financial services. Kenya does not yet produce oil but the country is known for its agriculture and tourism advantages. In the years following independence, agriculture, tourism, and manufacturing were the major contributors to the economy. Manufacturing grew in post-independence but the momentum was not sustained. As one of the tourism capitals of Africa, Vision 2030 aims to leverage this advantage by rapidly expanding its tourism industry. Specifically, it sets a target to quadruple tourism contribution to the GDP by increasing international visitors

98   *Kenya*

from 1.6 million in 2006 to 3 million by 2012. The document outlines a raft of steps that will be taken to achieve this including building three new resorts and increasing hotel beds.

Agriculture is undoubtedly the foundation of Kenyan economy. According to the Kenya National Bureau of Statistics (2012), agriculture contributes more than 60 per cent of the country's total export, accounts for 80 per cent of employment especially in the rural areas, about 30 per cent of the GDP and 45 per cent of government revenue. If there is an area in which Kenya has an economic advantage it is in the agricultural sector. However, the agricultural sector's contribution to the economy has been declining since the 1980s. For example its contribution declined from 22 per cent of the GDP in 2000 to 17 per cent in 2003. Many countries in the West such as the UK and USA started off as agricultural economies. Similarly, the success of agricultural reform and investment was an important catalyst for Chinese development. It is commendable, although hardly surprising, that Vision 2030 recognized the significance of agriculture and the need for further investment in this area in achieving the objective of long term economic growth in the country. Under the Medium Term Plan (MTP), it set a target of 6–8 per cent growth to be achieved by reducing the cost of farm inputs, improving farm prices, and irrigation of an additional 1.2 million hectares of land for crop production. Attention was also given to horticulture, fisheries, industrial crops and other subsectors. However, the downside is that Vision 2030 was silent about the land monopoly that was introduced during the colonial era and the necessary fundamental reforms required to address this structural injustice. The Vision barely mentions land policy without a clear outline of concrete steps for tackling the problem. Furthermore, there is little recognition or discussion about needed investment in technological development to advance the sector.

The manufacturing sector accounts for about 12 per cent of the GDP and is the second highest employer of labour after agriculture. Kenya has an advantage in manufacturing in that it boasts several agricultural raw materials that can be translated to intermediate value-added goods using low technology. Kenya's coastal location also provides the advantage of access to export markets through East African integration. Historically, however, these advantages have not been exploited and therefore the sector remains at a rudimentary level.

Vision 2030 served as a notice of the government's intent to remedy this situation by introducing two flagship projects to boost the manufacturing sector. First was the development of a strategy to establish two economic clusters, each consisting of closely related industries. The second was the establishment and development of five small and medium enterprise industrial parks. There was also a plan to reduce import in some areas by 25 per cent, grow market share of some produce from 7 to 15 per cent and attract at least 10 big strategic investors in the agro-processing industries by 2012. As a regional power and a pull for tourism and investment, Kenya has an

Kenya 99

economic advantage in the service sector and is promoting it with special attention to and investment in the expansion of Business Processing Offshore (BPO). This includes providing business services via the internet to international markets, particularly the UK, Canada and the USA. The aim is to attract IT investors and multinationals and the goal is to set up a BPO Park in Nairobi and create about 7,500 BPO jobs by 2012.

Building local capacity and institutions

Lack of capacity is a major constraint faced by many African countries. Therefore any development framework that does not prioritize investing in and building local capacity is unlikely to succeed. Moreover, local capacity legitimizes local ownership. A framework that is mostly crafted and implemented by external expertise will have serious legitimacy problems even if the reasoning is that the country is relying on external support because it lacks the requisite capacity.

As noted, Vision 2030 clearly states that the country's physical infrastructure such as transport and electricity distribution has been in bad shape, and pledges to invest in road repairs and building of more road networks as well as investing in the energy sector to generate electricity. Like most developing countries Kenya lacks adequate technical capacity and capability. This need is identified in Vision 2030 with a promise that government will invest in building more technical institutions to develop local technical expertise in science and technology. This objective, according to Vision 2030, was to be pursued under five key strategic thrusts:

1 Strengthening of technical capacities and capabilities by placing a strong emphasis on technical learning.
2 Creating a national critical skill development strategy to develop a highly skilled human resource base.
3 Encouraging the intensification of innovation in priority areas by conducting a biannual survey to determine the incidence of innovation and its impediments.
4 Enhancing science, technology and innovation awareness and strengthening performance.
5 Investing in general education to improve the country's literacy rate as well as protecting indigenous knowledge and technology as national heritage.

The government pledged to collaborate with industries to increase investment to Kshs (Kenya Shillings) 37 billion (over US \$420 million) by 2012. An interesting measure mooted in Vision 2030 is the establishment of a scheme to honour innovators through some form of national recognition in order to encourage innovation and other scientific endeavours (Kenya Vision 2030, 2010: 31).

100 *Kenya*

Furthermore, the authors of Vision 2030 recognize the need for public reform to promote good governance and rule of law as a necessary condition for achieving lasting success. Accordingly Vision 2030 proposes a number of reforms, prominent among which are the establishment of an independent Truth, Justice and Reconciliation Commission (TJRC) and a National Cohesion and Integration Commission to promote national unity and a commitment to raise awareness of corruption.

Yet, while these ambitions are lofty, Vision 2030 is generally weak in specifying concrete policies and mechanisms for achieving progress. For example, with respect to corruption it states:

> To strengthen the institutional framework for anti-corruption, ethics and integrity, the National Anti-Corruption awareness campaign will be expanded, as will the capacity of District Anti-Corruption Civilian Oversight Committees to monitor the management of devolved funds and stigmatize corruption.
>
> (Kenya Vision 2030, 2010: 27)

Indeed the need to strengthen the institutional framework to combat corruption is paramount in creating accountability and trust among the citizenry. However, the creation of an anti-corruption campaign and stigmatizing corruption without any concrete mechanism for enforcement and punishment of perpetrators will not go far in combating corruption.

Broad social development

Local imperatives include culture, history, political and social economic realities. Recognizing these local realities helps to deepen the understanding of a country's development challenges. This helps in finding ways of addressing them. Focus on the economy has been the trend of externally driven framework which has mitigated societal and human progress in most developing countries. Vision 2030 recognizes that economic development does not always automatically translate into social development. One of the three pillars of Vision 2030 is dedicated to social development with great emphasis on human resources and capabilities development through health and education, as well as access to clean water, sanitation and enabling environments to prosper. Having identified various challenges including the low percentage of teachers, gender gap in education, poor quality and adequate physical structures for schools, Vision 2030 set its flagship targets as follows: construction of more schools, recruitment of more teachers, a computer supply programme and introducing vouchers to bridge the inequality gap. In the health sector, the target for 2012 included rehabilitation of health facilities, introducing a community-based information system and de-linking the Ministry of Health from service delivery.

Vision 2030's goal is to create 'a just, cohesive and equitable social development in a clean and secure environment' through improved health, education, clean water and sanitation, and rehabilitation of physical infrastructure. This is a service project that demands significant funding and is dependent on the performance of the economy. Hence, we will critically examine the implication of the mixed economic performance in achieving the medium term goal of the social pillar: investing in the people and creating a healthy environment that will produce a better and productive society. In an attempt to improve human development through education, Vision 2030 proposed some measures including the continuation of free primary education and free secondary education that was introduced in 2003.

Ownership of ERS and Vision 2030 policy

Kenya continued its partnership with the Bretton Wood Institutions with the new PRSP framework introduced in 2000 as a conditionality for a loan. This is despite the critical view of the Institutions' framework as a failed policy for development. Following the election that ushered in democratic government in 2003, the government led by the National Rainbow Coalition (NARC), in an attempt to implement their election manifesto, established the National Economic Social Council (NESC) to provide an avenue for the formulation and monitoring of public policy. The NESC carried out a consultation process with various stakeholders that included local and international expertise of different sectors and international donors and partners. Through this process a preliminary document that integrated the PRSP, the NARC election manifesto and the Post-election Action Plan was used as basis for a series of workshops and seminars. The final outcome was approved by the Bretton Wood Institutes as the Kenya PRSP midterm programme known as ERS 2003–2007. Building on the ERS, the Vision 2030 development process was introduced in 2006 and was formally approved by the Bretton Wood Institutions in 2008 as the First Medium Term Plan (2008–2030). The relationship between international donors and Kenya took a more consultative approach in the crafting of Vision 2030. This relationship is facilitated via the Development Partnership Forum and Aid Effectiveness Group (AEG). The international donors continue to monitor the progress of the Vision 2030 implementation.

Despite the Vision 2030 process claiming an active participation of the broad stakeholder group via the collaborative structure of the private and public sector, the international partners and donors through the Bretton Wood Institutions still have some influence on the core sector of the policy. For example the Institutions influenced the macroeconomic pillar which determines government expenditure on the social pillar. Vision 2030 is also structured to meet the PRSP framework as Kenya is still dependent on international development institutions for loans and financing of some projects like the Energy Sector Recovery Project, and BPO. By the end of the first MTP implementation of Vision 2030, international donors through their various meetings agreed to be more involved in the implementation process of

102 *Kenya*

the second phase of Vision 2030 through the exercise of indirect centralized management. By implication, further implementation of Vision 2030 entails increased influence of donors in the asymmetrical relationship between the Kenyan government and international partners and donors. Hence, the limited ownership that existed during the crafting process is gradually declining.

Implementation and outcomes

The implementation of Vision 2030 is mostly carried out by relevant sectors while the different national agencies monitor and evaluate the implementation process. In general, however, the implementation process of the programme is coordinated by the Monitoring and Evaluation Directorate (MED) within the Office of the Prime Minister, which works closely with other government agencies, local agencies, the private sector and NGOs to ensure an inclusive implementation and effective monitoring and evaluation. The National Economic and Social Commission acts as a liaison between private, public sectors and civil society. In addition the Kenya National Bureau of Statistics (KNBS) develops technical capacities, and various surveys (like poverty and integrated household budget surveys) that are undertaken regularly over the period of the programme to provide information and input in monitoring the progress of the programme. The MED uses the survey data to publish a quarterly and annual report on progress in the implementation of the programme.

In terms of the economy, Kenya has recorded a mixed result since 2008. The average growth within the first review period (2008–2011) was 4.1 per cent which was significantly below the 9.7 per cent projected in Vision 2030. The inability to achieve the targeted goal is attributed to both external and internal shocks. As a commodity economy, the global economic crisis in 2008 directly impacted Kenya's economy. However, it is internal factors, especially post-election conflicts and adverse weather, that have had a more negative impact on key sectors, and specifically agriculture and tourism. In 2010 some key economic sectors started improving due partly to the macroeconomic expansion carried by the government to cushion the economy from both internal and external crisis (IMF, 2012a: 12).

The macroeconomic expansion and other monetary and fiscal policies that included increased credit to the private sector, however, later contributed to subsequent high inflation starting from 2010 and peaking in 2011 at 20 per cent from 3.8 per cent in 2009. The inflationary pressure now appears to have stabilized at 5 per cent (since 2012) but the overall outlook remains somewhat fragile especially with the percentage of investment of the GDP decreasing from 20.7 per cent in 2009 to 19.6 per cent in 2011.

In Kenya, the tourism sector remains a major source of foreign exchange earnings due to an increase in international tourism by 17.4 per cent in 2010 after a decline in 2007/2008 as a result of the post-election violence. However despite some improvement in performance, this key sector failed to meet the target set in Vision 2030. Interestingly the wholesale sector performed rather

Kenya 103

well. It grew by 7.8 per cent and contributed to about 10.3 per cent of the GDP. The newly introduced BPO sector is still going through the development phase but had generated 7,000 jobs by 2011 and is on course to meet the 7,500 target of the MTP.

Overall, the economic performance has been moderate. Critically, even this moderate growth did not translate to job growth, thereby defeating the fight against high unemployment and poverty. According to the Vision Report (IMF, 2012a), the target was an average job growth of 8.7 per cent annually, however the economy on average has only created 1.3 per cent annually from 2008 to 2011.

Conversely, performance in terms of social development even though improved in some areas did not meet targets. According to the Vision Report, primary school enrolment increased from 5.9 million in 2002 to 9.38 million in 2012. However, between 2007 and 2010 the net enrolment rate dropped slightly from 92.9 per cent to 91.4 per cent respectively. The transition to secondary school increased from 59.6 per cent in 2007 to 72 per cent in 2010 but is below the target of 88 per cent. Other targets such as improving the teacher to pupil ratio were not met. In addition the flagship programmes – establishment of a computer supply programme, construction and rehabilitation of boarding primary schools and the introduction of a voucher system in five of the poorest districts are yet to take off.

Similarly, the health sector did not make progress. Inadequate hospital facilities and health staff remain a dominant feature of the landscape. Although life expectancy has improved over the years, there has been no significant improvement in mortality rate. Immunization rates increased but this was due mostly to foreign sponsored and implemented programmes. There was some progress in the flagship programme of rehabilitation of health centres but most of the work is ongoing.

In a similar trend, access to water, waste management systems, water irrigation and sewage drainage did not improve. Access to pipe water only increased in urban areas while rural areas continue to be riddled with persistent poor access to clean water, exacerbating the rule/urban divide. Flagship programmes introduced in Vision 2030 to improve this sector such as rehabilitation of irrigation and drainage systems are yet to commence. As of the time of writing, China has signed a memorandum of understanding to fund one such project, however work has not started (IMF, 2012a). In summary, the weakest aspect of the ERS and Vision 2030 has been in the area of human development, suggesting that to the extent a departure from a SAP-like programme has occurred, such a shift has been minimal.

Kenya: providing leadership or dithering

We noted that through crafting and implementing ERS and Vision 2030 Kenya has managed to make some progress compared to where it was in 2002. For a medium term programme of four years, Vision 2030 to some

104   *Kenya*

degree has been able to articulate the general challenges facing the country and propose broad ideas for tackling these. The broad consultative approach taken in formulating the document is particularly commendable. Kenya's economy like other African countries is known to be narrow. Given this constraint the attempt made in Vision 2030 to offer some measures for economic expansion by utilizing the country's economic endowment in agriculture and tourism as well as its geographical advantage to promote sectors like services and manufacturing are also worthy of praise. After all it should not be forgotten that Vision 2030 is the first attempt to refocus and look within after decades of externally driven SAPs. It is therefore fair to say that Vision 2030 ticks some boxes in terms of its homegrown features.

However, there are far-reaching challenges. Overall, while Vision 2030 identified some of the country's advantages and measures to build on these, it was very weak in terms of articulating unique local challenges and concrete measures to tackle them. A prime example can be found in agriculture. Vision 2030 correctly identified agriculture as the country's main economic advantage. However, there is no systematic strategy to restructure this sector. Despite general knowledge that land is intrinsically linked to agriculture, there is no serious policy directed at breaking the monopolistic structure and extractive pattern that currently exists in the country. For example, according to Kenya Land Alliance, over 65 per cent of arable land in Kenya is controlled by 20 per cent of the population with the Kenyatta family controlling the largest acres of land in various regions of Kenya. In fact many sources suggest that the Kenyatta family owns more than half a million acres of prime land in Kenya. This is intriguing given that the majority of the populations are in the agricultural sector.

Furthermore, given the role of agriculture in the economy and its linkages to other sectors such as manufacturing, service and tourism, the country is still lacking an innovative way to develop technology for the agricultural sector locally or through technology diffusion. Although irrigation, which currently attracts the most focus, would greatly contribute to increased output, it is not enough to propel the sector to the level of development the country desires.

Moreover, the strategy for developing the agriculture sector seems to focus on encouraging production for the external market which tends to benefit the elite and middle class farmers. The consequence is that the main policies do not work in favour of the majority of the poor population who work in the agricultural sector. The post-independence programme recognized the need for self-reliance agriculture and developed the Harambee concept to support local farmers through local cooperative societies. Despite claiming to look inwards current development initiatives still harbour serious gaps in incorporating and adapting local culture and philosophy, as evidenced in the general economic strategy of Vision 2030. The implication is that even if Kenya effectively implemented the Vision programme, it is likely that development would be mostly lopsided creating further inequalities.

The development process in Kenya is still largely a top-down approach with little impact at the local level, especially in rural areas. The old guards still dominate the economic and political environment and that continues to impede real institutional reform. Consequently, inequality continues and the supposedly targeted groups are not impacted. Despite claims of the reports that Vision 2030 has improved social sectors and repaired damaged infrastructure, access to social services is still skewed towards the elites or those living in the urban areas, leaving the majority of the population living in rural areas with little or no access to social services. The informal economic sector continues to be the highest employer of labour. Yet little incentive has been provided to enable this sector to grow and to fully integrate the activities of this sector into the mainstream economy. This has led to the accusation that Vision 2030 remains just a text on paper for Kenyans, with many stressing the neglect of the social pillar. While it is commendable to aim high towards industrialization, the neglect in addressing basic social structure has been the source of major criticism. As one Kenyan academic pointed out, 'the government appears more interested in showing a lofty structure with the big "Vision 2030" tag than tackling huge problems of unemployment, poverty and absence of basic infrastructure facing the country' (Anonymous Source). The same source cited the government's plan to supply 700,000 computers to Standard One pupils by 2014 when the majority cannot even afford decent meals or ordinary pencils, as a prime example of such misguided loftiness.

Adams Oloo a political scientist at the University of Nairobi linked the underperformance of Vision 2030 to Kenyan politics. This negative perception is not isolated as most respondents do not think Vision 2030 has had an impact on ordinary Kenyans. This corresponds with surveys carried out by the National Survey of Kenya in 2009 which also indicate that Kenya populations have least trust in public institutions and political elites. The peaceful election process of 2013 restored some confidence in Kenya, but the action of the newly elected President, Uhuru Kenyatta the son of the first president of Kenya, in carrying out an effective implementation of the programme is yet to materialize.

Critically, Kenya's demography has been changing in the past decades creating some opportunities and threats that have been ill recognized in Vision 2030. Young people are moving away from farming to seek paid employment or start businesses. This means that the percentage of the productive population is increasing. If the economy is not turned to generate jobs, unemployment will continue to rise in the country. The implication will be persistent poverty and inequality which could translate into more social malaise. Growth in Kenya is mostly driven by the service sector and agriculture with little impact from manufacturing; if these sectors are not expanded enough as noted above, adding new jobs will be impossible. The public sector that absorbs most jobs is bloated with corruption and mismanagement which eventually spills over to the private sector and raises the cost of doing business. The World Bank argues that corruption is smothering jobs in Kenya.

106   *Kenya*

'If the private sector could redirect the money it now spends on corruption to creating jobs, it could create 300,000 jobs, sufficient to hire every unemployed urban Kenyan between the age of 15 and 34' (World Bank, 2012: ix).

Although Kenya has been able to stabilize its fiscal position, foreign financing of the budget increased by 2 per cent in 2012, as government prefers to borrow from the international monetary market through syndicated loans from a group of commercial banks (ibid.); consequently, the country debt is increasing steadily. And Kenya continues to struggle under a heavy weight of foreign and domestic debt. This leads to the vicious circle of borrowing more and spending heavily on interest payment with precious little revenue left for the pursuit of long term socio-economic development. Specifically, Kenya is faced with a structural problem that is embedded within poor governance and weak institutions both at the macro and micro levels which shapes the economic and social progress. This is in addition to the age old problem of sourcing high interest and stringent external funding without adequate accountability. The cost of development is high which is why these countries continue to depend on external funding through loans and aid that come back to hurt the economy. Instead of using external support as a short term strategy to expand the economy, Kenya like many countries, makes it a permanent trend thereby exacerbating dependency, a tendency that reduces opportunity for a country to independently seek a solution to its development challenges. Emphasis continues with the top-down approach of macroeconomic stabilization without full consideration of local imperatives. This is despite the government stressing the modelling of its development after the Asian Tigers including China. Even when there is enough economic revenue and resources, corruption mitigates economic diversification and distributive processes.

Summary

Vision 2030 appears to be different from ERS and other programmes implemented from 1980 up to 2002. This is because even though the Vision 2030 programme came with conditionality from Bretton Wood Institutions as with previous ones, its elaboration took a more consultative process. Through the process of broad stakeholder consultation, the government was able to identify some places where it had comparative economic advantages as well as relatively good measures to encourage growth and economic diversification. Nevertheless, Vision 2030 still placed macroeconomic stability far above efforts to diversify and build a self-reliant and sustainable economy. As a result, economic growth has not resulted in improved lives for the majority of the population, who continue to live in extreme poverty. The implementation of ERS and Vision 2030, so far, suggest that the leaders are more interested in pleasing the development partners than dealing with structural challenges confronting the country. These include widespread poverty, rising unemployment, poor infrastructure and widening inequality. A key problem here is

Kenya's over-dependence on external funding in the form of loans and aid. External dependence on development finance explains why Kenya continues to look outwardly rather than seriously setting its own priorities and pursuing HGD. Hence despite relatively active local involvement and comparatively less external meddling compared to the SAP years, Kenya still lacks local ownership over its own development agenda. To this extent the programme is not anywhere near as homegrown as the Harambee programme that was initiated and implemented by the founding fathers of the Kenyan nation immediately after independence.

7 South Africa
Reconstruction and Development Programme

Arriving at O.R. Tambo International Airport South Africa and driving towards Sandton neighbourhood, one gets a very strong impression that South Africa is a developed and truly industrialized country. Take away the billboards and signposts and one can easily mistake the city for British Colombia, Chicago or Melbourne.

However, less than seven kilometres away from Sandton is Alexandra or Alex for short – a well-known black township with a large number of hostels and informal dwellings known as shacks. With about 180,000 residents, 99 per cent of whom are black and mostly very poor, Alex is one of the largest informal settlements in South Africa. Most shacks are made from rusted zinc or cardboard and usually lack basic amenities such as sanitation facilities.

Of course, having a poor community that is closely situated to a wealthy neighbourhood is not peculiar to Alexandra. However, what makes this case stand out is that it is emblematic of an extreme type of rich–poor dichotomy that characterizes the whole of South Africa reflecting the country's history of apartheid where the black majority were racially segregated and denied basic social and economic rights by a ruling white minority. Hence, although South Africa is officially a middle income country and a member of the BRICS bloc, it has a very high poverty and unemployment rate comparable to other low income countries of Africa. With a Gini coefficient of 0.65, South Africa is about the most unequal society in the world. So stark is this rich–poor dichotomy that former president Thabo Mbeki, apparently taking cue from Oliver Twist, described it a tale of 'two nations'.

Since the end of apartheid, the South African government has introduced various transformation programmes in general to achieve economic development and in particular to address this 'two nations' legacy. These include the Reconstruction and Development Programme (RDP) of 1994, a macroeconomic framework known as the Growth, Employment and Redistribution (GEAR) programme, introduced in 1996, and the more targeted Broad-based Black Economic Empowerment programme (BBEE). Furthermore, the Accelerated and Shared Growth Initiative for South Africa (ASGISA) was introduced in 2006, and the New Growth Path (NGP) was initiated in 2010.

In this chapter our focus will be on the RDP and the GEAR programme because these are the foundational post-apartheid development framework upon which other initiatives are built. In fact, subsequent programmes such as the ASGISA and the NGP are mostly a combination of ideas from RDP and GEAR. The chapter also gives considerable attention to the Black Economic Empowerment (BEE) programme which was derived from the RDP core principles. The BEE programme merits special treatment because although it was not a comprehensive development framework, it was a crucial initiative designed to redress the vast inequalities in South Africa and lift the black population out of aching poverty. First however, we start by providing a short account of the history of South Africa and how it created the current socio-economic challenges in modern South Africa.

The Union, apartheid and development process in South Africa

South Africa is uniquely different from the previous three cases. The major difference lies in the fact that it was a settled colony where a significant share of the proceeds from economic extraction was invested in national development. The Union of South Africa was formed in 1910 after several years of three-way war between the Afrikaner groups (predominantly Dutch settlers), the English and the native Zulus. At the formation of the Union, the ethnic European colonists-*cum*-settlers held power with Britain granting nominal independence. This political compromise allowed the European settlers to commit significant resources to national development while also repatriating wealth to the mercantile state (Feinstein, 2005; Wilson and Thompson, 1969).

However, this act of national development was not evenly spread out. Rather, the colonizers introduced a system of racial segregation and discrimination against black African natives. A prime example was the Natives' Land Act of 1913 which severely restricted land ownership by blacks (more than 87 per cent of the population) to 13 per cent of the entire country, setting the foundation for the segregation development policies and deprivation of blacks' economic progress (Feinberg, 1993; Wolpe, 1972). The post war poverty in Europe and the discoveries of diamonds and gold all combined to cause an influx of European migrants which in turn increased the population of white settlers. In order to protect the correspondingly expanding white economic interests, further dispossessions were orchestrated through the 1936 Native Land Act which created secluded areas called the Native Reserves and mandated the forcible removal of blacks from their lands to these Reserves (Bundy, 1972).

In 1948 the National Party (NP), an Afrikaner political party which campaigned under the introduction of apartheid – which literally means separate development – was elected into government. Following their electoral victory, the NP intensified the racial segregation against blacks using a suite of penal government regulations and policies. The NP classified all peoples into racial categories and sought different development tracks for each. In principle it

110   *South Africa*

sought to secure a state of economic development and wellbeing for the white minority that is comparable to Western countries while consigning the black population to a state of poverty and servitude.

In accordance with the policy of apartheid, the social, political and economic development of Africans was confined separately within the so called 'homeland' (Bantu) through the Bantu Authorities Act of 1951 and the promotion of the Bantu Self-government Act of 1959. With the establishment of a separate institutional framework for development, the government proceeded to remove the right of blacks, coloured and Indians to run businesses outside their group areas as well as restricting the type of business in which they could engage. In 1957, black African entrepreneurs in the African homelands were further mandated to seek permission before establishing any business; they were also legally restricted on the type and number of businesses they could own (Beinart, 2001). In 1962, business opportunities in urban areas were opened up to Indians and coloureds, thereby strengthening the tripartite structure and laying the foundation for the widening inequality between them and black Africans (Iheduru, 2004).

Meanwhile, the situation deteriorated for the black African population during the 1960s to the late 1970s following a series of additional legal restrictions enacted by the NP. Not only were several business opportunities closed to blacks, blacks were also barred from apprenticeships. The only businesses permitted were those that provided the daily necessities of the Bantu, excluding dry-cleaning, running garages and selling petrol, among other activities (Hart, 1974). Job restrictions were intensified, with legal classifications of the jobs that Africans, Coloureds and Indians were allowed to have (Beinart, 2001; Hart, 1974). Given these restrictions the only means of livelihood available to many were working as a sharecropper, maids, mining (for men) and other manual labour with very little pay.

Black advancement was further deliberately hampered through the Bantu educational system (Act No. 47 of 1953). Africans were not allowed to train or be employed as skilled workers. They were also barred from studying science, business and engineering courses in school (Hirsch, 2005). Thus, for Africans the path to socio-economic progress and development was obliterated by the apartheid regime. In reality, then, apartheid was more or less a deliberate institutionalization of severe inhuman underdevelopment for black Africans. One of the proponents of the view D.G. Scholtz, was clear about the necessity for racial segregation, saying that 'economic integration must of necessity lead to political integration and eventual [black] political domination; hence there is the need to get rid of the non-white proletariat' (cited in Baldwin, 1975: 219).

Racial segregation and repressive rule in South Africa resulted in the formation of various oppositional socio-political movements, the most prominent of which was the African National Congress (ANC) formed in 1924 and its military wing, the Umkhonto we Sizwe (Spear of the Nation) created in 1961. Preoccupied with the liberation struggle, the ANC did not articulate a coherent strategy for development. However, the economic philosophy of the organization was decidedly socialist (some might argue communist) with equality, redistribution and social justice figuring as the favourite themes. By far the most important statement of the ANC's pre-1990 economic intentions was The Freedom Charter, adopted on 26 June 1955 at a 'Congress of the People' in Kliptown. Although the Charter lacked detail, it expressed commitment to national ownership 'by the people as a whole' of 'the mineral wealth beneath the soil, the Banks and monopoly industries'. It advocated state control of all industry and trade 'to assist the wellbeing of the people'. Land re-division and redistribution were to be undertaken in order to 'banish famine and hunger'. Other commitments included free medical care and a preventative health scheme run by the state, free compulsory and universal education, national minimum wage, the abolishment of contract labour and the right to 'full unemployment benefits'.

For as long as apartheid rule was in full force, anti-apartheid/liberation groups including ANC were not allowed to operate legally until 1985 with the formation of Congress of South African Trade Unions (COSATU). During this period, supportive business groups dominated by the corporate sector, especially foreign multinationals, were clamouring for the de-racialization of the economic environment. The underlying purpose was mainly the need to reverse the country's dearth of skilled labour and halt the declining economy, especially as many countries were boycotting South African goods and services. With the unbanning of the ANC and other liberation groups and the release of political prisoners including Nelson Mandela, South Africa's transition process began in earnest. Given the ANC prominence and the global fame of Mandela, it was obvious that the ANC would lead the transition negotiations. The ANC entered negotiations driven by the principles of the Freedom Charter which called for total freedom, equality and the sharing of the national wealth, among others.

Despite frequently rehearsing their commitment to the Freedom Charter principles, there was no practical strategy on how to carry them in such a complex and fragile environment (Nattrass, 1994) especially the critical challenge of accommodating the varied and conflicting interests of diverse stakeholders as the country transitioned from apartheid. Moreover, the full import of the fact that the powerful ally of the ANC from the private sector that controlled the economy was not comfortable with the Charter's call for nationalization of the core economic sectors had not yet dawned upon the ANC elite. In order to build a strong consensus for the first post-apartheid democratic election, the ANC formed a tripartite alliance with the South African Communist Party (SACP) and the COSATU. As the country entered independence in 1994, it was faced with the complex challenges of not only uniting the racially divided country, but also forging an integrated political and social economic development framework to revive the economy and rebuild the country.

112   *South Africa*

Post-apartheid reconstruction policies

By far the most prominent legacy of apartheid was the staggering inequality between the white minority and the black majority. At the fall of apartheid, 95 per cent of the poor in South Africa were black Africans while white and Indian poor constituted less than one per cent. Less than one third of black Africans had access to flush toilets, electricity and refuse removal and a vast proportion lived in shacks (Bond, 1996). Consequently, articulating a socio-economic policy reform that would regenerate the economy while alleviating the deprivation of the black population became (and still remains) the foundation on which the development policies in the new South Africa was (and is) framed.

The history of socio-economic development programmes in post-apartheid South Africa makes an interesting if challenging reading. It captures the tensions, struggles and compromises that have marked the ANC's attempt to restructure the economy and stimulate sustainable growth in a neoliberal era while addressing the inequality and injustice occasioned by their unique history. Following a landslide election victory in 1994, the ANC-led government introduced the Reconstruction and Development Programme (RDP) as the first comprehensive post-apartheid development framework. The document articulated the past injustices of apartheid and set the goal of addressing the many socio-economic challenges facing the country. However, the RDP was abandoned after two years following stiff opposition by the private sector which complained that it had a socialist bent. With the RDP abruptly discarded, the government was not able to muster enough consensuses to set out another comprehensive socio-economic programme until a full 10 years later when ASGISA was introduced. In the interim, the government filled the gap with two targeted programmes. One was GEAR, which focused on macroeconomic stabilization of the country. The other was BBEE – a targeted affirmative programme designed to correct the historical injustice against the black majority.

Given this unique history, subsequent sections will cover these four programmes making this chapter different from the previous ones where emphasis was on one or two programmes at the maximum. Furthermore, some references will also be made to the New Growth Path (NGP) initiated in 2010. Commentary on NGP will however be limited as the first evaluation of the programme is due to take place at the end of 2014.

Reconstruction and Development Programme

The ANC presented the RDP as an integrated socio-economic policy framework for a new beginning. The hope was that the framework would provide the basis for mobilizing people and resources towards the eradication of the negative legacies of the apartheid system and building a prosperous and united county. The RDP was based on six basic and interlinked principles that included integration and sustainability, peace and security, nation building, meeting basic needs of all and deepening the democratization process. Given the country's recent past, the programme also emphasized the need for institutional restructuring in moving the country forward. It stated, 'The Government and its institutions will be restructured to fit the priorities of the RDP. Here, especially, there is no "business as usual"' (African National Congress (ANC), 1994: 9). Achieving these objectives was seen as necessary in laying a solid foundation for an inclusive democratization of South Africa going forward.

The RDP was intrinsically linked to the goal of building a participatory democratic process that enabled everyone to contribute to the reconstruction and development of the country. Significantly, the RDP was seen as a compromise between the different ideologies of the tripartite alliance comprising the ANC, the outgoing apartheid government and the private sector (Bond, 1996). While it emphasized the need for inclusive growth based on enterprise, it also noted the important role of the state in economic management and driving growth. It also noted that some form of affirmative action would be needed to correct the past injustices due to apartheid.

Despite the huge effort devoted to making the RDP a balanced and comprehensive programme, the initiative eventually proved ill-fated as it was trapped in the high tide of mistrust and suspicion between the black dominated government and the white dominated private sector which prevailed in the transition period and which sadly continues to shape development in South Africa to date. While the RDP was well received by most South Africans, some of the power brokers in the private sector did not support the RDP despite its attempt to reach out. At the same time, there are some who claimed that the RDP represented a withdrawal from the previously idealistic ANC as the programmes did not go far enough to break the monopolistic structure of the economy that had concentrated power in the hands of a few white. Yet, others argued that the RDP attempted to please different interest groups and present a programme that was everything for everyone. The outcome, they saw was an economic nonsense which moved uncritically between a commandist central planning system, a mixed economy and an unfettered free market system (Allen, 2006; Mutua, 2011).

In any case, it was the powerful and well-resourced group in the private sector that reacted most angrily to the RDP. They mounted a powerful propaganda campaign against the initiative which instigated fear of economic collapse among the wider business and capital flight. This in turn led to inflation, devaluation of the Rand and a volatile macroeconomic environment. Under intense pressure from the economic elites, a very limited economic power to fight back and lacking the political will to forge ahead, the ANC eventually suspended RDP after two years and introduced GEAR.

Growth, Employment and Redistribution programme

Following the suspension of RDP the ANC introduced the Growth, Employment and Redistribution programme (GEAR). Supported by the

114 *South Africa*

World Bank and the section of the private sector that had ensured the discontinuation of RDP, the goal of GEAR was to set a strategy for rebuilding and restructuring the economy as set out in the RDP. It also highlighted its commitment to some of the other principles stated in the RDP such as increasing human resource capacity, meeting basic needs and increasing participation in the democratic institutions.

However, no one was left in doubt that GEAR was essentially a macroeconomic programme, and that the core objectives were to tighten spending in order to stabilize the fiscal environment, increase debt services, and restructure the monetary environment to reduce inflation. It also emphasized the centrality of promoting competiveness through tax incentives and advocated the need for further economic liberalization. Furthermore, the ANC government through GEAR pledged to encourage wage restraint, encourage competitive exchange rate system and implement tax reforms to raise revenue thereby ticking all the boxes prescribed as universal panacea for '"development" by the Bretton Woods institutions such as the World Bank and IMF' (cf. Chikulo, 2003). Hence, while RDP was seen as a compromise by the ANC's principled position on nationalization and redistribution, GEAR represented a complete a U-turn towards liberalization and the free market economy (Agupusi, 2011; Bond, 2004; Terreblanche, 1999). Although the majority of the population was forced to accept GEAR given that the ANC had presented it on as *fait accompli*, they continued to agitate that little was being done to address the racial divide since the suspension of the RDP. In response to this agitation, the ANC in 1997 started a process that led to the introduction of the BBEE.

The Broad-based Black Economic Empowerment

The Black Economic Empowerment (BEE) is a form of affirmative programme to help address the inequality that exists in the country as a result of the long history of apartheid penal laws. The core BEE strategies are to increase the number of blacks business owners, increase the number of blacks in senior management positions, reduce racial income inequality and increase land ownership and participation of blacks in productive economic activities. Originally, BEE was an integral part of RDP. In that context the focus was narrow and consisted mainly in encouraging businesses to try and promote racial balance in the private sector through a set of codes of good practice in equity ownership, promotions and management representation. Following, on the one hand, the minimalist and half-hearted response of the private sector, and on the other hand, the eventual discontinuation of the RDP, the need was felt to broaden and formalize the BEE as a full socio-economic affirmative programme This led to the introduction of BBEE – Broad-based Black Empowerment – with the aim of encouraging wide scale economic empowerment and wealth distribution to as broad a spectrum of previously disadvantaged South African society as possible through diverse but integrated

South Africa 115

socio-economic strategies (BBEE, 2003). The target population comprised all black people, including women, workers, youth, people with disabilities and people living in rural areas.

It is probably fair then to understand GEAR and BBEE as the outcome of the breaking up of RDP into two different targeted programmes with one focusing on macroeconomic stabilization and the other on addressing historical economic injustice through affirmative action. However, while GEAR was subsequently replaced in 2006 with a comprehensive socio-economic development framework – the Accelerated and Shared Growth Initiative for South Africa (ASGISA) – BBEE continues to operate as a separate government programme.

Accelerated and Shared Growth Initiative for South Africa

A decade after the suspension of the RDP, the government finally managed to introduce another comprehensive development programme that integrated some macroeconomic goals in GEAR with some broad socio-economic principles of RDP. The outcome was the Accelerated and Shared Growth Initiative for South Africa (ASGISA). The core goal of the initiative was to halve poverty by 2014. It was understood that such an objective could only be achieved with a stable and growing economy. At a deeper level, this signifies a desire to recognize and promote complementarity between macroeconomic stabilization with social and human development. The programme called for effective economic leadership from the government and active partnerships between the government and other key stakeholders such as organized labour and business. The programme identified macroeconomic stability, investment in infrastructure, education and skill development and elimination of the 'second economy' as core priorities.

In the following sections we will assess the extent of the *indigeneity* of the four programmes (RDP, GEAR, BBEE, and ASGISA) and their outcomes. However, because of space constraints and the relationship among the programmes, we do not separate out the discussions under different heading and subsections.

Broad stakeholder consultation and participation

The ANC has a history of grassroots consultation and participation in its decision-making processes. This commitment was taken in the framing of the 1955 Freedom Charter, the guiding principle of the ANC struggle. The Charter was the result of extensive grassroots consultations whereby people from all communities were represented as broadly as possible. The drafting of the RDP also involved similar extensive stakeholder sessions across South Africa. In addition, international experts were also invited to make contributions.

The process that led to the crafting of the RDP started in the late 1980s through secret meetings by various anti-apartheid movements – ANC,

116 *South Africa*

COSATU and SACP. One of those meetings was 'The South African Economy after Apartheid' held at York University in the UK in 1986 (Agupusi, 2011). With the release of Nelson Mandela in 1990 the process became more open and broadened to include a wider range of stakeholders. The consultation process included the active participation of various groups including the ANC alliance, Inthaka Freedom Party, the then ruling white minorities, members of private sectors, experts from different fields and civil society. They worked with external actors mostly from within academia who served as advisors and were directly involved in the research and drafting of policy documents. Research groups were also constituted to cover various policy areas. These included, for example, the Macro-Economic Research Group (MERG) and the Economic Trends and Research Group (ET), which was coordinated by Stephen Gelb and funded by British, Canadian and German foundations (Agupusi, 2011). Given the fragile state of South Africa at the time, it is not surprising that the process of RDP involved broad participation of different interest groups in the society.

Curiously, the ANC radically departed from the established and long tradition of broad consultation in the introduction of GEAR. The programme was more or less an adoption of a macroeconomic framework known as 'Growth for All' published by the South African Foundation (SAF) in February 1999. The SAF was an organization that comprised the 50 largest companies in South Africa, although more recently the Foundation's membership has increased to include large black-owned companies.

GEAR was introduced in June 1996 by the ANC leadership as a non-negotiable macroeconomic framework in a move that grossly undermined the traditional grass-root consultation and broad-based participation approach of the ANC. COSATU and the SACP argued that they were excluded and not consulted in the decision-making process. They noted that GEAR was the product of an exclusive group in the corporate sector which was informed by the World Bank's macroeconomic framework reminiscent of the SAP. Additionally, they pointed out that GEAR was a departure from the social transformation they had promised the people through the RDP. Consequently, even though they remained part of the tripartite alliance, COSATU, together with its external allies from the left, became major critics of GEAR and especially the privatization programme outlined in the initiative. Following pressure from the opposition within the alliance (SACP and COSATU) and the strong arguments that GEAR programmes were failing to improve the economy and address mounting social challenges, the ANC leadership reluctantly and gradually relaxed implementation.

Meanwhile, criticisms continued to mount over the lack of consultation before the introduction of GEAR and the narrow approach taken by the private sector in the implementation of BEE. These criticisms were particularly damaging for the ANC because commentators were keen to observe the peevish irony of entrusting BEE into the hands of the same private sector that had opposed the RDP and spearheaded the introduction of the SAP-oriented

GEAR. It was in response to these pressures that the government decided to change the institutional framework and broaden the mandate of BEE. The key event was the 1997 conference of the Black Management Forum in Stellenbosch that resulted in the creation of the Black Economic Empowerment Commission (BEECOM).

The BEECOM was subsequently formally established in 1998 under the auspices of the Black Business Council (BBC), an umbrella body representing 11 black business organizations with the commitment to contribute to the debate about the economic transformation of South Africa. BEECOM conducted research and had a wide range of consultations with key players including labour unions and the private sector through seminars and workshops. After this, it held a conference in 2000 to present its report on strategies for a new vision of BEE to the government, private sector, NGOs and representatives of unions. It can therefore be said that BBEE was a product of broad stakeholder consultation even though the extent of participation was not as extensive as what went into the articulation of the RDP. But this is understandable since BBEE has a more targeted focus rather than being a comprehensive development programme.

In 2006, ASGISA was introduced as the second overarching development framework in post-apartheid South Africa. Its introduction followed a two-year broad consultation process in what appears to suggest that the ANC had learnt bitter lessons from the internal rift caused by the way in which GEAR was foisted on the country. Keen to ensure high visibility and wide participation, ASGISA went through a wider consultation process headed by the then Deputy President, Phumzile Mlanbo-Ngcuka which involved extensive discussions and regular feedback from local stakeholders with active participation of civil society. Moreover, as with the RDP the government solicited advice, contributions from international experts included a review team from Harvard University in the USA.

In sum it is fair to say that the problem of lack of inclusiveness and broad consultation that occurred during the GEAR process had been corrected. It is notable that a nationwide consultation process was also followed in introducing the New Growth Path, which is the successor of ASGISA. Generally, post-apartheid South Africa performs quite well in terms of broad consultation and participation in designing its development programmes.

Economic diversification and sensitivity to local imperatives

We have consistently suggested that the recognition and harnessing of local economic advantages is a key element of any homegrown development approach (HGD) approach. South Africa at independence in 1994 was faced with a unique economic challenge. Unlike most African countries including those studied in this book, South Africa has a more diverse and developed economy. At the same time it has a very unequal society. Hence, its main economic challenge was more about achieving equality and inclusiveness. In

118   South Africa

addition, there was also a lack of human capital to propel a much needed economic expansion following decades of decline.

The RDP White Paper in its six point principles identified this crucial problem and promised to create a more inclusive economy. The Paper also noted that as the most industrialized economy in Africa, it needed to expand its market and pledged to integrate the country's economy more closely with the Southern African region. However, RDP lacked coherent concrete strategy for achieving the economic challenges identified. This has been attributed to the dynamics, and conflicts of ideology that characterized the negotiation process. In order to strike a compromise, the RDP took to vagueness and dropped a number of concrete policy proposals and hence left many key areas blurred. David Everatt points out that the programme even failed to define poverty eradication or provide specific details on its core economic policies. It also barely mentioned the word redistribution in a programme that had building an inclusive economy as its primary goal (Everatt, 2005). Incidentally, this lack in practical strategy for economic growth was in fact one of the criticisms of the private sector against RDP.

GEAR on its own did little to correct this weakness. Its main emphasis, as stated, was on macroeconomic stabilization based on fiscal prudence, competitive private sector, promotion of investment and trade as means of stimulating growth. The strategy did not take into consideration the structural economic problem that had created 'two economies', and completely ignored the major problem of the economy, which was its monopolistic nature. Although the programme noted the advantage of regional integration to Southern African economy and introduced 'an accelerated depreciation scheme for all new investments in manufacturing' (GEAR, 1996: 13) through trade liberalization, its focus remained on protecting the monopolistic structure of the economy and raising the bar to market entry. These are some of the reasons why GEAR was widely seen as a neoliberal take-over that does not take into account the local history and socio-economic challenges of the country (Bond, 2001). There was little surprise then that at the end of GEAR's implementation, South Africa's manufacturing had declined while unemployment had increased.

With the failure of GEAR to stimulate growth and generate employment as predicted, ASGISA was introduced. ASGISA through its consultation process and expert advice identified structural and administrative inefficiency, high barriers to market entry, low competition and shortage of skilled labour as some of the main economic challenges (Hausmann, 2008). In order to address these constraints, five objectives, which included investment in strategic sector, skills and education initiatives, intervention in the 'second economy', macroeconomic stabilization and restructuring of the public sector to reduce administrative bottlenecks were proposed. However, the programme emphasised investment in the service sector rather than manufacturing which is curious given that South Africa has better infrastructure and environment for manufacturing than other African countries. Also South Africa has the

South Africa   119

advantage of expanding its market especially within Africa. Even though this was emphasised in the RDP, it did not garner attention in ASGISA, thereby perpetuating the delay in the country's professed desire to achieve regional integration.

It would appear that the NGP has improved on ASGISA by identifying the need for increasing exports of manufactured value added goods given that its trade balance sheet is lopsided with commodity goods exports. Furthermore the current programme identifies that its focus on the Northern market has not yielded the right result for the country especially with the global economic crisis. As result there is renewed attention toward developing and expanding the African market. This approach has caused Fine (2012) to suggest that NGP seems to have ticked the right boxes needed to achieve diversified and sustainable economic growth in South Africa.

Human and social development

Since the end of apartheid, social and human development has been one of the core policy goals of successive development initiatives. From the RDP to the NGP, human and social development has been prioritized. The centrepiece of the RDP was an integrated development that focused on incorporating previously disadvantaged groups into the social and economic fabric of society. This is based on the assumption that departing from the separated development of the past will be achieved through investment in the majority of the population.

The apartheid system did not only affect the black population but it also stunted the social and infrastructural development of vast sections of the country. Noting this, the RDP stated that the government would be directly involved in the development of human resources and meeting basic needs. Recognizing the conditions of the majority of the blacks, the RDP extended the definition of basic need to job creation, land and agrarian reform, housing, water and sanitation, energy supply, health care, among others. Lack of access to housing with basic amenities had been a major challenge in South Africa. This is because of the Land Acts and socio-economic deprivation that condemned blacks to living in shacks with no basic sanitation. The welfare system was only beneficial to the white population during the apartheid; the RDP White Paper indicated the government intention to de-racialize the welfare system to reach the most vulnerable groups.

The GEAR programme barely recognized the local social and human development challenges and only mentioned education and health in general terms. The neglect of the social and human development problem plaguing the country in the programme was because, as already noted, GEAR was primarily a macroeconomic stabilization programme with the document boldly declaring: 'The focus of this document is the overall macroeconomic environment ... Social and sectoral policy development cannot be outlined comprehensively' (GEAR, 1996: 14). At the same time, while BEE touches

120   *South Africa*

on training and employment, its focus remains far too narrow as to comprehensively tackle the problem of social and human development in the country.

ASGISA recognized education as one of the biggest constraints on economic development:

> For both the public infrastructure and the private investment programmes, the single greatest impediment is shortage of skills – including professional skills such as engineers and scientists; managers such as financial, personnel and project managers; and skilled technical employees such as artisans and IT technicians.
>
> (ASGISA, 2006)

In response to this, the programme set out various projects such as further education training programmes, QIDS-UP (Quality Improvement, Development Support and Upliftment Programme) and the mathematics and science programmes for high schools to raise the level of skills in the country. However, as we shall see, later success in this area remains very marginal.

Building local capacity and institutions

The major transformation that ushered in new South Africa was the introduction of a new constitution in 1996. This in theory has given the country a strong institutional foundation. Even though the South African constitution has been hailed as comprehensive and modern, the country lacks human capacity. Lack of capacity in the public sector was attributed to the poor implementation of RDP (Agupusi, 2011; Luiz, 2002; Terreblanche, 1999). Capacity challenges in the country are endogenous to the local imperatives of its apartheid history. Hence, due to lack of skills South Africa has suffered from inadequate policy implementation. The constitution remains an abstract term without capacity for execution; hence the biggest challenges facing the country are not necessarily institutional arrangements but rather the capacity for effective institutions. South Africa's lack of skill has permeated into the entire political, economic and social system of the country. The inherited legacy of apartheid that institutionally subjugated the majority of its population to illiteracy was complicated by the brain drain of the educated white population.

There were an estimated 2.5 million children without basic education and only 3.7 per cent of the population with a Standard 9 and secondary school diploma (National Training Board, 1994 cited in Corder, 1997: 181) when ANC came into power. Also according to the National Training Board), there was a shortage of 473,000 teachers. Under RDP, the government attempted to introduce universal education that would make ten years of education compulsory, but faced huge obstacles for lack of trained teachers and poor facilities.

The acute shortage of skill at independence in 1994 is intrinsically linked to low capacity. As a result, the country's renowned constitution has not been translated into an effective institution. Since 1994, the government has invested heavily in education to improve capacity through the various policies but the problem is yet to be addressed. This is attributed to the inability of the government and its departments to articulate, conceptualize and link skills shortages to productivity (Daniels, 2007). Administrative bottlenecks, especially in the public sector, are also embedded in the problem of low capacity. According to research carried out by the Strategic Business Partnership (SBP) 'red tape' costs businesses R79 billion annually in South Africa (Drull, 2004). Shortage of qualified teachers and learning challenges of many has negatively affected quality of education amplifying the problem of institutional effectiveness.

Ownership

Although RDP was a local initiative with its roots in the ANC Freedom Charter, it is notable that inputs were made by various foreign experts in the final crafting of the framework. As the transitional process advanced, external influences on the policy process became more pronounced with significant involvement from the World Bank, the International Monetary Fund and a host of other foreign economists 'with different historical backgrounds and ideological leanings' (Agupusi, 2011: 35). The main group, Macroeconomic Research Group (MERG) that crafted the RDP framework was made up of a team of South African and Canadian economists, supported by the Canadian Government and coordinated by the Canadian Development Agency's International Development Research Centre (IDRC). The process, however, was closely monitored by South African's core stakeholder especially the ANC alliance. Even though external experts carried out research and gave advice, the final decision was in the hands of South African stakeholders. For example, when there was disagreement between the Economic Trends (ET) and COSATU over union rights during the drafting of RDP, the two groups deliberated widely and eventually arrived at a system that recognized and protected workers' rights in a balanced way (Padayachee and Sherbut, 2007).

The major contestation in transforming the RDP from an election manifesto to a coordinated development policy framework for new South Africa was due to the ideological differences between the old guard of South African political economy (i.e. the private sector and the outgoing apartheid government) on the one hand, and the ANC tripartite alliance, on the other hand. Adelzadeh and Padayachee summed this up in their commentary as 'conflicts and tensions between "pragmatists" and "socialists" allegedly battling for the soul of the ANC and of policy differences between "conservatives" and "interventionists"' (1994: 1). Some also refer to the intricacy of negotiation that took place as the battle for economic influence between World Bank led neoliberal ideology and the socialist-leaning ANC alliance (Bond, 2001). Despite the external involvement and structural constraints imposed by the neoliberal global economic framework, it would appear that a significant part of the final decisions were taken through negotiated agreement by various local stakeholders.

122 *South Africa*

The contestation between the political and economic elites can be best seen in the way the implementation of RDP was met with stiff resistance by the powerful cabal in the private sector leading eventually to its suspension after two years and the introduction of GEAR. With the economic resources of the private sector combined with the rising influence of globalization, government was forced to abandon its flagship economic policy in place of GEAR. Despite its lack of broad consultation and the strong influence of the World Bank economic model, GEAR did not have any external conditionality attached to it.

As noted above, BBEE was crafted and drafted by the BEECOM through broad consultation of various local interest groups. BBEE is one programme that is devoid of external input during the drafting process given that the programme was specifically for blacks and by blacks. The phrase Blacks here includes African, coloured and Indians. Whether this has actually broadened the impact of BBEE to the majority of the poor is of course a different subject. While BEE focuses on breaking the white economic monopoly and forging an integrated economy, ASGISA was introduced as an overarching development policy that would simultaneously address economic growth, job generation and poverty reduction. The programme framing followed a similar process of inviting external experts' advice and like the RDP decision remained in the hands of local stakeholders.

Implementation and outcomes

The implementation process in South Africa since the RDP in 1994 is considered to be decentralized at least in theory. The RDP emphasized an inclusive approach through the distribution of responsibility among the three tiers of government, private sector and civil society agencies. An RDP office headed by Jay Naidoo was established to coordinate the implementation process. The GEAR, implementation process followed a strict top-down approach through government coordination.

GEAR's top-down narrow implementation approach was because the policy was specifically centred on economic growth. However, subsequent policies improved on the RDP decentralization approach through the coordination of specific departments including that of Trade and Industry. There has also been increasing emphasis on feedback especially with the NGP. The creation of the Department of Performance Monitoring and Evaluation helped in collating data that would improve performance and accountability. Despite effort to improve the implementation process and coordination, low capacity due to skills shortages continue to be a constraint.

During the two years that RDP was implemented, there was a moderate improvement in the socio-economic outlook of South Africa, especially when compared to the magnitude of the problems inherited as well as the limited funding available to the new government. By far the most significant aspect of its success was the de-racialization of the country's welfare system, such as the national pension scheme that was previously reserved for the white population. There was also modest improvement in housing, electricity and water provision in some few areas.

However, by the time the programme was suspended, millions were still living in shacks and lacking basic services. At the same time, the campaign to reduce illiteracy and build human capacity among the black population also resulted in very limited success. With an estimated 2.5 million children without basic education and only 3.7 per cent of the population with a Standard 9 and secondary school diploma (National Training Board, 1994, cited in Corder, 1997: 189), the attempt to introduce universal education that would make ten years of education compulsory faced huge obstacles for lack of trained teachers and poor facilities. The government also embarked on training unemployed individuals for jobs, but despite this attempt, unemployment remained very high amongst black population due mainly to jobless growth. Generally, the South African human development index (HDI) improved from 53.4 in 1980 to 62.9 in 2012 as noted by the UNDP 2013 Report.

The improvement in the HDI could be attributed to de-racialization of the welfare system and social services such as the National Pension Scheme, education and health system. However, as noted, the economy is yet to be restructured in order to inverse the jobless growth that has plagued the country. Crucially there is a lack of political will to carry out some changes that would contribute to poverty and inequality reduction. For example, at the end of apartheid it was agreed that 30 per cent of agricultural land would be redistributed between the white and black communities – a very modest figure given the scale of dispossession that had taken place. Yet, 15 years after this agreement, even this modest distribution has not been accomplished and the entire programme has in fact been swept under the carpet. White land owners have campaigned vigorously against the programme often citing the case of Zimbabwe as an example of the inefficacy of land distribution programmes even though the two countries are on very different trajectories. What the new ANC government soon found out was that it is one thing to provide for minority that was less than 13 per cent of the population and another to cater for the entire population especially in the context of a lean purse and stiff opposition from the wealth-controlling private sector.

The GEAR programme which replaced RDP did not address itself to the major social issues facing the country such as poverty and inequality. Despite some mention of the need for job creation and reconstruction of society, the main goal of GEAR was tightening fiscal spending, rapid tariff liberalization and stabilizing the macroeconomic environment. Comparing targets to outcomes, GEAR made progress in its fiscal target by reducing budget deficit from -4.3 per cent of GDP by 1998, while inflation decreased from 7.3 to 5.5 per cent (Weeks, 1999). Meanwhile, the stabilization of inflation and deficit did not affect interest rates, which was the real purpose for reducing inflation and deficit. Instead interest rose from 4 to 10 per cent (ibid.). When GEAR was introduced, it predicted a growth rate of 4.2 per cent but the GDP barely grew

124   *South Africa*

at about 2.3 per cent. During the two years of aggressive implementation of GEAR, the private sector recorded negative job growth.

Critically, while every development framework since 1994 has consistently insisted on the need for unity and socio-economic integration, the country is still highly divided. Incidentally, in post-apartheid South Africa, it was macro-economic stabilization which took primacy over social aspects of the transformation and development programmes that could help redress the century of socio-economic imbalances. Even a programme such as BEE is modelled after the liberalized trickle down approach and so sluggishly implemented that its effect after ten years of implementation is minimal and mainly visible among the elite blacks in what is now commonly called the '*cappuccino effect*'. Poverty rates among blacks, especially Africans, have not declined. According to Bhorat (2008), the poverty rate using R322 per month poverty line among black Africans has slightly increased from 92.5 per cent in 1995 to 93.2 per cent in 2005 (R322 is about US $30). Indeed, one can argue that this is the direct consequence of programme designs and implementations which mostly took top-down approaches and neglected the reality of challenges facing the country.

A general outlook of socio-economic changes since 1994 indicates a very modest progress especially in comparison to the past apartheid regime. Through various government integration programmes, the public sector has been de-racialized, while the private sector remains less integrated. More blacks are venturing into small business but mostly in the informal sector. In comparison to the early stages of empowerment, more blacks are benefiting in the current process. The black middle class has increased from 1.2 million in 2005 to 3 million in 2008 (UNILEVER, 2008). The economy has been growing at an average 3 per cent, but the level and quality of growth has not been capable of reducing general poverty and unemployment. According to the International Labour Organisation (ILO) South Africa is among the top ten countries with the lowest level of employment. In addition, there is a low level of income which increases the level of poverty and inequality. The Presidential Development Indicator Report showed that the poverty rate was about 48 per cent, based on US $1 a day, while unemployment stood at 36 per cent (COSATU, 2011). Even though there has been an over one per cent increase in working age population, the dismal low employment rate has increased the percentage of dependency amongst the population.

The South African modest jobless growth trajectory has raised some questions about its economic potentials. The current slow growth has been linked to the EU crisis given that the Eurozone is South African's primary trade partner. Others have however attributed the country's persistence economic challenges to lack of skills, inequality and the two economies debate (Hausmann, 2008; Oosthuizen and Cassim, 2014). Not withstanding considerable investments in education and skill development since 1994, lack of skills continues to be one of the biggest socio-economic challenges. The International Panel of economist experts on South Africa pointed to a lack of competition and restricted market entry among major obstacles to growth:

South Africa 125

Many markets in South Africa suffer from limited competition. High margins and restricted entry are in theory an obstacle to growth … on average margins in South Africa are 50 percent higher than in other countries and this is strongly related to poor growth. Hence, there is evidence that lack of competition is a problem, limiting investment in activities that present large barriers of entry or that use inputs from activities with strong pricing power.

(Hausmann, 2008: 7)

However, the inability of the country to structure its economy in a way that would facilitate labour intensive manufacturing has raised serious questions about the logic and motivations driving the country's economic frameworks (Hausmann and Klinger, 2008; Rodrik, 2006).

The major sectors of the economy since 1994 are agriculture, financial services, manufacturing and mining. The various developmental policies have failed to stimulate growth in these sectors, and insufficient emphasis has been placed on manufacturing and the utilization of the African market as a dominant manufacturing country in the continent. Even when notable scholars like Rodrik (2006) have strongly suggested economic growth and unemployment would be significantly reduced by investing in the more labour absorbing manufacturing sectors, the country continues to do very little in this regard.

Ideology contestation and development challenges in South Africa

On balance, it would seem that the development frameworks in South Africa have mostly followed a homegrown approach. Even though many of these programmes had external input, the ownership rested with the South Africans who were largely responsible for initiating, crafting and implementing the policies. Evidence from the South African case strongly suggests that external intrusion and control from donors are limited when the recipient nation has the leadership, exposure and institutional capability to 'hold their own'. Yet the case also suggests that, even in such situations, the wider structural constraints imposed by the prevailing global economic framework or the ideological commitment by powerful internal actors could still result in the adoption of externally oriented and local-economy-damaging policies.

The extent to which its policies since the end of apartheid in 1994 have been able to identify local socio-economic advantages and challenges varies from one policy to another. Where it was able to capture its various local challenges and advantages as seen in the RDP, the programme came up short in strategies or mechanisms for implementation. Subsequent policies such as GEAR and BEE are not comprehensive development programmes but rather specific policies directed to a particular need. The ASGISA offered some improvement to RDP in developing a mechanism and strategy for broad-based economic growth but remained limited in terms of capturing core social and human developmental issues facing the country and radical policies for

126 *South Africa*

addressing those. Specifically, these initiatives have so far failed to address the number one challenge facing South Africa which is curbing persistent unemployment and eradicating poverty among the majority of the black population in the country.

Despite its HDI modest progress, South Africa is still blighted with low literacy, skill shortages and a high prevalence of HIV/AIDS. The South African development indicator noted that infant and maternity mortality has not improved and is not likely to meet the Millennium Development Goals target of 18 deaths per 1,000 by 2014 due to HIV/AIDS and persistent poverty. With about 14.5 per cent of households still living in shacks (Ziblim, 2013), housing problems still beset South Africa. To address this, the government through its housing programme since RDP has been building housing for the poor. Under the subsidized housing programme over 3 million houses have been provided with about 76.2 per cent of African households living in formal dwellings according to the South African Development Indication. There is progress in access to water and sanitation as the target set by the RDP has been met, but the 100 per cent target by 2014 will not be met. The South African Development Indicator shows that the number of households with electricity has more than doubled since 1994, but 25 per cent of the country's household are still without access to electricity; which is below the universal target for 2014. In fact the rate of new electricity connection is decelerating especially in rural areas.

The foregoing suggests the need for a closer look at identifying the core forces or dynamic holding down progressive development in South Africa, which many suggest is the ideological battle between the government and the private sector. Weeks (1999) observes that the government's ideologically generated neoliberal policy has been seen as undermining the goal of redressing the gross inequalities of the apartheid period. This ideological influence is evident in the way RDP was dropped, in the content and manner in which GEAR was introduced, and even in the outcome of BBEE despite an extensive consultation process of local black communities, interest groups and other stakeholders.

It is evident that while ANC has not completely lost its egalitarian flavour, its ideology has been shifting from the far left to the centre (and even right) since the assumption of power in 1994. It is also clear that while COSATU and SACP – the progressive wing of the ANC alliance – continue to exert some pressure, their influence has been all but completely eclipsed by the increasing influence of the corporate sector and the World Bank's free-market-oriented economic ideology in the policy process. So powerful is the influence of the private sector that some authors have described the introduction of GEAR as a form of self or internally imposed structural adjustment programme. Carmody puts it this way:

> While most of Southern Africa has experienced globalization as something externally imposed and mediated through World Bank/International

Monetary Fund (IMF) structural adjustment programmes (SAPs), in South Africa globalization has been largely internally generated. The two sets of actors that have most promoted globalization from within are the state and the country's major conglomerates.

(Carmody, 2002: 256)

The problem is not necessarily ideology; rather it is the blind adoption of ideology that is neither informed by nor promotes local imperatives. Even Hayek in his audacious promotion of the free market based his argument on the centrality of local information and local imperatives.

Some have wondered why the government cannot simply ride rough shod over the private sector to bring about the reforms and egalitarian society critical to addressing local challenges it so loftily spoke about during the days of struggle (Bond, 2001; Edigheji, 2007). However, while ANC can certainly do with some more political will, it is important to recognize the import of two critical factors that worked against the ANC. The first was the general ignorance about economic policies at the time of taking power and the second was the structural power of business. For example in discussing the economic changes proposed by the South African Communist Party (SACP), Essop Pahad, a leading member, explained that it:

> does not have concrete economic policies yet. What we have is a general understanding of what are the fundamental economic issues that have to be addressed ... The extent of the intervention must be determined by a whole lot of factors of which we are not even in control and for which we have no information.

(Pahad, 1990)

Hence, it is clear that the alliance admitted their limited grasp of the working of the economy and its implications. Apparently understanding the weakness of the ANC and other social political movements leveraged the position of the business sector in the transition bargaining process and helped in shifting the egalitarian view of the ANC.

But the second and perhaps most important point is the historical relationship between the government and private sector and how this has empowered the latter in relation to the former. The government's influence in the private sector dates back to the apartheid period and can be seen in the enactment of several pieces of legislation since 1913, peaking under apartheid. Thus, government intervention in the private sector through legislation created the socio-economic environment of post-apartheid South Africa. The government influenced the private sector not only through legislation but also through state-owned enterprises and patronage. In the 1980s, the state owned and managed about 40 per cent of all wealth-producing assets in all key sectors including mining, manufacturing and services (Byrnes, 1996). In addition, the agricultural sector was heavily dependent on the state for subsidies

128   *South Africa*

and other assistance, while government-owned parastatals were important to the private sector through procurement.

In post-apartheid South Africa, with the strong influence of the private sector the ANC has been moving to the orthodox market-oriented policy with little state intervention and reforming of the apartheid economic structure. Even though the state has some influence on mining regulations and procurement, it is the private sector that controls direction of the economy and has strengthened the monopolistic nature of the economy. The private sector, especially the big corporations continue to concentrate in the hands of a few whites who control the economy and who do not trust the economic views of some in the government alliance (Johnson, 2010; Randall, 1996; Southall, 2004; Tangri and Southall, 2008).

The way the South African political economy has been structured has given the private sector enormous power. Instead of using this power to partner with the government to effect real change, the private sector has continued to use their economic power to maintain the status quo. The government on its part lacks bold initiatives and the political will to carry out real reform or enforce the private sector partnership in transforming the country and eliminating apartheid legacies. As a result despite its homegrown approach to development, the South African development process since 1994 has at most been very minimal. Two economies still exist divided along racial lines, inequality has not been reduced, unemployment and poverty continue to cripple the country with many still living in shacks while land reform is a forgotten issue. This outcome is because local, imperatives have not been seriously considered and even when they are identified in the policy documents, there is inadequate strategy and political will for their implementation.

Instead of forming a synergy and forging ahead, the state and the private sector have shifted blame for progress or the lack of it since 1994. While many in the private sector did not trust the government handling of the reform, the government coalitions especially COSATU and SACP blamed the jobless growth on the private sector economic strategy:

> For the past 16 years, private-sector-led growth has worsened the conditions of the vast majority of South Africans. In almost all dimensions that are relevant to our Alliance's economic transformation programme, private-sector-led economic growth has failed South Africans, as we demonstrate in our document: A Growth Path Towards Full Employment (GPFE).
>
> (COSATU, 2010: 9–14)

Summary

Generally, South Africa has made some improvement in its socio-economic reforms through various policies. However, the imprint of the country's tortured past legacies still lingers. Poverty, inequality, shortage of skills and protracted unemployment remain the biggest challenges. The problem of slow and limited progress in South Africa is not for lack of a homegrown approach; rather the main obstacles are lack of political will, and the public/private sector dichotomy and ideological contestations between the public and private sectors which have limited the introduction of pragmatic programmes that reflect sensitivity to local imperatives. There are also problems of lack of technical and human capacity to actually address the structural economic problems. It does not help that when implementation actually happens, it is highly biased in favour of the upper strata of the population that accounts for just a fraction of the population.

Given its ideologically driven political economy, South Africa has been consistently laden with ideological contestations that affect policy content and implementation. In theory, some of these policies, such as ASGISA and NGP adopted a multidimensional approach, but implementation remains an ad hoc top down approach. Hence, despite having taken a HGD approach, 'the country has been unable to articulate a comprehensive development agenda around which it can mobilise all sectors of society' (Edigheji, 2007: 14). Unfortunately this assertion still reflects the situation in South Africa in 2014. The slow progress is an indication that HGD expressed solely in the form of control over development agenda is not a magical formula for achieving sustainable development. The case shows that without properly integrating basic general principles of development highlighted in the HDG features (see Chapter 3) it will be difficult for countries to realize lasting success.

8 Common trends and issues in African homegrown development efforts

In this chapter we aim to summarize the findings from the case studies and provide an analytical comparison of the four countries, Ghana, Nigeria, Kenya and South Africa. In addition we identify tensions, issues and patterns implicated in the search for homegrown development (HGD), not just in the case of these countries but also in Africa as a whole. We start by comparing the four countries on the basis of the HGD framework developed in Chapter 3 and on which the analysis in the empirical chapters were built. Based on the comparison we draw out some common trends and issues. Following, we present a model that shows the various degrees of 'ownership' of development strategies that can be found in different African (and other developing) countries. These range from outright policy imposition through a hybrid of policy adoption and modification to genuine ownership and HGD. This is to our knowledge the first taxonomy or model of its kind and we hope that scholars will find it useful as a template for studying development efforts in other developing countries around the world. To end, we discuss some of the imperatives needed for African HGD efforts to consolidate and succeed and examine some abiding tensions.

Comparing Ghana, Nigeria, Kenya and South Africa

In assessing the *indigeneity* and outcome of the proclaimed HGD initiatives in Africa, we took four countries – Ghana, Nigeria, Kenya and South Africa – as case studies. Selecting these cases was always going to be difficult because of the diversity of the countries on the continent. However, in the end, we believe that the four cases provided a rich representation of the similarities and differences among African countries in a way that allows for meaningful comparison. Kenya, Nigeria and South Africa are regional powers and have huge economic and political influence on the continent. Ghana is relatively small but its democracy is seen as one of the few exemplar ones in Africa. Ghana is also representative of the many African countries where there has been new discovery of natural resources. Kenya is the least endowed with natural resources among the four and therefore occupies a critical position – representing the many African countries that are not endowed

Common trends and issues 131

with oil, diamond, or gold. Colonialism played a key role in the current development trajectories of Africa but affected countries in vastly different ways. The four countries chosen represent important differences in the process, experiences and outcomes of colonialism on the continent.

That said, the very fact that the whole emphasis of HGD is local solutions to local problems or tailoring development plans to suit local context means that comparison is largely possible regardless of the unique situations of the individual countries. In fact the uniqueness of the different countries provides a perfect opportunity for observing how a HGD approach can be taken in different situations with different outcomes. At the same time, it allows one to pull out common threads that are internal characteristics of HGD which enable it to function effectively and deliver results regardless of the unique situations and circumstances in any given country.

Table 8.1 shows a summary of our interpretation of how the four countries have fared in terms of the essence and core features of HGD.

Ownership: the core of HGD

Our analysis suggests that only South Africa scores high in terms of ownership of development policy. Although the ANC-led tripartite alliance, with the South African Communist Party (SACP) and the Congress of South African Trade Union (COSATU), sought for and accommodated inputs from external stakeholders including international donors, the final content of the Reconstruction and Development Programme (RDP) was largely determined by national actors. Local stakeholders have also continued to exert a high degree of control in the design and implementation of subsequent post-apartheid development polices including the Broad-Based Black Economic Empowerment (BBEE), the Accelerated and Shared Growth Initiative for South Africa (ASGISA) and most recently the New Growth Path (NGP) initiated in 2010. The notable

Table 8.1 Calibrating homegrown development in the four case-study countries

	Ghana	Kenya	Nigeria	South Africa
Essence of HGD				
Policy ownership	Low	Low	Medium	High
Core features of HGD				
Economic diversification and sensitivity to local imperatives	Low	Low	Low	Medium
Broad stakeholder consultation and participation	Medium	Medium	Low	High
Building local capacity and institutions	Medium	Low	Low	High
Social and human development	Low	Low	Low	Medium

132 *Common trends and issues*

exception was the Growth, Employment and Redistribution programme (GEAR) where the World Bank exerted considerable influence.

The ability of South Africa to take control of its own development planning and implementation has a lot to do with the established tradition of local control over policies mostly because South Africa is a settled colony. Unlike other African countries, the white minority that ruled the country since the formation of the Union in 1910 until 1994 eschewed external meddling in internal policy processes. Also, the political consciousness of the black majority during more than a century of segregation instilled a nationalist tendency that abhors external control in anyway. The level of development and especially high level of public awareness are also important factors as is the country's unique history. That said, it should be noted that South Africa remains vulnerable to external pressures and influence as can be seen in the high degree of influence exerted by the World Bank in the design of GEAR in 1996. This vulnerability is accentuated by at least three factors including: (i) lack of economic experience of the ANC ruling party – although the ruling elite has been learning very quickly; (ii) the high integration between South Africa and European markets; and (iii) the distrust and ideological war between the black dominated government and the white dominated private sector. In Chapter 7 we detailed how this ideological war and the structural power of the neoliberal minded private sector hinder South Africa from effectively integrating local considerations in its development policy.

Policy ownership in both Ghana and Kenya is low. The relationship between international donors and national governments in these countries continue to be highly asymmetrical with the donors exerting heavy influence in the design and implementation of development programmes. Development policies in Ghana and Kenya are very closely tailored to the World Bank's and International Monetary Fund's Poverty Reduction Strategy Framework with its overriding focus on macroeconomic stabilization and debt repayment. The major factors shaping the asymmetrical relationship between these countries and International Financial Institutions (IFIs) are the extent of these countries' indebtedness and their current high dependence on external donors for development funding.

Ghana is a member of the Highly Indebted Poor Counties (HIPC) which allows it to borrow money under special conditions from the World Bank and IMF. Despite significant concessions under the HIPC initiative, which in any case, came with tough reform conditionality, Ghana is still heavily indebted with a total public debt stock of about US $22,737 billion representing about 49.25 per cent of GDP. Currently, Ghana still depends on international donors for up to 65 per cent of its development funding with the Ghana Poverty Reduction Strategy I (GPRS I) indicating that donor aid accounted for 90 per cent of energy, 86 per cent of agriculture and 76 per cent of roads' expenditure respectively (Government of Ghana, 2003: 2). Given Ghana's indebtedness and lean extra-aid resources, local politicians have little or no bargaining power against donors whose demands and influence have grown in

Common trends and issues 133

proportion to Ghana's increasing aid dependence (Whitfield and Jones, 2008). Ghana has attempted to use the little wriggle room it has under the Bank's Poverty Reduction Strategy Papers' (PRSP) framework to articulate national priorities that could lead to a more HGD approach such as great emphasis on quality education and human resource development. However, Ghana's degree of indebtedness robs the government of any meaningful leverage in deciding loan conditions and development policy. And this is despite Ghana's relatively good reputation in terms of political stability, institutions and democracy.

Although Kenya is not a HIPC country, it is heavily constrained by a huge burden of debt. Like Ghana, Kenya also has a very meagre source of extra aid revenue for development. There is currently no known commercial oil or mineral reserves or mining taking place in Kenya and the government's income is mostly through agricultural exports and tourism. Given this structural weakness Kenya's development policy is closely tailored to satisfy the conditionality of international donors. Influence of donors on Kenya's economic policy is further enhanced by weak institutions, poor governance and grossly inadequate human capacity. Critically Kenya has a 'reputation for being a "regime taker" among donor community' (Cumming, 2001: 284) – a term used to describe countries that are inclined to obey rules and aid conditionality handed down by donors. Kenya was one of the first countries in Africa to produce, in 1999, a full PRSP which it entitled Poverty Reduction and Growth Facility (PRGF). Hanmer, Healey and Naschold (2000) commented that 'the Kenya PRGF had the dubious distinction of having the toughest conditionalities ever imposed by the IMF board'. There is a perception that donors see tough loan conditionality as a way of helping to enforce accountability and good governance which are severely lacking in Kenya (Hanmer and Shelton, 2001; McGee, Leven and Hughes 2002). While, however the intention may be good, there is also a recognition that the impact of donor control has led to the erosion of local ownership of Kenya's development agenda. At the same time the insistence of broad stakeholder participation as a precondition for loans has also resulted in greater recognition and sensitivity to local imperatives, such as poverty among the pastoralists, nature resource management and gender disparity in development planning (Hanmer *et al.*, 2000; McGee, 2002; Oversea Development Institute (ODI), 2004). Nevertheless, Kenya's development priorities remain for the most part dictated by external donors with very limited ownership exerted by the national government.

Policy ownership in Nigeria hovers between medium and low. Nigeria is well-endowed with oil resources and less dependent on international donors for development funding compared to many other African countries. However, in an attempt to reconnect with the international community after decades of military regime and being regarded as a pariah nation, the new democratic president was keen on gaining external legitimacy and in doing so surrendered a lot of control over the nation's development agenda to IFIs. Our analysis reveals that although the economic planning committee headed

134 *Common trends and issues*

by Ngozi Okonjo-Iweala enjoyed some autonomy and respect from the donor community, this high regard produced a rather paradoxical effect with the economic minister manifesting a high level of zeal to please her ideological demagogues in the World Bank and IMF mostly in a bid to retain her hard-earned reputation as a good manager. The result was that while the economic policy was authored mostly by Nigerians without undue direct pressure from the World Bank and IMF, both the 'letter and spirit' of the programme became almost indistinguishable from a World Bank's imposed initiative.

The foregoing raises several tensions and issues regarding policy ownership in African development especially in the context of the PRS. At least three of these are very potent. First, does ownership mean a commitment by a country to do as it is told (implement reforms) by the IFIs or does it mean total autonomy and control over development priorities? The evidence is that the IFIs subscribe to the former definition while many African governments prefer the latter. A vague definition of ownership might be necessary to retain its broad appeal within the aid and development discourse. In practice, however, there is serious tension in the various and contradictory interpretations harboured by the different stakeholders. Second, it is very difficult to ascertain how much ownership (understood in terms of total policy control) that can be realistically expected from countries in the context of an appalling state of technical, human and institutional capacity. In other words, even if the IFIs were to be minded to eschew meddling in the internal affairs of borrowing African countries (which they are not), there would still be legitimate questions about the ability of the aid recipient countries to articulate and implement a set of coherent HGD plans.

Third and related, there is a tension about how to balance the need for total policy autonomy with the need donors feel to provide accountability for their lending. There are some who advocate absolute autonomy based on arguments around sovereignty (e.g. Whitfield and Fraser, 2009). However, the IMF is often quick to remind critics of conditionality that many borrowing countries are like 'intensive care patients' implying that it would amount to irresponsible lending for the IMF and World Bank to not subject such countries to a strong regime of policy prescription and micro-management. A few have mooted the idea to restrict lending only to those countries that have good governance with great growth potential. However, such a measure would not only mean that some of the most needy countries are denied aid which would be morally perverse; there is also a question of how and who is to define what accounts for good governance. Moreover, the idea to tightly link lending to good governance ignores the fact that the misuse of aid can be just as much due to poor administrative machinery as it is to wilful corruption.

There is no doubt that the situation presents a dilemma both for governments who would rather avoid external tutelage and the IFIs who are well aware that high-handed policy prescriptions have not often resulted in the recovery and subsequent discharge of their patients. Speaking from the perspective of a recipient nation, President Kaunda of Zambia, way back in

Common trends and issues 135

1966, described the situation as being in a 'desperate strati' and suggested that the answer was for donors 'to provide alongside the aid, the professional and technical skills needed to train nationals to control it wisely' (Kaunda, 1966: 123). Still, how to strike a balance between policy advice and policy prescription especially in a condition of huge resource, knowledge and information asymmetry between donor and recipients remains a challenge to which no simple solution exists.

Economic diversification and sensitivity to local imperatives

Economic diversification is one of the basic principles of economic development. Undiversified economic structure is a major impediment to economic growth and stability in Africa. We postulated that a key feature of HDG is economic diversification and close attention to local imperatives whether these are advantages, threats or potential future opportunities. Our analysis reveals that African economies are still trapped in single commodity exploitation and exportation. Despite historical growth rate and positive noises about reforms, neither meaningful nor fundamental structural transformation has yet taken place. Specifically, countries have made minimal progress with regards to reinvesting windfall from commodity boom to enhance economic diversification and self-sustaining growth. In Nigeria, oil still accounts for over 95 per cent of total export while manufacturing accounts for less than 2.1 per cent. In Ghana three primary products – cocoa beans, gold and timber – account for about 72 per cent of export earnings. In Kenya, agriculture contributes more than 60 per cent of the country's total exports and 80 per cent of employment especially in the rural areas. Kenya's agricultural sector is responsible for about 30 per cent of its GDP and 45 per cent of government revenue.

Development polices analysed indicate strong recognition that overdependence on a few traditional commodities for export revenue places African countries in a vulnerable and precarious position especially given a rapidly changing climate and the high volatility in the international prices of these commodities (Okereke, 2014). This view is widely shared by scholars, African policy makers and their international development partners, all of whom stress that diversifying the economy is critical in order to leverage the current growth for development (Noman *et al.*, 2012). Yet, the empirical analysis and a quick survey of the general landscape in Africa suggest that progress is still very slow and that many countries are not leveraging their unique potentials to increase their competitive advantages.

South Africa is the most diverse and competitive economy of the four countries studied and arguably on the whole of the continent (Schwab, 2013). It is also the most developed and largest manufacturer. However, for decades now, the country has been recording jobless growth in part because of a failure to invest in increasing its manufacturing base. Instead of expanding the manufacturing sectors where it has the technology, economic environment and the regional market advantage, it is stemming its manufacturing sectors

136 *Common trends and issues*

while expanding mostly the service sector apparently in a bid to become more like Western European countries. According to Statistic South Africa (StatSA), manufacturing sector contribution to the GDP has declined from 19 per cent in 1993 to 17 per cent in 2010. This has contributed to jobless growth and booming unemployment in the country. As a country, South Africa has a high population of low skilled workers who could benefit in a labour intensive manufacturing sector that absorbs low skilled labour. Failure to expand the manufacturing base through concerted policies and incentives indicate a lack of sensitivity to local imperatives despite considerable local ownership of development agenda.

The gap left by South Africa especially in soft manufacturing could easily be filled by Nigeria given its high entrepreneurial culture and large market. Several portions of Nigeria's National Economic Empowerment and Development Strategy (NEEDS) and its successor, Vision 2020 are dedicated to the importance of encouraging diversification away from oil and towards agriculture, manufacturing and servicing. Nevertheless, the country remains ambivalent to investing in its declining manufacturing sector and creating a viable environment for the private sector. Investment in the manufacturing sector continues to be grossly inadequate and the government has not been able to create a viable environment to stimulate innovation and industrial growth. Hence in spite of Nigerian entrepreneurial culture, a combination of hostile business environment, poor economic policies and lack of infrastructure continue to stifle even the best of many individual efforts.

Nigeria's dependence on oil has been a major factor affecting economic diversification since the 1970s. Agricultural produce that gave the country its initial wealth has long been abandoned. In the 1960s Nigeria was the world's highest exporter of palm oil and groundnut. It also accounted for 18 per cent of the world's cocoa exports. During this period, Nigeria also produced most of its food and supplied 65 per cent of tomatoes on the West African market (Aregheore, 2005). However following the discovery of oil, Nigeria has allowed its agricultural and manufacturing sector to collapse and has gradually become a net importer of food despite its vast arable agricultural land. A renewed emphasis now seems to be devoted to revitalizing the agricultural sector but how far reaching and sustainable this endeavour will be remains to be seen.

Kenya and Ghana are making some attempts at economic diversification but again the pace is very slow. Like Nigeria and South Africa, Kenya is a regional power with strong potential in the agricultural sector. Kenya also has good prospects in the tourism sector. Kenya's Economic Restructuring Strategy (ERS) articulated ways of diversifying the economy. These included quadrupling tourism contribution to the GDP, promoting horticulture and fisheries, and establishing small and medium sized industrial parks to translate agricultural produce to intermediate value-added goods using low technology. Other big ideas were to attract ten big strategic investors in the agro-processing industries and to invest in the expansion of Business Processing Offshore (BPO) including the provision of business services via the internet to international markets, particularly the UK, Canada and the USA. Kenya's coastal location also provides important advantage of access to export markets via shipping and the East African integration. However, despite some improved performance in these areas compared to the situation during the SAP years, progress remains slow and many of the targets set in the policy documents remain unachieved. Crucially, despite correctly identifying agriculture as the country's main economic advantage, successive government policies have evaded the necessary if painful task of breaking the monopolistic land ownership structure that has stifled agricultural industrialization for decades.

Ghana has pledged not to go the way of Nigeria, Angola and Guinea, and other oil-rich countries on the continent following recent discovery of oil. This vow has seen the country record some impressive results in its efforts to increase economic diversification. Between 2001 and 2004, Ghana's earning from non-traditional export (NTE) grew by 40 per cent – a figure which represented a 100 per cent increase within a decade. Some of the notable commodities have included cassava chips, fruits and vegetable products, handicraft, canned fish, garment, and aluminium products. But as the list reveals, the country's economy remains at a rudimentary level and diversifying into intermediary goods continues to pose a major economic challenge for Ghana. Different governments have bemoaned the fact that manufacturing is the slowest growing sector of the economy, however, Ghana does not have a history of facilitating indigenous entrepreneurs.

Other countries of Africa are not faring much better. Overall, Sub-Saharan Africa remains dependent on a few primary commodities – mostly cocoa, cotton, sugar, tea and tobacco – for a large share of its export earnings. Several countries have remained almost exclusively dependent on one or two of these commodities for more than four decades. Cocoa, which is Africa's number one export product, accounted for 34 per cent of the continent's exports in 2010 (World Bank, 2013). While global trade (in current prices) has increased from US $13 trillion in 2000 to an estimated $30 trillion in 2010, Africa's share in world trade has been in decline since 1980 and currently stands at about three per cent (UNECA, 2014). While the share of exports of manufactures of East Asia Pacific has been growing since 1995, increasing from 15 per cent in 1995–1997 to 25 per cent in 2006–2008, the African share has remained low, even declining from 1.2 per cent in 1980 to less than 0.9 per cent in 2008. According to Africa Report (2011: 18) in 2008, Vietnam alone exported more manufacturing products than all sub-Saharan African countries combined. Despite being endowed with large areas of arable land, sub-Saharan Africa countries are said to be importing about $50 billion worth of processed food, and this amount is projected to reach $150 billion by 2030 (UNECA, 2014).

The continued lack of economic diversification in Africa may lead to a repeat of what happened from 1950 to the early 1970s when most African countries experienced high growth based on increases in commodity prices

138 *Common trends and issues*

only to quickly descend into deep economic crises at the onset of the international economic crunch of the 1970s. Unless African countries transit from commodity based economies to economies focused on manufacturing and value-added services, growth will remain superficial while sustainable development will be an elusive quest. Accelerating economic diversification was the key theme of the World Economic Forum held in Cape Town South Africa in August 2013. This is an indication that African leaders are aware of the importance of diversification in sustaining the ongoing economic growth. How far policy makers will go to put this awareness into action and create an economic infrastructure that would promote durable growth is yet to be seen.

Broad stakeholder consultation and participation

The scope and quality of stakeholder participation in the design and implementation of development programmes in Africa have been on the rise. Our analyses indicate that in all the four case study countries, governments made some effort to widen participation. South Africa scores high in the quality of stakeholder participation. Through the tradition of grass root consultation established during the process that led to the ANC Charter, the ANC-led government has maintained broad consultation in policy process. The notable exception was the Growth, Employment and Redistribution (GEAR) programme which was introduced by government as a *fait accompli* by the ANC on the pretext that it was urgently needed to save a rapidly degenerating economy. Enshrining inclusive participation in its constitution and consistently declaring the country a participatory democracy have both helped to institutionalize broad stakeholder participation. The strong and active civil society has also helped in getting the public to be actively involved in policy. The fact that the attempt to create a culture of inclusiveness policy formation had been broadly internalized was demonstrated by the level of outrage shown by many when GEAR was introduced in 1996 without broad consultation.

Ghana also has a history of promoting stakeholder participation especially since its return to democracy in 1993. Like South Africa, Ghana has also enshrined broad consultation and inclusive participation in its constitution, saying 'The State shall enact appropriate laws to ensure the enjoyment of rights of effective participation in development processes' (37.2a). This constitutional provision had a positive effect in spurring the high degree of consultation and participation that led to the Vision 2020 document. While the extent of consultation for the Ghana PRSP was considerably less extensive and less well organized than what went into the preparation of Vision 2020, the effort nonetheless represented a step away from the exclusive policy making that marked the SAP era.

While Kenya's effort at widening participation has so far been less than that of Ghana and South Africa, the country has nonetheless made decent progress. Both with respect to its Economic Restructuring Strategy (ERS) and

Common trends and issues 139

Vision 2030, Kenya made attempts to elicit contributions from stakeholders through the National Economic Social Council (NESC). The level of stakeholder consultation in Nigeria remains very low. Nigeria's NEED was mainly a product from a few technocrats and these only sought a limited consultation after the programme has gotten its external stamp of approval. Nigeria has not necessarily had a tradition of broad stakeholder consultation but rather a culture of top-down technocratic policy process. However, there has been an improvement in public consultation in the context of Vision 2020 which is the country's latest development framework.

Impetus for the improvement in stakeholder consultation in development planning comes from at least three main sources. Firstly stakeholder participation is one of the main requirements of the World Bank and the IMF's PRSP. Countries wishing to access loans and grants under the PRSP are expected to demonstrate that they have broadly consulted with key stakeholders including the public. The second factor responsible for increased participation is democratic institution and constitutional requirements. This is most applicable in the case of Ghana and South Africa. In general the nature of parliamentary democracy makes it imperative that a government should make development programmes more inclusive. However, democratic institution and requirement for the World Bank do not necessarily translate to broad and inclusive participation in policy process as much stills depends on institutional capacity, socio-cultural conditions and the willingness of governments to genuinely broaden the participatory process. For example, Nigeria carried out a limited consultation process despite being a democracy and regardless of this being a PRSP requirement.

The third impetus, which is related to the above, is pressure from below coming mostly from civil society organizations demanding more openness and participation from the government. Active participation also increases a sense of ownership and general awareness of policies by the majority of the population. We observed that in three countries with a strong and active civil society, the quality of the consultation process was fairly decent. In Ghana, Kenya and South Africa, to different degrees, governments have encouraged the active participation of civil society organizations and in some cases used them to organize public debates on policy. Nigeria is weakest in this case; hence it not surprisingly scored the lowest in terms of inclusiveness and broad consultation.

Participation has a complex relationship with HGD especially in the context of institutionally weak developing countries as found in Africa. The empirical analysis reveals at least six key issues, some of which are interrelated. The first is that while broad participation might in principle increase policy ownership, it could also throw up populist and unworkable economic policies. Second, there are questions about the quality of participation that can be expected in the context of limited capacity, knowledge and information flow. Third, there is tension about the extent to which or whether in fact participation can help increase ownership. Fourth, it is not clear what exactly the point of participation is, when the final decision is ultimately taken by a

140 *Common trends and issues*

few officials at the centre. Similarly one wonders why people should take the trouble to participate in policy making process given the fact that it is external donor agencies and not the citizens themselves that eventually ratify the plan. Fifth, there is tension related to the role of sponsored and well-resourced groups in hijacking participation and unduly influencing policy agenda. Finally there are serious questions about whether the types of consultation promoted by donor agencies undermine the constitutional mandate and role of countries' parliaments in formulating national development plans. Some of these issues have been highlighted by insightful commentaries on PRSPs and aid politics in Africa (Booth, 2001; Bugingo, 2002; Hearn, 2001; McGee *et al.*, 2002; Stewart and Wang, 2004; Whitfield, 2009). Let us examine some of these in a bit more detail.

Regarding the first tension, it is notable that Ghana in drafting Vision 2020 followed a very inclusive and participatory approach. However, the outcome was deemed unworkable as it promised a lot more than government budget could afford. In the end it had to be abandoned in favour of a belt-tightening economic policy emphasizing fiscal prudence and macroeconomic stability. Similarly, South Africa's Recovery and Development Programme (RDP) was a product of very extensive consultation and a wide stakeholders' participation. However, driven by the need to make compromises to accommodate diverse interests, the RDP ended up with a very long list of idealistic and poorly sequenced objectives which proved difficult to implement especially in the light of prevailing economic circumstances. And, just like Ghana's Vision 2020, the outcome was that the RDP had to be abandoned, again in favour of an austerity framework, in this instance GEAR. In contrast, Nigerian's National Economic Empowered and Development Strategy (NEEDS) may not have involved extensive consultation but there is no reason to suggest that it necessarily fell short in the analysis of the economic situation of the country or the set of interventions needed to promote sustainable growth. In fact the commitment to its implementation – at least the macroeconomic aspects of the plan – may be due to the fact that the few bureaucrats that crafted it felt a deep sense of ownership towards the plan.

This tension is felt not only by African governments by also by donor agencies like IMF and the World Bank who on the one hand cherish the 'good old days' when they could work with a few but knowledgeable bureaucrats in government to drive through reforms quickly, and on the other hand duly recognize that participation is a desirable normative goal even though it could lead to less streamlined policy or hinder needful reforms. This tension is aptly revealed in the case of Ghana where the World Bank, following the serious problems encountered in the implementation of Vision 2020, wrote:

> In the 1980s, the Bank dealt with a small group of leaders and technocrats accountable to an unelected head of state. In the 1990s, Ghana has an increasingly active parliament ... and new forms of decentralized organization and accountability. The political reforms may slow decision-making

Common trends and issues 141

and policy implementation in the short-term. But insofar as they broaden the 'ownership' … they will serve to deepen and to speed development over the long-term.

(World Bank Report, 1997, cited in Hearn, 2001: 46)

Similarly a USAID report also cited by Hearn (2001) equally reveals the ambivalence of donor organizations in this regard. In the report, USAID praised the SAP induced reforms in Ghana for their 'swiftness' and 'success'. It went on to attribute the good performance 'to the mandate given to a small and well qualified group of presidential and ministerial advisors' by the military regime. At the same time, however, it acknowledged that 'the maturing of democratic institutions means that a much more intensive process of consultation and consensus-building is required' (USAID, 1997, cited in Hearn 2001). This is not of course to suggest that stakeholder participation cannot or does not improve the quality of development plans. It is simply to say that it cannot be presumed that it will do so at all times and in all circumstances.

Although broad consultation can enhance policy ownership and a better understanding of local imperatives, inclusiveness does not necessarily translate into effective and impactful policy. A lot here depends on the quality of participation, which in turn depends on several factors and not least institutional capability. There is little doubt that the quality of participation in Africa is hampered by the low level of capacity and knowledge both of government and the large number of the citizens (Darko-Mensah and Okereke, 2013). Governments are known to boast that farmers, artisans, and housewives were consulted in crafting national development plans. There is of course no doubt that this sort of consultation can help broaden the understanding of different dimensions of poverty. However, it is also difficult to escape the judgment that these exercises are often rushed and superficial insofar as the majority of the local people that are involved in the process lack the broader knowledge to critique the proposals tendered by government.

IFIs mandated participation as a requirement for PRSPs under the supposition that it will help increase country ownership (Khan and Sharma, 2001; Stewart and Wang, 2004). However, this may have been presumptuous. Evidence suggests that participation can increase ownership where the culture of consultation already exists, where the civil society is strong and where governments genuinely believe in the merits of such an exercise. If however, governments believe consultation is forced upon them by the World Bank or that it is what they must do to tick a box needed to access loans, then consultation, under such circumstances, may well undermine ownership. Either way, there are questions about the relevance of participation when the final decision is always made by a few bureaucrats. The impression which came out strongly in the case of Ghana and Nigeria – but was also evident in Kenya – is that at the end of the day, the primary goal of the authors of these development plans is usually to satisfy the donors rather than the ordinary citizens of the countries.

142 *Common trends and issues*

In the same vein, our analysis, and many before us, have revealed that parliamentarians have shown low participation in formulating these putative development plans, with the government being more mindful of satisfying donors and meeting their deadlines. In the cases of Ghana and Kenya, for example, the governments routed the draft plans to the World Bank, and the parliament merely rubber stamped them. Stewart and Wang (2004) citing various sources provide ample statistics to demonstrate the minimal involvement of parliaments in Africa. According to them less than 10 per cent attended consultations, only six out of 83 MPs participated in Benin, and only five MPs were involved in Malawi. This is not to say that more active involvement by parliaments would have necessarily affected the plans since in many cases these are subservient to the executive arm. Yet it is telling that the representatives of the people could be virtually ignored when the World Bank's emphasis is on consultation with civil society organizations.

It may be that the focus on civil society actors has something to do with the fact that Western donors actually feel they might through these organizations exert some influence in the shape of the plan for which they give aid. Although our analysis did not necessary uncover evidence to this regard, Hearn (2001) has marshalled proof to show that there is a section of Western-sponsored civil society whose objective is often to promote neoliberal economic reform without consideration of how it fits into the local socio-economic structure. The implication is that participation here is used as a means of legitimizing rather than challenging the status quo.

Despite these shortcomings, there is evidence that, on the balance, broad consultation and widespread public participation can help broaden understanding of poverty types, consensus through public dialogue and improve the quality of the development plan. However, as noted, for the full potential of broad stakeholder consultation and participation to be realized, 'considerably higher intensity and better quality will be needed' (McGee *et al.*, 2002: ix).

Social development

One of the key fault-lines that stand out on studying the HGD attempts of African countries is the tension between the pursuit of social development and macroeconomic stabilization. This tension is evident regardless of the degree of policy ownership and stakeholder participation in the respective countries.

By far the most important criticism levelled against SAP was that it forced borrowing governments to focus almost solely on fiscal prudence and macroeconomic stabilization at the expense of social development. The 'Consensus' behind SAP-based lending was that economic predicaments of poor, aid-seeking African countries were caused by a combination of fiscal recklessness, state-led socialist policies and unwarranted protectionism. Adjustment lending was therefore intended to compel aid-seeking developing countries to 'adjust' or rebalance their economies through public spending cuts,

Common trends and issues 143

privatization, deregulation, increased tax, and similar other such structural reforms. However, it turned out that while SAPs did help a few countries achieve some measure of macroeconomic stability, it was only temporarily and resulted in job cuts, a rise in unemployment, reduction in social spending and ultimately more poverty and mostly economic decline.

However, despite the increasing recognition that both economic growth and social development are necessary components for improving wellbeing, combining these two objectives effectively continues to prove one of the defining challenges in African socio-economic development endeavours. Nigeria's marketing slogan for its development plan was 'meeting everyone's needs' and the plan emphasized wealth creation, employment generation, poverty reduction and value orientation as central goals. A sound macroeconomic framework, it was said, was necessary only as a means of achieving these wellbeing enhancing goals. In practice, however, the attention quickly turned primarily towards fiscal prudence and debt repayment, while employment creation, health services and education related objectives were relegated to the background. As we saw in the analysis chapter this lopsided focus of macroeconomic stabilization, eventually manifested in very poor performance in social development aspects of the plan such as provision of education, healthcare and sanitation. For example in 2012 Nigeria recorded the highest out-of school children on the continent according to the UNESCO 2012 Report.

In South Africa, the balance between economic growth and poverty reduction was touted as the defining feature of the RDP. In practice, however, it proved difficult for the government to convince all the stakeholders that it was able to juggle the two. Again one of the consequences, as in the case of Nigeria, was that South Africa recorded the highest drop-out rate with only 39 per cent of enrolled students completing grade 12 according to the South African Department of Basic Education. After abandoning Vision 2020, Ghana introduced GPRS with emphasis on macroeconomic stabilization and poverty reduction; however, the implementation reveals that, like the SAP, Ghana reverted back to macroeconomic focus while neglecting social issues. Generally, Ghana performs modestly in some areas especially health access and education. Ghana's cumulative drop-out rate is lower at 11 per cent for junior secondary school.

Unfortunately, the situation in the countries studied mirrors the general trend in Africa. Overall, Africa has recorded a high growth average since 2000. After a brief period of decline between 2007 and 2009 caused by the world economic recession, most African countries are bouncing back. Since 2001, the average economic growth in Africa has been higher than that of the rapidly emerging economies including Brazil, China and India (*The Economist*, 2012). The macroeconomic environment has relatively stabilized although there are fluctuations during national election processes. Encouragingly, it is predicted that Africa's average growth rate will continue to rise with seven countries in Africa including Ghana and Nigeria, recording the fastest growth by 2015 (*The Economist*, 2012).

144 *Common trends and issues*

However, the positive economic performance of the four case studies, as in the rest of Africa, is severely blighted by the abject social conditions of the vast majority of the citizens. Although, there has been a general decline in poverty on the continent, the level of poverty in Nigeria has risen and Ghana, Kenya, and South Africa do not fare much better. Overall, while the percentage of African population living on US $1.25 per day has decreased, African share of global poverty has risen since the 1990s. It is true that the accuracy of statistics is contested due to data and measurement challenges. However, it is generally accepted that the rate of growth does not correspond to the rate of poverty reduction on the continent.

The level of poverty is directly linked to the state of basic services like housing, education, health, electricity and water, where overall, Africa continues to lag far behind the rest of the world. The child mortality rate has declined, however Africa still tops the table on high child mortality rate when compared to other regions. High mortality rate in Africa is attributed to high prevalence of preventable diseases such as malaria, HIV/AIDS and typhoid. This is complicated by poor access to health and quality health service. With the exception of South Africa, basic functioning infrastructures, such as transportation and electricity, are still at a dismal level. Although South Africa generates enough power for electricity distribution, large numbers of the population still lack access to electricity. Water access remains a big challenge. This trend is also reflected in various countries in Africa which recorded a decline in social conditions according the 2013 UNICEF report. Africa remains the poorest and the most underdeveloped region in the world. Based on Gross National Income (GNI) only seven out of 54 countries in Africa are upper middle income countries. There is only one higher income country – Equatorial Guinea – while the rest hover between middle lower and lower income countries (World Bank Report, 2014). The same trend is seen in social indicators whereby African countries populate the bottom of the Human Development Indicator (HDI) scale. Even a high income country like Equatorial Guinea scored very low in the HDI. Africa has the highest prevalence of hunger in the world despite being rich in land and water resources according to the United Nations Development Programme's 2014 Report. There is a renewed optimism that 'Africa is rising' but the available data and reality in the different countries show there is still plenty of catching up to be done.

Another striking observation is the increase in the urban middle class as seen in these four case studies, which is reflected in other African countries as noted in the Mutual Review the Development Effectiveness in Africa (MRDE, 2012). Generally, while Africa's middle class is growing, the poverty rate is also increasing which means inequality is on the rise. According to the African Development Bank, the African rich (over US $ 20/day) control 18.8 per cent even though this group accounts for only 4.8 per cent of the population. Conversely the poor (less than US $2/day) who constitute 60.8 per cent of Africa's population hold just 36.5 per cent of total income in Africa. In some of the most unequal countries such as Mozambique and South Africa, the mean share of the lowest 20 per cent of the population is about 6 per cent of total income while the top 20 per cent has a share of 51.5 per cent. According to the African Development Bank, the middle class accounts for 33 per cent of the population in the region, compared with 56 per cent in developing Asia and 77 per cent in Latin America. Even the majority of the so-called middle class in Africa remain very vulnerable to external shock and could easily slip back into poverty if growth slows. South Africa is viewed as the most developed country but still has a majority of its population in poverty and is still haunted by two economic structures divided along racial lines. Equatorial Guinea has the highest per capita income on the continent but lacks infrastructure and ranks 139 on the UNDP HDI due to uneven distribution of oil wealth. According to the UNDP, the country's infant mortality rate is 20 per cent and less than half of the population has access to clean water. On the other hand, the Seychelles have the highest standard of living but also the highest income inequality. This increasing inequality on the continent coupled with high youth unemployment is a potent social time bomb. It is putting the whole growth in danger and creating a groundswell of discontent among those that have been left behind, which could result in mass uprising and even violent conflict.

Building local capacity and institutions

We hypothesized in Chapter 3 that building local capacity and effective institutions is one of the core features of HGD. There we observed that no country yet has been able to develop without investing in its human capital and organizing its core institutions to promote efficiency. This implies essentially having a strong and effective state, good environment for business, rule of law and, crucially, local human capacity building through high quality education, science and technology. Other keys aspects are organizing activities and incentive structures in ways that reward hard work, and promote innovation.

Several scholarly analyses suggest that the level of institutional sophistication and effectiveness corresponds with the level of governance and developmental progress (Acemoglu and Robinson, 2012; Rodrik, Subraminian and Trebbi, 2004). From the four cases studied, it is clear that the level of institutional capacity is seen as a key determinant for progress. For example, the most stable and progressive of the countries, South Africa and Ghana, are set apart by the level of institutional stability and to a large extent governance. It is not surprising that the Mo Ibrahim governance index rated South Africa and Ghana in the top ten, while Kenya and Nigeria are rated 21 and 41 in Africa respectively. The Ibrahim Index of African Governance provides a framework for citizens, governments, institutions and businesses to assess the delivery of public goods and services, and policy outcomes, across Africa.

Our analysis reveals that for a putative HGD approach to take place in Africa there is a need to recognize the value of good institutions in enhancing sustainable development. African countries have recognized this and are

146 *Common trends and issues*

making a commitment to progress. For example, the four cases are making progress in reforming institutions. South Africa's 1996 constitution which lays the foundation for other institutions has been hailed for its inclusiveness (Heller, 2001). Ghana introduced a new constitution in 1992 that ushered in democratic institutions and has continued with various institutional reforms that have made it a beacon of democracy in the region. Ghana is also improving its economic environment thereby attracting foreign investment. The prevalence of weak institutions is one of the biggest challenges facing Kenya and Nigeria. Both countries score low in this area even though there have been some notable improvements in recent years. After the 2008 post-election conflict Kenya took a step further in addressing institutional problems in the country through institutional reform that resulted in a constitutional referendum in 2010. Nigeria while still crippled with corruption and a dysfunctional public sector has embarked on some reforms in the financial sector and established the Economic and Financial Crimes Commission (EFCC) to tackle corruption. However, in general, institutions remain very weak and human capacity continues to constitute a serious challenge to sustainable development.

Yet, there is still a long distance to go even for the more progressive countries. In various ease of doing business rankings, most African countries perform very poorly. In the World Bank Groups Index 2013, Mauritius is the highest ranking African country and is the only African country in the top 20 in the world. A few other African countries that did well are Rwanda at position 32, and South Africa at 42. Meanwhile Kenya and Nigeria rank 129 and 147 respectively. Although individually many African countries have better record than the BRIC countries (Brazil, Russia, India and China), the average cost of doing business is still highest in Africa due mainly to high cases of violent conflicts on the continent when compared to other regions and the wide-spread poor state of economic infrastructures.

Obtaining credit facility is one of the major impediments for local entrepreneurs in many African countries with loan interest as high as 40 per cent. When these obstacles are added to the problem of infrastructure, a weak justice system, bureaucratic bottlenecks and external competition, finding a HGD approach that promotes local entrepreneurs through self-reliance becomes more complicated. Other biding constraints include improper functioning financial, legal, economic systems, and complex trading regulations. Countries in Africa, including South Africa, scored very low in business administrative processes that includes number of days it takes to start a business, registering property and enforcing contract. In addition to this, there is the problem of corruption. Many African countries still score very low in the Transparency International Corruption Perception Index. Ghana and South Africa scored highest among the four cases explored (in band 40–49 per cent country-groups) while Kenya and Nigeria scored lowest (in band 20–29 per cent group of countries). These scores correspond with institutional and ease of doing business rankings shown above. The foregoing suggests there are at least three key points about the relationship between institutions and HGD. First, good institutions are not simply about what is best for free market; rather effective institutions are those that enhance the synergy between the state, market and civil society in their respective roles to promote societal development.

The foregoing suggests that at least three key points about the relationship between institutions and HGD. First, institutions are simply what is good for the market rather effective institutions are those that enhances the synergy between the state, market and civil society in societal development. Hence while Easterly (2006a, 2006b) is correct for stressing the importance of the homegrown approach to development, he repeats a common mistake made by many Western scholars by attempting to strongly link self-reliant growth with market-enhancing institutions. Evans (2004) presses this point well when he argues that 'institutional effectiveness does not depend on ... the more specific premise that idealized versions of Anglo-American institutions are optimal developmental instruments, that their applicability transcends national cultures and circumstances' (ibid.: 33). Second and related, effectiveness of any institutions is dependent on the extent to which local culture, histories and characteristics are integrated. Hence in their pursuit of HGD, African countries have no reason to be ashamed of or disown their culture and local economic advantages. Third, institutions are dynamic and evolve over time to enhance the capacity of a country in carrying out developmental processes and maintaining existing institutions as well as creating complementary new ones. Kalinowski (2009) is therefore spot on when he identifies institutional learning as one of the vital ingredients of a country's ability to effectively adopt HGD.

Evidence from countries like China, India and Brazil shows the critical importance of education and human capital in capacity building for socio-economic development. From a point of severe disadvantage compared to the West, these countries have made tremendous progress in the last decades and have in fact caught up in some areas. Today China is the biggest exporter in the world and attracts huge foreign direct investment because of skilled cheap labour. India is the biggest exporter of human resources especially in science and technology due to early investment in these areas. Given the growing young population, Africa has the demographic advantage to enhance its productivity if it can prioritize investment in education and human capital. Critically, many African countries barely invest in research and development (R&D), neither do they invest enough in science and technology. The average proportion of investment in R&D is only 0.3 per cent of GDP. Only South Africa allocates up to one per cent of its GDP towards investment in R&D. It is hardly surprising that the amount of R&D spend correlates directly with the number of scientific publications. Again, South Africa leads the pack with 46 per cent of the continent's entire share of scientific output while Nigeria and Kenya account for 11.4 and 6.6 per cent respectively (UNESCO, 2012). As noted earlier in Chapter 3, human resource development is a critical condition for social economic development.

148 *Common trends and issues*

The homegrown development pyramid

An important outcome from the case studies and the research as a whole is that the alternative to HGD is not always outright imposition by foreign donors. The picture is rather complex with a number of variants or 'models' possible. Drawing from the conceptualization of HGD in Chapter 3 the findings from the analysis of the four cases and observation of the development strategies applied by different countries, we argue that there are at least four development approaches that can be discerned in the spectrum. These are (i) homegrown development strategies (HGDS), (ii) adapted development strategies (ADS), (iii) adopted development strategies (AoDS); and (iv) imposed development strategies (IDS). These four development strategies can be identified all over the world. However, in describing these strategies below we provide examples mostly from Africa in keeping with the focus of the book.

1: Homegrown Development Strategies (HGDS)

This is a holistic approach to homegrown development – one could call this mature HGD. In a country where such mature HGDS obtains, one can expect to see strong policy ownership or autonomy. This does not mean that such a county cannot borrow ideas or accommodate advice from external

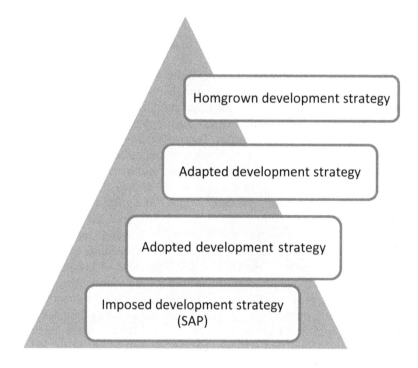

Figure 8.1 Pyramid of self-reliant growth

sources. It means there is no conditionality and that local stakeholders have full control over policy agenda and priorities. In HGDS, economy is diversified and due cognizance of local imperatives is taken whether these are unique economic advantages or any other cultural and historical imperative. In countries practising HGDS, institutional improvement is a priority and a continuous process. It is hard to see how a country can attain the HGDS status without strong institutions and human capacity. We would expect that strong participation – whether through parliament and/or involving the civil society – would characterize HGDS. Based on all of the above, we cannot judge that any African country has HGDS. South Africa comes very close with a high degree of policy autonomy. However it falls slightly short in integrating local imperatives, social development and human resource capacity development.

2: Adapted Development Strategies (ADS)

In ADS, there is some sense of policy ownership and decent effort to articulate national priorities. However, this is done in the context of aid conditionality. In other words the defining feature of ADS is that even though it is undertaken within an externally recommended framework with conditionality, conscientious effort is made by countries to adapt such a framework to local realities. In other words, even though such countries are given (or chose to take) a template from donors, they still exert considerable agency in deciding their national priorities. Rwanda and Ethiopia are some of the notable examples of African countries where ADS obtain. Through their agency, these countries bargain, re-negotiate, stretch and redefine the boundaries of the template or loan conditionality they are presented. Unlike in IDS and AoDS, where the aspiring country is mostly a 'rule taker', here, the country is a more dynamic 'player' – taking rules but also helping to define and set the rules. Evidence suggests that strong leadership is a central factor for a country to adopt ADS especially if such a state is heavily dependent on aid. However, there are a number of other factors such as the structural condition of a country, political stability and reasonably effective institutions.

3: Adopted Development Strategies (AoDS)

In an AoDS setting, there is limited policy ownership and integration of local imperatives. This is the approach taken by most African countries under the HIPC initiative, including Malawi, Zambia and Mali. Here, the overriding emphasis is to tick boxes that help fulfil the World Bank's loan conditionality. Countries employing AoDS model their development agendas tend to stick very closely to a template received from IFIs such as the World Bank and IMF's Poverty Reduction Strategy Papers (PRSPs) and show very limited initiative in imposing their own national priorities. Here, there is very limited ownership of policy if any at all. A condition of AoDS would suggest lack of

150   *Common trends and issues*

creative, visionary and dynamic leadership. However, there are other factors that exert huge influence, the topmost of which is structural disadvantage usually expressed in limited internal revenue and massive public debt overhang.

4: *Imposed Development Strategy (IDS)*

This is an imposed policy model plus condition and minus local imperatives. This approach is when external agency has a strong influence on local policy with total disregard to local needs and challenges. This approach reflects the Structural Adjustments of the 1980s and is different from the PRSP framework which even though it is externally driven with conditionality encourages inclusiveness and integration of local realities.

HDG is not a magic bullet

Even though we have strongly argued that there is ultimately no alternative to self-reliance for any country that wishes to ensure sustainable development, it needs to be duly recognized that HGD is not a magic bullet. First, while simply seizing control over its development plan may lead a country to having high policy autonomy, there is no guarantee that such an action will necessarily result in enhanced and sustainable development for such a country. In fact although autonomy remains the most important feature, in deed the essence of HGD does not equal isolation. Rather, a country must assiduously seek out the best policies for engaging with the rest of the world while nurturing its own priorities and endogenous growth. Julius Nyerere captured this imperative well way back in 1969 when he said:

> We used many different roads to independence; we shall probably need to use many different routes to reach the one goal of economic and social well-being for our peoples. It is not up to any one of us to imagine that we have a God-given answer for all places, and all circumstances, and all stages of a national struggle; each country must work out these things for itself.
>
> (Nyerere, 1969)

Secondly HGD is not static. It is a process. To be successful, a country would need to constantly evaluate both its development approach and specific policies in the light of prevailing circumstances and conditions. We have repeatedly stated the need to integrate local imperatives and economic advantages – but these too are not constant. Changes in demography (ageing population, number of youth, and percentage of urban dwellers), discovery or exhaustion of mineral resources, technological breakthroughs, are a few of the multitude of factors that can alter the economic calculus and a country's competitive advantage in a matter of months. Specific approaches that work today may be less effective tomorrow. Again, success resides not simply in taking ownership but in having the correct mindset and putting in place mechanisms to enable the anticipation and response to emerging challenges that can hinder development.

Summary

Today's Africa is in many ways different from the one that existed in the 1980s when SAPs reigned supreme. Africa now boasts some of the world's economically fastest growing countries and predictions are that the continent's average growth rate may well be the highest in the coming decades. However, there has also been remarkable improvements in policy interventions, institutions, public participation, and good governance, all of which has contributed to growth. Many African countries have genuinely sought to take greater ownership of their development agenda and articulate their own national priorities. However African nations have not yet fully succeeded in this endeavour. External meddling and control are still rife. The economy is still not diversified and while more strides have been made, participation remains shallow. There is wide-scale infrastructural deficit and institutions are still hobbled with corruption and patronage. Far too much of jobless growth is occurring. The percentage of unemployed is growing and poverty is still rampant. A lot still requires to be done to create an enabling environment that will help nations and individuals to achieve their capability through self-reliant growth. Critically the share of the growth is not equitably distributed as wealth is increasingly concentrated at the top. Rather than HGD, what obtains in many African countries is a mixture of adapted and adopted development strategies based on the template provided by IFIs. This is not good enough. A lot more effort needs to be made towards embracing HGD by African people and their governments. This is a critical requirement for converting the current commodity-boom-based-growth into long term sustainable development. Perhaps the first step in this regard is good and responsive national leadership. However, at the same time, the structural constraints facing many Africans also requires that donors work harder to provide better policy space to allow African leaders to operate.

Conclusion

From an idea that was once derided as illusory, naïve and socialist, the concept of homegrown development (HGD) for Africa has of late pushed its way back again into the frontline of both African and international development discourse. HGD alongside its many variants – 'endogenous growth', 'self-reliant growth', and 'African solutions to African problems' – are now widely seen, not as one of the several alternatives, but as the *only* viable option for long term sustainable African development. There is a general consensus among scholars, African leaders, donors, civil society and the international community that externally driven development frameworks tied to conditions have not worked for Africa. The future, as is frequently said, lies in local articulation, ownership and accountability of development strategies. In the context of development, peace and security and environmental protection, the concept of HGD has become a potent tool for political mobilization and a focus of action. As Nathan (2013: 22) aptly puts it, 'The concept of "African solutions" evokes a sense of self-reliance, responsibility, pride, ownership and indigeneity, at once a rallying cry and a neat amalgam of politics, agency and geography'.

However, while the idea of HGD has captured the imagination of stakeholders across the spectrum, the concept remains very poorly defined. In the absence of a rigorous conceptualization of HGD, many connotations and interpretations have emerged resulting in much confusion and misguidance. Some of the many questions that have arisen about HGD in Africa relate to its definition – what exactly it is, how it may be operationalized, how much it has taken hold, its relationship with existing development paradigms and its utility as a vehicle for ushering in sustainable development (Apuuli, 2012; Nathan, 2013; Whitfield, 2009). Furthermore, does it have a normative content? Does HGD involve borrowing ideas from the West or solely leveraging local knowledge and assets? Does it entail broad-based participation that involves more civil society organization development planning or merely the more direct involvement of parliaments?

The book has aimed to contribute to the understanding and practice of HGD in Africa. The specific focus was to critically analyse the development initiatives that have coincided with the period of an increasing call for and

Conclusion 153

emphasis on local ownership of development in Africa, which was the late 1990s. The study was based on the assumption that African countries are now beginning to eschew policy rent and external meddling from donors and are seriously looking inwards for homegrown solutions. The uniqueness and contribution of the approach taken was in looking closely at these initiatives covering their conception, design and implementation, to see first, how truly endogenous they are, and second, how well or not they have served in facilitating sustainable development in the continent. In other words, we have attempted to explore what, if anything, differentiates these 'new wave' programmes from the previous approaches; the challenges they have faced and their prospects and limits as the vehicles of achieving a lasting socio-economic transformation of Africa.

The different 'levels' of homegrown development in African countries

In theory, a development strategy is either homegrown or not. But we live in a grey world. From general observation and based on our conceptual framework we can surmise that development approaches could fall anywhere in a spectrum from no HGDs at all to fully mature and operational HGDs. Looking more closely, we suggested that this continuum could be heuristically divided into four levels. We have called this the pyramid of development (Chapter 8). At the bottom of the pyramid is the Imposed Development Strategy (IDS) where countries have little or no say over their development agenda but do exactly as they are told by external agents, whether these are foreign states or international financial institutions (IFIs). Typical examples of IDS are the development approaches that characterize the Structural Adjustment Programmes (SAPs) of the1980s. We noted in Chapter 1 and Chapter 2 that SAPs were the focal point of anti-foreign-meddling anger in the 1980s and conversely the cause of agitations for African Solutions to African Problems. Next, are Adopted Development Strategies (AoDS) where countries model their development agendas very closely to a template received from IFIs such as the World Bank and IMF's Poverty Reduction Strategy Papers (PRSPs). Here, there is very limited ownership of policy and little or no coordination of aid strategies from recipients. A condition of AoDS would suggest lack of creative, visionary and dynamic leadership. However, there are other factors that exert huge influence, the topmost of which is structural disadvantage usually expressed in limited internal revenue and massive public debt overhang.

The third level in the pyramid is the Adaptive Development Strategy (ADS). Here, countries are given (or choose to take) a template from donors but they exert considerable agency in deciding their national priorities. Such countries do their best to give attention to unique local imperatives such as history and social economic structures. Through their agency, these countries bargain, re-negotiate, stretch and redefine the boundaries of the template or loan conditionality they are presented. Unlike in IDS and AoDS, where the

154 *Conclusion*

aspiring country is mostly a 'rule taker', here, the country is a more dynamic 'player' – taking rules but also helping to define and set the rules. Finally at the topmost level are Homegrown Development Strategies (HGDS). This is the approach we have in mind when we speak of HGD in the book. At this level, the *core* and the *features* of HGD as defined in the previous section are operating at a fairly advanced level. There is complete policy autonomy, institutions are mostly effective, economy is diversified, policies faithfully incorporate local imperatives and social development is advanced.

In examining the development strategies of four African countries – Ghana, Nigeria, Kenya, and South Africa – through the prism of our conceptual framework, we found that while Africa may have started the journey towards HGD, it is yet to arrive at the desired destination. South Africa is the only country of the four cases analysed that operates HGDS – but *only just*. The policy autonomy is sufficiently high, institutions are moderately advanced and there is a deep culture of broad-based public participation. The severe drawback for South Africa is that it does not yet sufficiently implement local imperatives in its development strategies. Another serious issue for South Africa is the persistence of the so called 'two economies' problem that sees the minority white population enjoying a high state of wellbeing while the vast majority of the black population lives in abject poverty. Mostly, as a result of the legacy of apartheid, South Africa continues to have a very high poverty and unemployment rate comparable to other low income countries of Africa even though it is officially a middle income country.

Effective HGDS will see South Africa investing a lot more in manufacturing where it has comparative advantage given its fairly advanced infrastructure especially when compared to other African countries. Investment in manufacturing is also an imperative for the absorption of the large population of young employed in the country. In addition to strengthening its manufacturing sector, South Africa will have to work harder to take advantage of its regional power status by expanding its market within Africa.

Ghana, Kenya and Nigeria do not score high in policy ownership although Nigeria performs marginally better than the first two. These countries are implementing World Bank/IMF PRSPs with varying degrees of success in their attempt to adapt. Although all have made significant progress compared to what obtained in the SAP era, aid dependence is still a big challenge especially for Ghana and Kenya. Despite its reputation as the trailblazer of democracy in Africa, a huge public debt overhang has ensured that Ghana remains bound by the IFIs' development model formulated through PRSPs frameworks and the Highly Indebted Poor Countries (HIPC) conditionality. Kenya is less dependent on aid than Ghana but still suffers from high loan conditionality. The perception is that IFIs are using harsh conditionality to help correct bad governance in Kenya, but this constitutes a hindrance to ownership. Nigeria presents a strange case. Despite being resource rich, and on paper, with great potential to throw its weight, it has consistently demonstrated far less dynamism in terms of taking control over its own priorities for

Conclusion 155

development agenda. We determined that this has to do with the bureaucrats at the helm of affairs who seem too keen to satisfy the IFIs for their own reputational reasons.

All the three countries have sought to identify and articulate national priorities that integrate local imperatives in the context of the PRSP template received from the IFIs. Nigeria identified the need for economic diversification and job creation, Ghana put emphasis on poverty alleviation and human resource development, and Kenya's bold ideas are quadrupling tourism contribution to GDP and expanding its Business Processing Offshore (BPO). All countries identify the need to modify and transform their agricultural sectors as an urgent priority. However the overriding emphasis of these countries remains macroeconomic stabilization.

Public participation is medium in Kenya and Ghana but low in Nigeria which continues to adopt a top down approach. The key reasons for moderately good participation in Ghana and Kenya are constitutional requirements and a strong civil society. However the need to satisfy the requirements of the PRSPs is also an important factor. Participation has a complex relationship with HGD especially given weak institutional capacity (McGee, 2003). Although in theory public participation can help broaden understanding of poverty types and build consensus around policy, these benefits are nowhere being fully realized because of the currently low quality of participation. Crucially, participation can also undermine policy ownership if it is undertaken purely for the sake of fulfilling donors' requirements.

By far the biggest challenge in these countries – including South Africa – is effective implementation. A combination of weak institutions, low political will and the inadequacy of development finance result in the poor implementation of many aspects of countries' development strategies. Specifically, the urgency to satisfy conditions imposed by the IFIs means that when the need for hard choices arises, stabilizing the macro economy is prioritized over poverty alleviation and social development components of the development strategies. This lopsided focus on macro stabilization explains the gap between moderately good economic growth rates on the one hand, and rising poverty on the other hand. For example, while the percentage of African population living on US $1.25 per day has decreased, African share of global poverty has risen since the 1990s. The level of poverty is directly linked to the state of basic services like housing, education health and water, where overall, Africa continues to lag far behind. The child mortality rate has declined but Africa still tops the table on high child mortality rate in comparison to other regions.

There has been much talk about economic diversification by African leaders and this rhetoric is abundantly reflected in the strategies (Government of Ghana, 2003; 2007; National Planning Commission, 2004; African National Congress, 1994). Economic diversification was the theme of the first African Economic Summit held in Johannesburg in 2010. But economic diversification does not just spring up in the absence of an enabling environment that

156   *Conclusion*

fosters production capability, investment and infrastructure. Our analysis strongly shows that with the exception of South Africa, the state of physical and social infrastructures in many African countries – such as water, transportation system and health services – is woeful. Over 547 million Africans out of a population of about a billion do not have access to electricity but depend on biomass for their basic energy needs (IEA, 2011; Okereke and Yusuf, 2013) and businesses spend up to 45 per cent of their recurrent expenditure on electricity – mostly private diesel generators. The high cost of electricity, poor access to credit and graft ridden institutions combine to strangle business, suffocate the entrepreneurial culture and choke innovation. The World Bank Group's *Ease of Doing Business Index 2013* shows Kenya and Nigeria rank 129 and 147 respectively while South Africa posts a decent rank of 42.

Many African countries recognize that one of the most critical impediments to decent self-sustaining growth development in the continent is weak institutions. Since the turn of the millennium, many countries have invested effort in institutional reform. Ghana, which has long pursued the policy of decentralization (Okereke, 2011), has made even more progress in this area – granting more autonomy and funding to District Assemblies. Governance has improved in Kenya with greater democratic checks and balances between the various arms of government. The notion of 'open society' and a stronger role for civil society in decision making is taking root. Nigeria has passed a Freedom of Information Bill and instituted anti-corruption agencies. The government publishes the allocations given to state and local governments and has strongly promoted a more open and transparent approach to contract tendering popularly known as 'due process'. However, bribery, corruption, graft and patronage are still endemic.

Aid conditionality and homegrown development

While the need for good governance remains high, a lot of obstacles to policy ownership in Africa are also linked to external conditions including its colonial history, position in the global economic structure, debt overhang and aid conditionality. National development does not come cheap. Despite a record growth in the last decade, for example, most African countries still fall far short of the money needed to fund development. Shortfall is exacerbated by a number of factors including capital flight (by multinationals and local cronies), limited internal revenue stream, increasing population, and crucially the debt burden. Unfortunately, the inability to carry the cost of development leads countries to borrow more which in turn leads to bigger debt liability and again to stricter borrowing conditions and control. This problem is grossly exacerbated because, ironically, poor countries borrow money on conditions much harsher than their developed countries counterparts. This not only severely limits public investment in infrastructure and poverty alleviation; it also makes it difficult for countries to impose themselves and define their own priorities and development agenda.

Conclusion 157

Many African countries are burdened with heavy debt, and in most cases export earnings are used for debt interest service instead of investment. For instance, Ghana's value of total public debt is at around 52 per cent of GDP, public debt service absorbs about 40 per cent of government revenue (Bräutigam and Knack, 2004: 257). The implication is these countries are perpetually at the mercy of lending institutions and their conditionalities thereby denying countries the freedom to manage their economy and propel development. The debt burden of African countries is strangulating. Even though debt is declining, debt service continues to drain huge percentages of countries' export earnings which could be diverted to social needs and expanding the economy.

This vicious cycle of debt and poverty has received much attention in the literature and development discourse but precious little effort has been made by donors to break it. One of the interventions trumpeted as destined to solve this problem was the HIPC initiative which promises debt scheduling or in some cases cancelling as reward for structural reform. But while the HIPC initiative is often branded as another act of benevolence by the Organisation for Economic Co-operation and Development, it turns out, on closer examination, that the package comes with conditions, which in practice worsen poverty situations and deepen dependence on the West. For example studies carried out by the US Jubilee Debt Campaign in 2008, shows that in order to access debt, Zambia had to privatize its national bank despite stiff opposition from parliament and public. The same Zambia was forced to implement a wage and hiring freeze which restricted the government from employing 9,000 needed teachers. Similarly, Mali with about 90 per cent of its population living on less than a dollar a day was forced to privatize public enterprises and utilities including electricity. It was also made to accept price liberalization of the cotton sector according to artificially low market prices. This led to a 20 per cent drop in cotton price for the farmers. Ironically, cotton farmers in the USA and EU are highly subsidized by their governments. Other countries such as Democratic Republic of Congo, Sierra Leone and Burundi were required to keep their budget deficit lower as a percentage of GDP (Jubilee USA, 2008). This is despite experience from the EU and other countries showing that pegging deficit to percentage of GDP is hardly a pragmatic policy, even for more developed countries. These cases apply to many other African countries that are subscribed to the HIPC initiative.

It is understandable that some kind of conditions may be required for loan or aid, but there is need to distinguish between conditions that help a country to pay its loan and those that merely lead countries further into poverty and underdevelopment. It is interesting, for example, that while PRSPs mandated reforms regularly include good governance, health and literacy targets, the poverty reduction aspects of the requirement are never used in assessing countries' debt cancellation. In almost all cases the key considerations have been the fiscal and market liberalization conditions. There is no record or evidence whereby IFIs used poverty reduction, education targets, or even

158　*Conclusion*

participation and ownership to determine a country's debt cancellation or qualification for loan. A study of countries within the HIPC initiative carried out by Angela Wood of Jubilee UK noted that 'it was either a failure to comply with PRGF programs or to reach agreement with the IMF on a new PRGF program that lengthened the time countries remained in the HIPC process' (Jubilee USA, 2008: 4). Even a report from an Independent Evaluation Office of the IMF confirms that its straightjacket conditionality does not work. John Weeks and Terry McKinley have argued that the fiscal gain from debt relief has been marginal because of conditionality attached to loan and aid by Overseas Development Agencies. They linked poor performance of MDG in most countries to stringent conditionality (Weeks and McKinley, 2009).

The Washington Consensus is not dead

Subscription to HGD would suggest the freedom to choose whichever path a country deems best. In a condition where countries are practising HGD one would expect to see several varieties of policy tools and approaches. Encouragement of variety was in fact one of the principles behind the introduction of the PRSPs in 1999. It was based, as Sanahuja Perales (2004: 415) puts it, 'on efforts to widen the political, economic, and social opportunities available to the poor, leaving behind reductionist approaches that insisted solely on economic growth'. However in practice, the orthodoxy of neoliberalism remains unchanged. The impact of decades of *imposition* of adjustment reforms is that the Bretton Woods Institutions (BWI) development models have come to be viewed as the universal mainstay for development, especially in African countries. Hence even when African countries purport to be moving away from the World Bank PRSPs and crafting their own development plan, the popular practice continues to follow the externally prescribed neoliberal model without adequate consideration of local imperatives.

It does not help that African countries have continued to adopt the orthodox free-market economic ethos even when it does not help their economic challenges. Contrarily, developed countries never apply the economic liberalization model in the same way they mandate that it should be applied in developing countries. For instance, during the recent economic crisis, the Western countries led by the USA and the UK quickly set aside the long venerated 'invisible hand of the market' and bailed out the banks that are headquartered in their countries. Developed countries have various economic policies that go against the so-called free-market ethos to protect their economies. There is heavy subsidy of the agricultural sectors by Japan, the USA and EU, but BWI macroeconomic models discourage this in less developed countries. The USA bailed its 'too big to fail' banks and corporations, and the UK nationalized some of its banks to save them in the wake of the 2008 economic crisis, while aggressive privatization is promoted in countries across Africa through the PRSPs. Today, African countries measure economic progress by the level of privatization – as seen in Nigeria and Kenya – without adequately considering how it is carried out or its effect to societal development.

Taking a homegrown approach means taking what works for a particular country. Some of the economic models which have been the mainstay of the BWI framework have not worked for African countries. This is mainly because of the aggressive way in which they are applied in these countries, which is not practical and which is harmful to economic development. Instead of African countries latching onto these economic models, there is a need to consider the suggestion of Rick Rowden:

> Africa should be encouraged to use industrial policies – even to the extent they violate free market precepts. To this end, donor agencies, free trade agreements and bilateral investment treaties should refrain from denigrating the use of industrial policies so that Africa has the policy space it needs to truly rise.
>
> (Rowden, 2013: 4)

Leadership and the problem of policy ownership

Many countries in Africa, as noted, are characterized by weak institutions that breed poor rule of law and a lack of accountability leading to a structural corruption of leaders. Countries are laden with capital flight through cronyism and use of public funds for private pockets. Provision of public goods and services and the creation of a viable environment for citizens to thrive are neglected. As a result leaders end up depending on external funding and legitimacy. While not diminishing the importance of the external factors discussed in the preceding section, it remains the case that ultimately the way a government responds to developmental challenges at a national level and in relations to external influence determines whether a country will take a homegrown approach. If a government lacks public accountability and depends on external funding, there is likelihood that funders will have stronger leverage over local policies and there is also a high probability that the government will defer more to the external funders' conditions at the expense of its population, even when the general public and parliament oppose them, as we have seen in the case of Zambia. In this case it does not depend on strong or weak leadership but more on the vision of the leader. Nigeria under Obasanjo and Rwanda under Kagame provide examples of the role of visionary leadership in securing ownership space. Obasanjo was viewed as a strong leader with an equally strong leverage in international politics. In addition, Nigeria is also the least dependent on aid. Similarly Kagame is viewed as the strong man of Rwanda although his country is highly dependent on external funding. However, these two leaders took a different path in their involvement with BWI with Kagame clearly exerting more control even though he operates from a structurally weaker position.

160　*Conclusion*

Due to the colonial legacy and postcolonial meddling, governance in Africa has been externally structured. This has created an external dependency rather than framing development through an organic process of local imperatives. African leaders, in an attempt to solidify power with limited options, tend to maintain this external approach to solving local problems. These leanings play out more in terms of the development process. Even when African leaders fought to take a homegrown approach through the promotion of self-reliance, it only lasted for a short period. Due to the foundational structure of the state and governance system in Africa, most leaders tend to look for external approval and legitimacy more than internal loyalty and accountability (Okereke, 2011). This plays a role in the degree of dependency on and relationship with external funders in determining policy autonomy. Some leaders have been able to either extricate themselves from deepening dependency, or, even when there is need for external funding, maintain policy independence. Rwanda is one example of a country that depends on external funding for its development and still manages to maintain policy independence. Hence, normative or conceptual, policy ownership to some extent is dependent on a country's government providing leadership space that can be respected by external funders.

Leadership and governance are intrinsically embedded in overarching development ownership. A country with stable and effective leadership gains more trust in managing a country's development plan even when external loan and aid are heavily involved. According to the World Bank Report, countries perceived with weak institutions and leadership attract more external involvement in both policy framing and implementation. This suggests that sometimes it is not the degree of aid or loan but government capacity and capability that makes the difference. For example, Rwanda is one of the most aid dependent countries on the continent but has strong autonomy over its development plan. Nigeria, however, one of the least aid dependent countries on the continent has less governance trust. The four cases also show that lack of bold initiative from the government has often stalled development progress, even in South Africa with its homegrown and stable institutions. With a strong and visionary leader a country has a better chance of initiating and carrying out a bold development framework with primary focus on the country.

Africa rising; Africa at a crossroads

Since the millennium there has been a renewed hope that Africa is rising. Internal conflicts and civil war have drastically reduced. More African countries have transited into democratic forms of government and African average growth has been positively steady since 2000 with the world's six fastest growths coming from African countries – Angola, Nigeria, Rwanda, Ethiopia, Mozambique and Ghana. These positive economic and social indices have given impetus to a dramatic turn on the Western narrative of Africa from the Dark Continent to a 'Continent of Hope', 'African Renaissance' and 'Africa is rising'. *The Economist* which labelled the continent 'hopeless' in 2000 is now calling it the 'Hopeful Continent' and has been championing the 'Africa is rising' debate. The IMF recently organized a conference on the same theme where its Managing Director Christine Lagarde emphasized that 'Rising Africa is not just a buzz word but something that has been seen in reality' (IMF, 2014).

There is no question that Africa has made some positive strides since the millennium but the questions one need to ask are what is rising, to what extent, and who is benefitting? Even the most pessimistic have been forced to accept that change is in the air. The key question has been whether this trend is transitory or one which can be sustained and how that might be made to happen. This book began with the assumption that there is a better chance for development if a country takes control of its development process. This is achieved by looking within and articulating a comprehensive broad-based framework of what could work with the understanding of local realities and the rapid globalizing world – homegrown. It turns out that although some progress is being made much of the development in Africa remains controlled by external factors and their agents. Despite the consensus call for Africa to develop a crafted homegrown socio-economic framework to foster its developmental challenges, many countries have continued to be dependent on IFIs for their development model.

Africa stands at a crossroads. What it does now will go a long way in defining its future. Effort is needed from all stakeholders to encourage deep transformation and help sustain the progress being made. Donors must provide more policy space. There is need to move away from the type of loan and straightjacket aid conditionality that constrain agency. Africa needs to be unburdened from the strangulating debt that holds most of its states down. There is need to devise better and less intrusive ways of making aid more effective. Furthermore there is a need to encourage a move away from 'institutional mono cropping' and rabid liberalization. African leaders, on their own, must show greater will to fight corruption and be more accountable to their people. They must do more to demonstrate to both donors and their own people that they are committed to doing what is the best for their nations. If they do so, they will gain the prestige and legitimacy needed to drive negotiations and hard bargains in the international donor community. HGD is not a magic bullet. In theory it is the only way for long lasting development. Getting it right in practice requires dedication and calls for tough choices and collective action from the government and citizenry.

Bibliography

Abdoulaye, W. (2001) *Omega Plan for Africa*. Addis Ababa, Ethiopia: Economic Commission for Africa (ECA).

Abrams, F.W. (1951) Management's Responsibilities in a Complex World. *Harvard Business Review*, 29(3), 29–34.

Abugre, C. (2001) *PRSP Monitoring and Information in Ghana*. Available at www.isodec.org.gh/Papers/prspmonitoringin-ghana.pdf (accessed 27 June 2005).

Acemoglu, D. and Angrist, J. (2000) How Large Are Human Capital Externalities? Evidence from Compulsory Schooling Law. In B. Bernanke and K. Rogoff (eds), *NBER Macroeconomics Annual*. Cambridge, MA: MIT Press, pp. 9–59.

Acemoglu, D., Johnson, S. and Robinson, J.A. (2001) The Colonial Origins of Comparative Development: An Empirical Investigation. *American Economic Review* 91: 1369–1401.

Acemoglu, D., Johnson, S. and Robinson, J.A. (2002) Reversal of Fortune: Geography and Institutions in the Making of the Modern World Income Distribution. *Quarterly Journal of Economics*, 117: 1231–1294.

Acemoglu, D., Johnson, S. and Robinson, J.A. (2003) An African Success Story: Botswana. In D. Rodrik (ed.), *In Search of Prosperity: Analytical Narratives on Economic Growth*. Princeton, NJ: Princeton University Press.

Acemoglu, D., Johnson, S., Robinson, J. and Thaicharoen, Y. (2003) Institutional Causes, Macroeconomic Symptoms: Volatility, Crises and Growth, *Journal of Monetary Economics*, 50: 49–123.

Acemoglu, D. and Robinson, J. (2012) *Why Nations Fail: The Origins of Power. Prosperity and Poverty*. London: Crown Publisher.

Adamolekun, L. (1983) *Public Administration: A Nigerian and Comparative Perspective*. Lagos: Longman.

Adedeji, A. (1981) *Indigenization of African Economies*. London: Hutchinson Publishing Group.

Adedeji, A. (ed.) (1999) *Comprehending and Mastering African Conflicts: The Search for Sustainable Peace and Good Governance*. London: Zed Books.

Adedeji, J.L. (2001) The Legacy of J.J. Rawlings in Ghanaian Politics. *African Studies Quarterly*, 5(2).

Adekanye, J.B. (1995) Structural Adjustment, Democratization and Rising Ethnic Tensions in Africa. *Development and Change*, 26(2): 355–374.

Adelabu, N.S. (2012) The Political Economy of Oil Deregulation in Nigeria's Fourth Republic: Prospects and Challenges. *Journal of Emerging Trends in Educational Research and Policy Studies*, 3(3): 193–198.

Bibliography   163

Adelzadeh, A. and Padayachee, V. (1994) The RDP White Paper: Reconstruction of a Development Vision. *Transformation*, 25: 1–18.

Adogamhe, P. (2007) *The Nigerian National Economic Empowerment and Development Strategy (NEED): A Critical Assessment*. A paper delivered at the 48th Annual Convention of International Studies Association, 28 February to 3 March 2007, Chicago, IL.

Afigbo, A.E. (1986) *Federal Character: Its Meaning and History. Nigeria*. Portsmouth, NH: Heinemann Educational Books.

Afigbo, A.E. (1991) Background to Nigerian Federalism: Federal Features in the Colonial State. *The Journal of Federalism*, (21): 40–52.

African National Congress (ANC) (1994) *The Reconstruction and Development Programme: A Policy Framework*. Umanyano, Johannesburg.

Agupusi, P. (2011) Trajectories of Power Relations in Post-Apartheid South Africa. *The Open Area Studies Journal*, 4: 32–40.

Agyei-Mensah, S. and de-Graft Aikins, A. (2010) Epidemiological Transition and the Double Burden of Disease in Accra, Ghana. *Journal of Urban Health*, 87(5): 879–897.

Ajulu, R. (2001) Thabo Mbeki's African Renaissance in a Globalising World Economy: The Struggle for the Soul of the Continent. *Review of African Political Economy*, 28(87): 27–42.

Ake, C. (1981) *A Political Economy of Africa*. London: Longman.

Ake, C. (1982) *Social Science as Imperialism: The Theory of Political Development*. Ibadan: Ibadan University Press.

Ake, C. (1991) Rethinking African Democracy. *Journal of Democracy*, 2(1): 32–44.

Ake, C. (1995) Is Africa Democratising? In O. Mimiko (ed.), *Crises and Contradictions in Nigeria's Democratization Programme, 1986–1993*. Akure: Stebak Ventures.

Ake, C. (1996) *Development and Democracy in Africa*. Washington, DC: The Brookings Institution.

Akpor, O.B. and Muchie, M. (2011) Environmental and Public Health Implications of Wastewater Quality. *African Journal of Biotechnology*, 10(13): 2379–2387.

Alechenu, J. and Josiah, O. (2007) PTDF: Panel Blames Obasanjo, Indicts Atiku. *The Punch*. Wednesday 28 February.

Alesina, A. and Spolaore, E. (2003) *The Size of Nations*. Cambridge, MA: MIT Press.

Allen, C. (1995) Understanding African Politics. *Review of African Political Economy*, 22(65): 301–320.

Allen, M.H. (2006) *Globalization, Negotiation and the Failure of Transformation in South Africa: Revolution at a Bargain?* London: Palgrave Macmillan.

Almond, G.A. and Coleman, J.S. (1960) *The Politics of the Developing Areas*. Princeton, NJ: Princeton University Press.

Almond, G.A. and Powell, C.P. (1966) *A Developmental Approach*. Boston, MA: Little Brown & Co.

Amanze-Nwachukwu, C. (2007) Nigeria Local Content-Oil Firms May Miss 2010 Target. *Thisday Newspaper*, 12.

Acemoglu, D. and Robinson, J. (2012) *Why Nations Fail: The Origins of Power. Prosperity and Poverty*. London: Crown Publisher.

Africa Report (2011) World Economic Forum, the World Bank and the African Development Bank.

Amjadi, A. and Yeats, A. (1995) *Have Transport Cost Contributed to the Relative Decline of Sub-Saharan African Exports? Some Preliminary Empirical Evidence*. World Bank Policy Research Working Paper No. 1559.

164   Bibliography

Amjadi, A. *et al.* (1996) *Did External Barriers Cause the Marginalization of Sub-Saharan.* World Bank Policy Research Working Paper WPS 1586.

Amin, S. (1972) Underdevelopment and Dependence in Black Africa-Origins and Contemporary Forms. *The Journal of Modern African Studies*, 10(4), December: 503–524.

Anamuah-Mensah, J. and Towse, P. (1995) Bringing Industry into the Science Classroom–Problems, Concerns and Prospects Associated with a Paradigm Shift. In J. van Trommel *Science and Technology Education in a Demanding Society.* Enschede Netherland: National Institute for Curriculum Development, pp. 165–180.

Anger, B. (2010) Poverty Eradication, Millennium Development Goals and Sustainable Development in Nigeria. *Journal of Sustainable Development*, 3(4): 138–151.

Angus, D. (1999) Commodity Prices and Growth in Africa. *Journal of Economic Perspectives*, 13(3): 23–40.

Anyanwu, J. (1991) President Babangida's Structural Adjustment Programme and Inflation in Nigeria. *Journal of Social Development in Africa*, 7(1): 5–24.

Apuuli, K.P. (2012) The African Union's Notion of 'African Solutions to African Problems' and the Crises in Côte d'Ivoire (2010 –2011) and Libya (2011). *African Journal on Conflict Resolution: Special Issue on the African Union*, 12(2): 135–160.

Aregheore, E.M. (2005) *Country Pasture/Forage Resources. FAO Country Files.* Available at www.fao.org/ag/AGP/AGPC/doc/counprof/nigeria/nigeria.htm

Arora, A. and Gambardella, A. (2006) *From Underdogs to Tigers: The Rise and Growth of the Software Industry in Brazil, China, India, Ireland and Israel.* Oxford: Oxford University Press.

Arrighi, G. and Saul, J.S. (1968) Socialism and Economic Development in Tropical Africa. *The Journal of Modern African Studies*, 6(2), August: 141–169.

Aryeetey, E. and Harrigan, J. (2000) Macroeconomic and Sectoral Developments since 1970, in *Economic Reforms in Ghana–The Miracle and the Mirage.* Trenton, NJ: African World Press, pp. 5–31.

ASGISA (2006) *Accelerated and Shared Growth Initiative for South Africa (ASGISA) Transformation Document Report.* Available at www.nelsonmandela.org/omalley/index.php/site/q/03lv02409/04lv02410/05lv02415/06lv02416.htm.

Awal, M. (2012) Ghana: Democracy, Economic Reform and Development, 1993–2008. *Journal of Sustainable Development in Africa*, 14(1): 97–118.

Awoonor, K. (1990) *Ghana: A Political History from Pre-European to Modern Times.* Accra, Ghana: Sedco Publishing.

Ayelazuno, J. (2012) Development Economics in Action: A Study of Economic Policies in Ghana. *Canadian Journal of Development Studies/Revue canadienne d'études du développement*, 33(3): 388–391.

Ayittey, B.N.G. (2006) *Nigeria's Struggle with Corruption.* A testimony before the Committee on International Relation's Sub-Committee on Africa, Global Human Rights and International Operations House Committee on Africa, US House of Representatives, Washington, DC, Thursday 18 May.

Ayo, E.J. (1988) *Development Planning in Nigeria.* Ibadan: University Press Ltd.

Ayoade, J.A.A. (1983) The Administration of Development Plans in Africa: A Comparative Perspective. *The Nigerian Journal of Economic and Social Studies*, 25(1): 61–97.

Baah, A. (2003) *History of African Development Initiatives.* Africa Labour Research Network Workshop, 22–23May, Johannesburg.

Baiocchi, G., Heller, P. and Silva, M.K. (2011) *Bootstrapping Democracy: Transforming Local Governance and Civil Society in Brazil.* Stanford, CA: Stanford University Press.

Bibliography 165

Baldwin, A. (1975) Mass Removals and Separate Development. *Journal of Southern African Studies*, 1(2): 215–227.

Barkan, J.D. (2004) Kenya After Moi. *Foreign Affairs*, 87–100.

Bates, R.H. (2008) *When Things Fell Apart: State Failure in Late-Century Africa.* Cambridge: Cambridge University Press.

Battersby, B. (2006) Does Distance Matter? The Effect of Geographic Isolation on Productivity Levels. *OECD Economic Studies*, 42: 206–225.

Beinart, W. (2001) *Twentieth Century South Africa*. Oxford: Oxford University Press.

Beaulier, S.A. (2003) Explaining Botswana's Success: The Critical Role of Post-Colonial Policy. *Cato Journal*, 23(2): 227–240.

Beckman, B. (1982) Whose State? State and Capitalist Development in Nigeria. *Review of African Political Economy*, 23: 37–51.

Beswick, D. (2010) Peacekeeping, Regime Security and 'African Solutions to African Problems': Exploring Motivations for Rwanda's Involvement in Darfur, *Third World Quarterly*, 31(5): 739–754.

Bhorat, H. (2008) *Unemployment in South Africa: Descriptors and Determinants.* Unpublished Mimeo.

Biney, A. (2008) The Legacy of Kwame Nkrumah in Retrospect. *The Journal of Pan African Studies*, 2(3): 129–159

Biney, A. (2011) *The Political and Social Thought of Kwame Nkrumah*. London: Palgrave Macmillan Publishers.

Bloom, D.E., Sachs, J.D., Collier, P. and Udry, C. (1998) Geography, Demography and Economic Growth in Africa. *Brookings Papers on Economic Activity*, 207–295.

Bloomberg (2011) *Foreign Direct Investment in China in 2010 Rises to Record $105.7 Billion.* Available at www.bloomberg.com/news/2011-01-18/foreign-direct-investm ent-in-china-in-2010-rises-to-record-105-7-billion.html.

Blumenfeld, J. (2003) From Icon to Scapegoat: The Experience of South Africa's Reconstruction and Development Programme. *Development Policy Review*, 15: 65–91.

Boafo-Arthur, K. (1999) Structural Adjustment Programs (SAPS) in Ghana: Interrogating NDC's Implementation. *West Africa Review*, 1(1): 1–19.

Boeckelman, K. (1996) Governors, Economic Theory and Development Policy. *Economic Development Quarterly*, 10(4), November: 342–335.

Bond, P. (1996) Neoliberalism Comes to South Africa. *Multinational Monitor*, 17: 8–14.

Bond, P. (2000) *Elite Transition: From Apartheid to Neoliberalism in South Africa.* Pietermaritzburg, South Africa: University of Natal Press.

Bond, P. (2001) *Against Global Apartheid: South Africa Meets the World Bank, IMF and International Finance*. Cape Town: UCT Press.

Bond, P. (2004) The ANC's 'Left Turn' and South African Sub-imperialism. *Review of African Political Economy*, 31(102): 599–616.

Bond P. (2006) *Talk Left Walk Right: South Africa's Frustrated Global Reforms.* Scottsville, South Africa: University of Kwazulu Natal Press.

Booth, D. (2001) PRSP Processes in Eight African Countries: Initial Impacts and Potential for Institutionalization (No. 2001/121) WIDER Discussion Papers//World Institute for Development Economics (UNU-WIDER).

Booth, D. (2012) Aid Effectiveness: Bringing Country Ownership (and Politics) Back. *Conflict, Security & Development*, 12(5): 537–558.

Booth, L., Aivazian, V., Hunt, A. and Maksimovic, D. (2002) Capital Structure in Developing Countries. *Journal of Finance*, 56(1): 87–130.

166   Bibliography

Botchwey, K. (2010) Contemporary Political Economy. Lecture given by Kwesi Botchwey in the Kwame Nkrumah Memorial Lecture series University of Cape Coast, Ghana, September.

Bowmaker-Falconer, O. and Searl, P. (1996) Human Resource Development and Managing Diversity in South Africa. *International Journal of Manpower*, 17: 134–151.

Branch, D. (2009) *Defeating Mau Mau, Creating Kenya: Counterinsurgency, Civil War and Decolonization* (No. 111). Cambridge: Cambridge University Press.

Bräutigam, D.A. and Knack, S. (2004) Foreign Aid, Institutions, and Governance in Sub-Saharan Africa. *Economic Development and Cultural Change*, 52(2): 255–285.

Breslin, S. (2004) *Capitalism with Chinese Characteristics: The Public, the Private and the International*. Working Paper No. 104. Asia Research Centre.

BBEE (2003) Broad-Based Black Economic Empowerment Act, No. 53 of 2003. *Government Gazette*, 463, 9 January.

Brown, S. (2004) Theorising Kenya's Protracted Transition to Democracy. *Journal of Contemporary African Studies*, 22(3): 325–342.

Bugingo, E. (2002) *Missing the Mark? Participation in the PRSP Process in Rwanda*. Christian Aid Research Report.

Buira, A. (ed.) (2003) *Challenges to the World Bank and IMF: Developing Country Perspectives*. London: Antherm Press.

Bundy, C. (1972) The Emergence and Decline of a South African Peasantry. *African Affairs*, 369–388.

Byrnes, R.M. (ed.) (1996) *South Africa: A Country Study*. Washington, DC: Federal Research Division.

Carmody, P. (2002) Between Globalisation and (Post)Apartheid: The Political Economy of Restructuring in South Africa. *Journal of Southern African Studies*, 28(2): 255–275.

Carroll, A.B. and Buchholtz, A.K. (1996) *Ethics and Stakeholder Management*. Cincinnati, OH: South-Western.

Central Bureau of Statistics (1999) *National Poverty Eradication Plan 1999-2015*. Nairobi: Government House.

Chabal, P. (1991) Africans, Africanists and the African Crisis: Africa. *Journal of the International African Institute*, 61(4): 530–532.

Chen, Q. (2012) The Sustainable Economic Growth, Urbanization and Environmental Protection in China. *Forum on Public Policy: A Journal of the Oxford Round Table*, 1 (March).

Chenery, H.B. (1961) Comparative Advantage and Development Policy. *The American Economic Review*, 51(1): 18–51.

Cheow, E.T.C. (2005) Strategic Relevance of Asian Economic Integration. *Economic and Political Weekly*, 40(36): 3960–3967.

Cheru, F. (1999) *The Silent Revolution in Africa: Debt, Development and Democracy*. London: Zed Books.

Chikulo, B.C. (2003) Development Policy in South Africa: A Review. *DPMN Bulletin*, 10(2): 7.

Chomsky, N. (2003) *Hegemony or Survival: America's Quest for Global Dominance*. New York: Henry Holt.

Chossudovsky, M. (1998) Global Poverty in the Late 20th Century. *Journal of International Affairs-Columbia University*, 52: 293–312.

Chow, G.C. (1994) *Understanding China's Economy*. Hong Kong: World Scientific.

Cline, W. (2005) *The United States as a Debtor Nation*. Institute for International Centre for Development.

Coase, R.H. (1960) The Problem of Social Cost. *Journal of Law and Economics*, 3: 1–44.

Coase, R. (1988) The Problem of Social Cost. In R.H. Coase (ed.), *The Firm, the Market and the Law*. Chicago, IL: The University of Chicago Press.

Coase, R.H. (1988) *The Firm, the Market and the Law*. Chicago, IL: The University of Chicago Press.

Coase, R. (1991) The Nature of the Firm. In O. Williamson and S. Winter (eds), *The Nature of the Firm: Origins, Evolution and Development*. Oxford: Oxford University Press.

Coase, R. (1994) *How Should Economists Choose*. In R.H. Coase (ed.), *Essays on Economics and Economists*. Chicago, IL: The University of Chicago Press, pp. 15–33.

Cole, R.E. (1980) Learning from the Japanese: Prospects and Pitfalls. *Management Review*, 69(9): 22–28.

Coleman, J. (1958) Nigeria: Background to Nationalism. *Modern African Studies*, 15(2): 163–169.

Collier, P. (1995) Marginalization of Africa. *The International Labour Review*, 134: 541–547.

Collier, P. (2000) Conditionality, Dependence and Coordination: Three Current Debates in Aid Policy. In C.L. Gilbert and D. Vines (eds), *The World Bank: Structure and Policies*. Cambridge: Cambridge University Press.

Collier, P. (2007) *The Bottom Billion: Why the Poorest Countries are Failing and What Can Be Done About It*. Oxford: Oxford University Press.

Collier, P. and Gunning, J. W. (1999) Explaining African Economic Performance. *Journal of Economic Literature*, 64–111.

Collier, P. and Lal, D. (1985) *Labor and Poverty in Kenya. 1900–1980*. London: Oxford University Press.

Cooke, B. and Kothari, U. (eds) (2001) *Participation: The New Tyranny?* London: Zed Books.

Corder, C.K. (1997) Reconstruction and Development Programme: Success or Failure. *Social Indicators Research*, 41(1–3): 183–203.

COSATU (2010) *A Growth Path towards Full Employment*. Policy Perspectives of the Congress of South African Trade Unions. Draft Discussion Document.

COSATU (2011) *Secretariat Report to the 5th COSATU Central Committee*, Congress of South African Trade Unions.

Crawford, D. (2000) Chinese Capitalism: Cultures, the Southeast Asian Region and Economic Globalisation. *Third World Quarterly*, 21(1): 69–86.

Crooks, V.A., Turner, L., Snyder, J., Johnston, R. and Kingsbury, P. (2011) Promoting Medical Tourism to India: Messages, Images and the Marketing of International Patient Travel. *Social Science & Medicine*, 72(5): 726–732.

Cumming, G. (2001) *Aid to Africa. French and British Policies from the Cold War to the New Millennium*. Aldershot: Ashgate.

Daniels, R. (2007) *Skills Shortages in South Africa: A Literature Review*. Working Paper. Development Policy Research Unit. University of Cape Town.

Dante, I. (2003) Aid Coordination and Donor Reform, in *Africa Report: Assessing the New Partnership*. Ottawa: The North-South Institute, pp. 37–53.

Darko-Mensah, A. and Okereke, C. (2013) Can environmental performance rating programmes succed in Africa?: An evaluation of Ghana's AKOBEN project, *Mangement of Environmental Quality*, 25(5): 599–618.

Datta, A. and Young, J. (2011) Producing Homegrown Solutions: Think Tanks and Knowledge Networks in International Development, *Development Outreach*.

168   Bibliography

Available at http://wbi.worldbank.org/wbi/devoutreach/article/1303/producing-home-grown-solutions-think-tanks-and-knowledge-networks-internati.

De Soto, H. (2003) *Mystery of Capital: Why Capitalism Triumphs in the West and Fails Everywhere Else.* New York: Basic Books.

Deaton, A. (1999) Commodity Prices and Growth in Africa. *The Journal of Economic Perspectives,* 13(3): 23–40.

Demographic and Health Survey (DHS) (2008) National Population Commission. Abuja, Nigeria

Deng, X. (1991) Build Socialism with Chinese Characteristics. In The Research Department of Party Literature, Central Committee of the Communist Party of China (ed.), *Major Documents of the People's Republic of China – Selected Important Documents since the Third Plenary Session of the Eleventh Central Committee of the Communist Party of China* (December 1978 and November 1989) Beijing: Foreign Languages Press, pp. 1–5.

Devarajan, S., Dollar, D. and Holmgren, T. (2001) *Aid and Reform in Africa.* Washington, DC: World Bank Publications.

Diamond, J. (1997*) Guns, Germs and Steel.* New York: W.W. Norton & Co.

Dijkstra, G. (2004) Debt Relief from a Donor Perspective: The Case of the Netherlands. In J.J. Teunissen and A. Akkerman (eds), *HIPC Debt Relief: Myths and Reality.* The Hague: FONDAD.

Dollar, D. and Kraay, A. (2004) Trade, Growth and Poverty. *The Economic Journal,* 114: 22–49.

Dolowitz, D. and Marsh, D. (1996) Who Learns What From Whom: A Review of the Policy Transfer Literature. *Political Studies,* 44(2): 343–357.

Dolowitz, D.P. and Marsh, M. (2000) Learning from Abroad: The Role of Policy Transfer in Contemporary Policy-making. *Governance,* 13(1): 5–23.

Domatob, J. (1998) *Contemporary Issues in Sub-Saharan African Political and Economic Development.* Lanham, MD: Rowman & Littlefield Publishers.

Donli, J.G. (2004) An Overview of Nigeria's Economic Reforms. *NDIC Quarterly,* 1(4): 62–82.

Donovan, J.F. (1974) Nigeria after 'Indigenization': Is There Any Room Left for the American Businessman? *The International Lawyer,* 600–605.

Drull, C. (2004) *Counting the Cost of Red-tape for Business in South Africa.* Johannesburg: Strategic Business Partnership.

Dunning, T. (2004) Conditioning the Effects of Aid: Cold War Politics, Donor Credibility and Democracy in Africa. *International Organization,* 58(2): 409–423.

Easterly, W. (2001) The Lost Decades: Developing Countries' Stagnation in Spite of Policy Reform 1980–1998. *Journal of Economic Growth,* 6(2): 135–157.

Easterly, W. (2002) How Did Heavily Indebted Poor Countries Become Heavily Indebted? Reviewing Two Decades of Debt Relief. *World Development,* 30(10): 1677–1696.

Easterly, W. (2006a) *The White Man's Burden: Why the West's Efforts to Aid the Rest Have Done So Much Ill and So Little Good.* New York: Penguin.

Easterly, W. (2006b) Reliving the 1950s: The Big Push, Poverty Traps and Takeoffs in Economic Development, *Journal of Economic Growth,* 11(4): 289–318.

Easterly, W. (2009) How the Millennium Development Goals are Unfair to Africa. *World Development,* 37(1): 26–35.

Easterly, W. and Levine, R. (1997) Africa's Growth Tragedy: Policies and Ethnic Divisions. *Quarterly Journal of Economics,* 112: 1203–1250.

Bibliography 169

Easterly, W. and Levine, R. (2003) Tropics, Germs and Crops: How Endowments Influence Economic Development. *Journal of Monetary Economics*, 50: 3–40.

Eboe, H. (1979) A Tale of Two Regimes: Imperialism, the Military and Class. Ghana. *Review of African Political Economy*, 14: 36–55.

Economic Commission for Africa (ECA) (1991) *Progress Report on the Strengthening of Sub-regional Economic Integration Process and the Establishment of the African Economic Community*. UN/E/ECA/CM.17/12. 1 February.

Edigheji, O. (2007) Rethinking South Africa's Development Path: Reflections on the ANC's Policy Conference. Special edition of *Policy Issues & Actors*, 20(10).

Egbetokun, S.A. (2010) Assessment of Innovation and Capability in the Cable and Wire Manufacturing Industry in Nigeria: A Case Study Approach. *International Journal of Learning and Intellectual Capital*, 7(1): 55–74.

Eggertsson, T. (1990) *Economic Behavior and Institutions: Principles of Neoinstitutional Economics*. Cambridge: Cambridge University Press.

Eicher, C.K. (1967) The Dynamics of Long-Term Agricultural Development in Nigeria. *Journal of Farm Economics*, 49(5): 1158–1170.

Ejere, E.S.I. (2011) Human Capital Formation as Catalyst for National Development: Nigeria in Perspective. *International Business & Management*, 2(2). Available at www.cscanada.net/index.php/ibm/article/view/j.ibm.1923842820110202.011.

Ejimofor, C. (1987) *British Colonial Objectives and Policies in Nigeria: The Roots of Conflict*. Onitsha: African-Fep.

Ekundare, R.O. (1971) Nigeria's Second National Development Plan as a Weapon for Social Change. *Journal of African Affairs*, 70(279): 146–158.

Ekundare, R.O. (1973) *An Economic History of Nigeria 1860–1960*. New York: Holmes and Meir Publishers.

Elkins, C. (2005) *Imperial Reckoning: The Untold Story of Britain's Gulag in Kenya*. New York: Henry Holt and Company, LLC.

Energy Information Administration (2011) International Energy Statistics. Available at www.eia.gov/ipdbproject/IEDIndex3.cfm (accessed 20 November 2012).

Englebert, P. (2002) *State Legitimacy and Development in Africa*. Boulder, CO and London: Lynne Rienner Publishers.

Esseks, J.D. (1971) Political Independence and Economic Decolonization: The Case of Ghana under Nkrumah. *The Western Political Quarterly*, 24(1): 59–64.

Evans, P. (1996) Introduction: Development Strategies across the Public-Private Divide. *World Development*, 24(6): 1033–1037.

Evans, P. (2004) Development as Institutional Change: The Pitfalls of Monocropping and the Potentials of Deliberation. *Studies in Comparative International Development*, 38(4): 30–52.

Evans, P. (2005) The Challenges of the Institutional Turn: New Interdisciplinary Opportunities in Development Theory. In V. Nee and R. Swedberg (eds), *The Economic Sociology of Capitalism*. Princeton, NJ: Princeton University Press.

Everatt, D. (2005) The Politics of Poverty. *Bangladesh Journal of Sociology*, 2(1): 16–31.

Ezeife, E. (1981) Indigenization: The Case Study of Nigeria. In A. Adedeji (ed.), *Indigenization of African Economies*. London: Hutchinson Publishing Group, pp. 164–186.

Fagbadebo, O. (2007) Corruption, Governance and Political Instability in Nigeria. *African Journal of Political Science and International Relations*, 1(2): 28–37.

Fapohunda, T.M. (2013) Reducing Unemployment through the Informal Sector in Nigeria. *International Journal of Management Sciences*, 1(7): 232–244.

170 *Bibliography*

Federal Government of Nigeria (1956) Statement of Policy of the Government of the Federation on the Nigerianisation of the Federal Public Service and the Higher Training of Nigerians, 1956–1960, Sessional Paper, No 4. Lagos: Federal Government Printer.

Federal Government of Nigeria (2012) *Nigeria's Path to Sustainable Development through Green Energy*. Country Report to the Rio+20 Summit. June. United Nations Conference on Sustainable Development.

Feinberg, H.M. (1993) The 1913 Natives Land Act in South Africa: Politics, Race and Segregation in the Early 20th Century. *The International Journal of African Historical Studies*, 26(1): 65–109.

Feinstein, C.H. (2005) *An Economic History of South Africa: Conquest, Discrimination and Development*. Cambridge: Cambridge University Press.

Few, R., Brown, K. and Tompkins, E.L. (2007) Public Participation and Climate Change Adaptation: Avoiding the Illusion of Inclusion. *Climate policy*, 7(1): 46–59.

Fine, B. (2012) Assessing South Africas New Growth Path: Framework for Change? *Review of African Political Economy*, 39(134): 551–568.

Floyd, S.W. (2009) 'Borrowing' Theory: What Does This Mean and When Does It Make Sense in Management Scholarship? *Journal of Management Studies*, 46(6): 1057–1058.

Foster, V. and Pushak, N. (2011) *Nigeria's Infrastructure: A Continental Perspective*. Policy Research Working Paper 5686. The World Bank Africa Region Sustainable Development Department.

Frank, A.G. (1966) *The Development of Underdevelopment*. Boston, MA: New England Free Press.

Frank, A.G. (1969) *Latin America and Underdevelopment*. New York: Monthly Review Press.

Frank, A.G. (1974) Dependence is Dead, Long Live Dependence and the Class Struggle: An Answer to Critics. *Latin American Perspectives*, 1(1): 87–106.

Frankel, J. and Romer, D. (1999) Does Trade Cause Growth? *American Economic Review*, 89: 379–399.

Frankel, J.A. (1974) *Cocoa in Ghana: The Cocoa Farmers, the Cocoa Marketing Board and the Elasticity of Supply*. Cambridge, MA: MIT Department of Economics.

Fraser, A. (2005) Poverty Reduction Strategy Papers: Now Who Calls the Shots? *Review of African Political Economy*, 32(104–105): 317–340.

Frimpong-Boateng, K. (2011) *Ghana: Vision 2020 Minus 2015 Minus Vision 2010*. Available at www.modernghana.com/news/320465/1/ghana-vision-2020-minus-2015-minus-vision-2010.html.

Fukuyama, F. (1992) *The End of History and the Last Man*. New York: Free Press.

Furedi, F. (1989) *The Mau Mau War in Perspective*. Athens: Ohio University Press.

G8 Statement on Africa (2005) Available at www.fco.gov.uk/Files/kfile/PostG8_Gleneagles_Communique.pdf (accessed 2 August 2005).

Gallup, J.L. and Sachs, J.D. (1998) The Economic Burden of Malaria. *Journal of Tropical Medicine and Hygiene*, 64(1).

Gallup, J.L., Sachs, J.D. and Mellinger, A.D. (1998) *Geography and Economic Development*. National Bureau of Economic Research Working Paper No. w6849.

Gayi, S.K. (1991) Adjustment and 'Safety-netting': Ghana's Programme of Actions to Mitigate the Social Costs of Adjustment (PAMSCAD). *Journal of International Development*, 3(4): 557–564.

Bibliography 171

GEAR (1996) *Growth, Employment and Redistribution: A Macroeconomic Strategy.* Republic of South Africa Pretoria, Ministry of Finance.

Gebe, B.Y. (2008) Ghana's Foreign Policy at Independence and Implications for the 1966 Coup D'état. *Journal of Pan African Studies,* 2(3).

Gentilini, U. and Webb, P. (2008) How Are We Doing on Poverty and Hunger Reduction? A New Measure of Country Performance. *Food Policy,* 33(6): 521–532.

Gertzel, C., Goldschmidt, M. and Rothschild, D. (1969) *Government and Politics in Kenya: A Nation-Building Text.* Nairobi: East African Publishing House.

Gibbon, P. (1993) *Social Change and Economic Reform in Africa.* Uppsala, Sweden: Nordiska Afrikainstitutet (Scandinavian Institute of African Studies).

Gocking, R. (2005) *The History of Ghana.* Portsmouth, NH: Greenwood Publishing Group.

Godfrey, S. and Sheehy, T. (2001) Civil Society Participation in Poverty Reduction Strategy Papers. Report to the Department for International Development (DFID). Vol I: *Overview and Recommendations,* SGTS & Associates, October.

Government of Ghana (2003) *Ghana Poverty Reduction Strategy (2003–2005): An Agenda for Growth and Prosperity National Development Commission*

Government of Ghana (2007) *Growth and Poverty Reduction Strategy (GPRS II).* Accra: National Development Commission.

Government of Ghana (2010) *Ghana Shared and Growth and Development Agenda (GSGDA), 2010–2013.* September. Accra: National Development Planning Commission.

Government of Ghana (2012) *The Implementation of the Ghana Shared Growth and Development Agenda (GSGDA) 2010–2013.* Accra: National Development Planning Commission 2012 Annual Report.

Government of Ghana (2012) *All Children in School by 2015: Global Initiative on Out-of-School Children. UNICEF Country Report.*

Government of Kenya (2003) *Kenya Economic Recovery Strategy for Wealth and Employment Creation 2003–2007.* June. Ministry of Planning and National Development. Available at http://siteresources.worldbank.org/KENYAEXTN/Resources/ERS.pdf.

Government of Kenya (2012) *Second Annual Progress Report.* Monitoring and Evaluation Directorate, Ministry of State for Planning, National Development and Vision 2030.

Goldsmith, E. and Hildyard, N. (1984) *The Social and Environmental Impacts of Large Dams.* Cornwall: Wadebridge Ecological Centre.

Grindle, M.S. (2007) Good Enough Governance Revisited. *Development Policy Review,* 25(5): 533–574.

Grischow, J.D. (2011) Kwame Nkrumah, Disability and Rehabilitation in Ghana, 1957–66. *The Journal of African History,* 52(2): 179–199.

Guest, R. (2013) *The Shackled Continent.* London: Pan Macmillan.

Gyimah-Boadi, E. (2008) Ghana's Fourth Republic: Championing the African Democratic Renaissance? *CDD-Ghana Briefing Paper,* 8(4).

Gyimah-Boadi, E. and Rothchild, D. (1982) Rawlings, Populism and the Civil Liberties Tradition in Ghana. *A Journal of Opinion* 12(3): 64–69.

Habib, A. and Padayachee, V. (2000) Economic Policy and Power Relations in South Africa's Transition to Democracy. *World Development,* 28(2): 245–263.

Hall, P.A. (1993) Policy Paradigms, Social Learning and the State: The Case of Economic Policymaking in Britain. *Comparative Politics,* 275–296.

172   *Bibliography*

Hall, P.A. and Soskice, D. (eds) (2001) *Varieties of Capitalism: The Institutional Foundations of Comparative Advantage*. Oxford: Oxford University Press.

Hamelink, C. (1983) *Cultural Autonomy in Global Communications*. New York: Norwood Press.

Hamid, K.T. (2010) *Global Financial Crisis, African Trade and Revival of African Economies*. Delivered at The Renaissance of African Economies organized by Council for the Development of Social Science Research in Africa (CODESRIA) Conference.

Hanmer, L., Healey, J. and Naschold, F. (2000) *Will Growth Halve Global Poverty by 2015?* ODI Policy Briefing Paper 8. London: ODI.

Hanmer, L. and Shelton, R. (2001) *Sustainable Debt: What Has HIPC Delivered?* Paper for the WIDER Conference on Debt Relief, Helsinki.

Hanushek, E. and Wößmann, L. (2007) *The Role of School Improvement in Economic Development*. NBER Working Paper 12832. Cambridge, MA: National Bureau of Economic Research.

Harbeson, J. (1973) *Nation-building in Kenya: The Role of Land Reform*. Evanston, IL: Northwestern University Press

Hart, G.P. (1974) Some Socio-Economic Aspects of African Entrepreneurship. *Man, New Series*, 9(2): 339–340.

Harvey, C. (1991) Recovery from Macroeconomic Disaster in sub-Saharan Africa. *States or Markets*, 121–147.

Hausmann, R. (2008) *Final Recommendations of the International Panel on ASGISA*. CID Working Paper No. 161.

Hausmann, R. and Klinger, B. (2008) South Africa's Export Predicament. *Economics of Transition*, 16(4): 609–637.

Hayman, R. (2009) Rwanda: Milking the Cow. Creating Policy Space in Spite of Dependence. In. L. Whitfield (ed.), *The Politics of Aid. African Strategies for Dealing with Donors*. Oxford: Oxford University Press, pp. 156–184.

Hayter, T. (1971) *Aid as Imperialism*. London: Penguin.

Hearn, J. (2001) The 'Uses and Abuses' of Civil Society in Africa. *Review of African Political Economy*, 28(87): 43–53.

Helleiner, G.K. (1964) The Fiscal Role of The Marketing Boards in Nigerian Economic Development 1947–1961. *Economic Journal*, LXXIV(295): 582–610.

Helleinner, G.K. (1966) *Peasant Agriculture, Government and Economic Growth in Nigeria*. Homewood, IL: Richard D Irwin.

Heller, P. (2001) Moving the State: The Politics of Democratic Decentralization in Kerala, South Africa and Porto Alegre. *Politics and Society*, 29(1): 131–163.

Herbst, J. (1990) War and the State in Africa. *International Security*, 117–139.

Herbst, J. (1991) *Economic Crisis and Reform in Ghana*. Unpublished Paper. Washington, DC.

Herbst, J. (1997) Responding to State Failure in Africa. *International Security*, 21(3): 120–144.

Hettne, B. (1980) Soldiers and Politics: The Case of Ghana. *Journal of Peace Research*, Special Issue on Imperialism and Militarization, 17(2): 173–193.

Hickey, S. and Mohan, G. (eds) (2004) *Participation–From Tyranny to Transformation? Exploring New Approaches to Participation in Development*. London: Zed Books.

Hirsch, A. (2005) *Season of Hope; Economic Reform under Mandela and Mbeki*. University of KwaZulu-Natal Press/IDRC.

Hjort, J. (2010) Pre-colonial Culture, Post-colonial Economic Success? The Tswana and the African Economic Miracle. *The Economic History Review*, 63(3): 688–709.

Bibliography 173

Holmquist, F.W., Weaver, F.S. and Ford, M.D. (1994) The Structural Development of Kenya's Political Economy. *African Studies Review*, 37(1): 69–105.

Hoogvelt, A. (1979) Indigenisation and Foreign Capital: Industrialisation in Nigeria. *Review of African Political Economy*, 14: 56–68.

Htun, M. (2004) From 'Racial Democracy' to Affirmative Action: Changing State Policy on Race in Brazil. *Latin American Research Review*, 39(1): 60–89.

Hu, G. (2009) Borrowing Ideas Across Borders: Lessons from the Academic Advocacy of 'Chinese-English Bilingual Education in China'. In J. Fegan and M.H. Field (eds), *Education Across Borders*. Netherlands: Springer, 115–136.

Hunt, D. (1984) *The Impending Crisis in Kenya: The Case for Land Reform*. Aldershot: Gower.

Hutchful, E. (1979) A Tale of Two Regimes: Imperialism, the Military and Class in Ghana. *Review of African Political Economy*, 6(14): 36–55.

Hutchful, E. (2002) *Ghana's Adjustment Experience: The Paradox of Reform*. Geneva: United Nations Research Institute for Social Development.

Ibhawoh, B. and Dibua, J.I. (2003) Deconstructing Ujamaa: The Legacy of Julius Nyerere in the Quest for Social and Economic Development in Africa. *African Journal of Political Science*, 8(1): 59–83.

Ibietan, J. and Ekhosuehi, O. (2013) Trends in Development Plan in Nigeria: 1962 to 2012. *Journal of Sustainable Development in Africa*, 15(4).

Idemudia, U. (2009) Oil Extraction and Poverty Reduction in the Niger Delta: A Critical Examination of Partnership Initiatives. *Journal of Business Ethics*, 90(1): 91–116.

IEA (2011) *Africa Energy Output: A Focus on Energy Perspective in Sub-Sahara Africa*. International Energy Agency World Energy Outlook Special Report.

Iheduru, O.C. (2004) Black Economic Power and Nation-building in Post-apartheid South Africa. *The Journal of Modern African Studies*, 42(1): 1–30.

Ikeanyibe, O.M. (2009) Human Resource Management for Sustainable Microfinance Institutions in Nigeria. *Global Journal of Social Sciences*, 8(1): 119–134.

Ikeanyibe, O. M. and Imhanlahimi, J.E. (2007) Credit Provision and Rural Development in Nigeria: Problems and Prospects of the Micro Finance Bank. *Nigerian Journal of Business Administration*, 9(1&2): 38–55.

Ikoku, E.U. (1980) *Self-reliance, Africa's Survival*. Enugu: Fourth Dimension Publishers.

Ikpeze, N.I., Soludo, C.C. and Elekwa, N.N. (2004) Nigeria: The Political Economy of the Policy Process, Policy Choice and Implementation. In C. Soludo, O. Ogbu and H.J. Chang (eds), *The Politics of Trade and Industrial Policy in Africa: Forced Consensus?* Trenton, NJ: Africa World Press/IDRC.

IMF (2008) *Nigeria Needs Sustained Reforms to Build on Success*. Available at www.imf.org/external/pubs/ft/survey/so/2008/car021508a.htm.

IMF (2012) *Ghana: Poverty Reduction Strategy Paper*. IMF Country Report No. 12/203.

IMF (2012a) *Kenya: Poverty Reduction Strategy Paper: Progress Report*. Washington, DC: International Monetary Fund.

IMF (2013) *Poverty Reduction Strategy Papers (PRSP) Factsheet*, 30 September. Available at www.imf.org/external/np/exr/facts/prsp.htm (accessed 11 November 2013).

IMF (2014) *Africa Rising IMF Conference*, 29–30 May. Mozambique. Available at www.africa-rising.org.

Irvin, R.A. and Stansbury, J. (2004) Citizen Participation in Decision Making: Is It Worth the Effort? *Public Administration Review*, 64(1): 55–65.

Iwuagwu, O. (2009) Nigeria and the Challenge of Industrial Development: The New Cluster Strategy', *African Economic History*, 37(1): 151–180.

174 *Bibliography*

Izibili, M.A. and Aiya, F. (2007) Deregulation and Corruption in Nigeria: An Ethical Response. *Journal of Social Science* 14(3): 229–234.

Ja'afaruBambale, A. (2011) National Economic Empowerment Development Strategy and Poverty Reduction in Nigeria: A Critique. *Economics and Finance Review* 1(1): 15–24.

Jerve, A.M. and Hansen, A.S. (2008) Conceptualising Ownership in Aid Relations. In A.M. Jerve, Y. Shinomura and A.S. Hansen (eds), *Aid Relationships in Asia. Exploring Ownership in Japanese and Nordic Aid*. Basingstoke and New York: Palgrave MacMillan.

Jerven, M. (2011) Revisiting the Consensus on Kenyan Economic Growth 1964–1995. *Journal of Eastern African Studies*, 5(1): 2–23.

Johnson, O. (2005) *Country Ownership of Reform Programs and the Implications for Conditionality*. G24 Discussion Paper Series, No. 35. Available at http://unctad.org/en/Docs/gdsmdpbg2420052_en.pdf.

Johnson, R.W. (2010) *South Africa's Brave New World: The Beloved Country since the End of Apartheid*. London: Penguin.

Joseph, N. (2012) Colonial Capitalism and the Making of Wage Labour in Kimilili, Kenya: 1900–1963. *International Journal of Humanities and Social Science*, 2(23).

Joseph, R.A. (1983) Class, State and Prebendal Politics in Nigeria. *Journal of Commonwealth & Comparative Politics*, 21(3): 21–38.

Jubilee USA (2008) *Are IMF and World Bank Economic Policy Conditions Undermining the Impact of Debt Cancellation?* Washington, DC: Jubilee USA Network.

Kagwanja, P.M. (2006) 'Power to Uhuru': Youth identity and generational politics in Kenya's 2002 Elections. *African Affairs*, 105(418): 51–75.

Kalinowski, T. (2009) From Developmental State to Developmental Society? The Role of Civil Society Organizations in Recent Korean Development and Possible Lessons for Developing Countries. *International Studies Review*, 10: 53–71.

Kanbur, R. (2000) Aid, Conditionality and Debt in Africa. In F. Tarp (ed.), *Foreign Aid and Development: Lessons Learnt and Directions for the Future*. London: Routledge.

Kanogo, T. (1987) *Squatters and the Roots of Mau Mau 1905–63*. Athens: Ohio University Press.

Kaunda, K.D. (1966) *A Humanist in Africa: Letters to Colin M. Morris from Kenneth D. Kaunda*. Nashville, TN: Abingdon Press.

Kaunda, K.D. (1968) Speech at the National Council of the United National Independence Party, Mulungushi, 19 April.

Kaufmann, D., Kraay, A. and Zoido-Lobatón, P. (2002) Governance Matters II – Updated Indicators for 2000/01, World Bank Policy Research Department Working Paper No. 2772. Washington, DC.

Kenya Vision 2030 (2010) *Poverty Reduction Strategy Paper First Medium Term Plan 2008–2012*. IMF Country Report No. 10/224.

Kenya National Coordinating Agency for Population and Development (NCAPD) (2010) March.

Kew, D. (2006) Nigeria. In S. Tatic (ed.), *Countries at the Crossroads*. New York: Freedom House.

Khan, M.S. and Sharma, S. (2001) *IMF Conditionality and Country Ownership of Programs*. IMF Working Paper No. 01/142. Available at http://ssrn.com/abstract=286968 or http://dx.doi.org/10.2139/ssrn.286968.

Killick, T. (1978) *Development Economics in Action*. London: Heinemann.

Bibliography   175

Killick, T. (1993) *The Adaptive Economy: Adjustment Policies in Small, Low-income Countries.* Washington, DC: World Bank.

Killick, T. (1998) *Aid and the Political Economy of Policy Change.* London: Routledge.

Killick, T. (2010) *Development Economics in Action: A Study of Economic Policies in Ghana,* 2nd edn, Routledge Studies in Development Economics. London: Routledge.

Killick, T. and Abugre, C. (2001) Institutionalising the PRSP Approach in Ghana. Report submitted to the Strategic Partnership with Africa. *PRSP Institutionalisation Study: Final Report.* London: ODI.

Kim, K.S. (1986) *Issues and Perspectives in Tanzania Industrial Development – With Special Reference to the Role of SADCC.* Kellogg Institute Working Paper 87, December.

Kirk-Greene, A.H.M. (1991) His Eternity, His Eccentricity, or His Exemplarity? A Further Contribution to the Study of HE the African Head of State. *African Affairs,* 163–187.

Kohli, A. (2004) *State Directed Development, Political Power and Industrialization in the Global Periphery.* Cambridge: Cambridge University Press.

Koledoye, T.O., Jumah, A.A., Phillips, D.A. (2012) The Current and Future Challenges of Electricity Market in Nigeria in the Face of Deregulation Process. *African Journal of Engineering Research,* 1(2): 33–39.

KonaduAgyemang, K. (2000) The Best of Times and the Worst of Times: Structural Adjustment Programs and Uneven Development in Africa: The Case of Ghana. *The Professional Geographer,* 52(3): 469–483.

Krugman, P. (1998) *The Role of Geography in Development.* Paper prepared for the Annual World Bank Conference on Development Economics, Washington, DC.

Kwan, K.S. (1986) *Issues and Perspectives in Tanzanian Industrial Development: with Special Reference to the Role of SADCC.* Working Paper 87, The Helen Kellogg Institute for International Studies.

LaFraniere, S. (2005) Africa Tackles Graft, With Billion in Aid in Play. *The New York Times,* 6 July. Available at www.nytimes.com/2005/07/06/international/africa/06lagos.html?pagewanted=all&_r=0.

Lambo, E. (1989) Perspective Planning in Nigeria with Specific Reference to Social (Health) Sector. *The Nigerian Journal of Economic and Social Studies,* 31: 206–320.

Lazarus, J. (2008) Participation in Poverty Reduction Strategy Papers: Reviewing the Past, Assessing the Present and Predicting the Future. *Third World Quarterly,* 29(6): 1205–1221.

Leite, S.P., Pellechio, A., Zanforlin, L., Begashaw, G., Fabrizio, S. and Harnack, J. (2000) *Ghana: Economic Development in a Democratic Environment.* Occasional Paper 199. International Monetary Fund.

Leith, J.C. (1996) *Ghana: Structural Adjustment Experience.* International Center for Economic Growth, Country Studies Series, No. 13. San Francisco, CA: ICS Press.

Leith, J.C. and Soderling, L. (2003) *Ghana – Long Term Growth, Atrophy and Stunted Recovery.* Nordiska: Afrikainstitutet.

Leo, C. (1984) *Land and Class in Kenya.* Toronto: University of Toronto Press.

Letseka, M. and Maile, S. (2008) *High University Drop-out Rates: A Threat to South Africa's Future.* HSRC Policy Brief.

Levinsohn, J. (2008) *Two Policies to Alleviate Unemployment in South Africa.* CID Working Paper No. 166. Available at www.cid.harvard.edu/cidwp/166.htm.

Lewis, P. (1996) From Prebendalism to Predation: The Political Economy of Decline in Nigeria. *The Journal of Modern African Studies,* 34(1): 79–103.

176   *Bibliography*

Li, G. (ed.) (1995) *A Glossary of Political Terms of the People's Republic of China.* Hong Kong: Chinese University Press.

Liebenberg, I. (1998) The African Renaissance: Myth, Vital Lie, or Mobilising Tool? *African Security Review*, 7(3): 42–50.

Linehan, D. (2007) Re-ordering the Urban Archipelago: Kenya Vision 2030, Street Trade and the Battle for Nairobi City Centre. *Aurora Geography Journal*, 1: 21–37.

Livingstone, I. (1991) A Reassessment of Kenya's Rural and Urban Informal Sector. *World Development*, 19(6): 651–670.

Loewenson, R. (1993) Structural Adjustment and Health Policy. *Africa International Journal of Health Service*, 23(4).

Luiz, J.M. (2002) South African State Capacity and Post-apartheid Economic Reconstruction. *International Journal of Social Economics*, 29(8): 594–614.

Lumumba, O. (2004) *The National Land Policy in Kenya: Addressing Historical Injustices.* Issue Paper. Kenya Land Alliance.

Mambula, C. (2002) Perceptions of SME Growth Constraints in Nigeria. *Journal of Small Business Management*, 40(1): 58–65.

Martin, M. (2004) Assessing the HIPC Initiative: The Key HIPC Debates. In J.J. Teunissen and A. Akkerman, *HIPC Debt Relief Myths and Reality.* The Hague: FONDAD.

Martins, S. Da Silva, Medeiros, C.A. and Nascimento, E.L. (2004) Paving Paradise: The Road From 'Racial Democracy' to Affirmative Action in Brazil. *Journal of Black Studies*, 34: 787–816.

Mays, T.M. (2003) African Solutions for African Problems: The Changing Face of African-Mandated Peace Operations. *Journal of Conflict Studies*, 23(1).

Mbaku, J.M. (2004) *Institutions and Development in Africa.* Trenton, NJ: Africa World Press.

Mbeki, T. (2002) *Africa Define Yourself.* South Africa: Tafelberg.

Mboya, T. (1965) *African Socialism and its Application to Planning in Kenya.* Nairobi, Kenya: Ministry of Economic Planning.

McFarlane, A.G. (2000) When Inclusion Leads to Exclusion: The Uncharted Terrain of Community Participation in Economic Development. *Brooklyn Law Review*, 66: 861.

McGann, J.G. (2012) *Global Go To Think Tanks Index Report.* University of Pennsylvania: Think Tanks and Civil Societies Program.

McGee, R. (2002) Participating in Development. In U. Kothari and M. Minogue (eds), *Development Theory and Practice: Critical Perspectives.* Basingstoke: Palgrave.

McGee, R. (2003) Poverty Reduction Strategy Papers: A Role for Civil Society? In D. Potts, P. Ryan and A. Toner (eds), *Development Planning and Poverty Reduction* Houndsmill: Palgrave Macmillan.

McGee, R., Levene, J. and Hughes, A. (2002) *Assessing Participation in Poverty Reduction Strategy Papers: A Desk-based Synthesis of Experience in Sub-Saharan Africa.* IDS Research Report 52, Sussex: Institute of Development Studies.

Melamed, C. (1996) *Adjusting Africa: Structural Economic Change and Development in Africa.* Tampa, FL: WorldView Publications.

Meng, J. (2004) Ghana's Development: Miracle or Mirage. *History*,107, 6 December.

Meredith, M. (2005) *The State of Africa: A History of Fifty Years of Independence,* London, New York, Sydney and Toronto: Free Press.

Meredith, M. (2011) *The Fate of Africa: A History of the Continent Since Independence.* New York: Public Affairs.

Millennium Partnership for the African Recovery Programme (2001) *African Vision.* Paper. Pretoria, SA.

Bibliography 177

Miller, F.P., Vandome, A.F. and McBrewster, J. (eds) (2009) *History of Ghana. United Kingdom and Germany.* Beau Bassin, Mauritius: Alphascript Publishing.

Migot-Adholla, S.E. (1984) Rural Development Policy and Equality. *Politics and Public Policy in Kenya and Tanzania,* 199–232.

Minondo, A. (2011) Does Comparative Advantage Explain Countries Diversification Level? *Review of World Economics,* 147(3): 507–526.

Mkandawire, T. and Soludo, C. (1998) *Our Continent, Our Future: African Perspectives on Structural Adjustment.* Trenton, NJ: African World Press.

Mkandawire, T. and Soludo, C.C. (2003) Introduction: Towards the Broadening of Development Policy Dialogue for Africa. In T. Mkandawire and C.C. Soludo (eds.) *African Voices on Structural Adjustment.* Trenton, NJ: Africa World Press.

Mogalakwe, M. (2003) Botswana: An African Miracle or a Case of Mistaken Identity? *Botswana Journal of African Studies,* 17(1).

Mohan, G., Brown, E., Milward, B. and Zack-Williams, A. (2000) *Structural Adjustment: Theory, Practice, Impacts.* London: Routledge.

Monye, S. (2010) *2008 Survey on Monitoring the Paris Declaration: Making Aid More Effective by 2010.* OECD. Available at www.oecd.org/dac/effectiveness/2008sur veyonmonitoringtheparisdeclaration.htm.

Morgan, J.Q., Lambe, W. and Freyer, A. (2009) Homegrown Responses to Economic Uncertainty in Rural America. *Rural Sociological Society,* 3(2).

Morishima, M. (1982) *Why Has Japan 'Succeeded'? Western Technology and the Japanese Ethos.* Cambridge: Cambridge University Press.

Morris, M.D. (1963) Towards a Reinterpretation of Nineteenth-Century Indian Economic History. *Journal of Economic History,* 606–618.

Morrison, L. (2007) The Nature of Decline: Distinguishing Myth from Reality in the Case of the Luo of Kenya. *Journal of Modern African Studies,* 45(1): 117–142.

Mosley, P. (1992) Policy-Making without Facts: A Note on the Assessment of Structural Adjustment Policies in Nigeria 1985–1990. *African Affairs,* 91(363): 227.

Mosley, P., Harrigan, J. and Toye, J. (1991) *Aid and Power: The World Bank and Policy Based Lending.* London: Routledge.

Mosse, D. (2005) *Cultivating Development: An Ethnography of Aid Policy and Practice* (Anthropology, Culture and Society Series). London: Pluto Press.

Moyo, D. (2009) *Dead Aid: Why Aid is not Working and How there is a Better Way for Africa.* London: Macmillan.

MRDE (2012) *The Mutual Review the Development Effectiveness in Africa: Promise & Performance.* A joint report by the Economic Commission for Africa and the Organization for Economic Co-operation and Development.

Muganda, A. (2004) *Tanzania's Economic Reforms (and Lessons Learned).* Case Study for the World Bank Shanghai Conference on Scaling up Poverty Reduction, Shanghai, China, 25–27 May.

Mutiso, G. and Rohio, S. (eds) (1975) *Readings in African Political Thought.* London: Heinemann Educational.

Mutua, M. (2008) *Kenya's Quest for Democracy: Taming Leviathan.* Boulder, CO: Lynne Rienner Publishers.

Mutua, M. (2011) *Human Rights: A Political and Cultural Critique.* Philadelphia: University of Pennsylvania Press.

Nathan, L. (2013) African Solutions to African Problems: South Africa's Foreign Policy. *WeltTrends: Zeitschrift für internationale Politik,* 92(21), September/October: 48–55.

178 *Bibliography*

National Development Planning Commission (NDPC) (1995) *Ghana – Vision 2020. The First Step: 1996–2000*. Available at www.ndpc.gov.gh/GPRS/Ghana's%20Vision%202020%20-%20First%20Step.pdf.

National Planning Commission (NPC) (2004) *National Economic Empowerment and Development Strategy (NEEDS)*. Abuja, Nigeria.

Nattrass, N. (1994) Politics and Economics in ANC Economic Policy. *African Affairs*, 343–359.

Nelson, R. and Phelps, E. (1966) Investment in Humans, Technological Diffusion and Economic Growth. *The American Economic Review*, 56(1/2): 69–75.

NEPAD (2001) The New Partnership for Africa Development Framework Document, October. Available at www.nepad.org/system/files/NEPAD%20Framework%20(English)pdf (accessed 30 August 2014).

Ng, F. and Yeats, A.J. (2002) *What Can Africa Expect from Its Traditional Exports?* Washington, DC: World Bank.

Ninsin, K.A. (2007) Markets and Liberal Democracy. In K. Boafo-Arthur (ed.), *Ghana: A Decade of the Liberal State*. Dakar: CODESRIA.

Nkrumah, K. (1957a) *Ghana Is Free Forever*. Kwame Nkrumah's Speech at Independence. Available at http://panafricanquotes.wordpress.com/speeches/independence-speech-kwame-nkrumah-march-6-1957-accra-ghana (accessed November 2014).

Nkrumah, K. (1957b) On Freedom's Stage. *Africa Today*, 4(2), March/April: 4–8.

Nkrumah, K. (1957c) *The Autobiography of: Kwame Nkrumah*. London: Nelson Publishers.

Nkrumah, K. (1962) *I Speak of Freedom: A Statement of African Ideology*. London: Mercury Books.

Nkrumah, K. (1963) *Africa Must Unite*. London: Heinemann.

Nkrumah, K. (1964) *Blueprint of our Goal: Launching the Seven Year Development Plan*. 11 March. Ministry of Information and Broadcasting. Available at http://nkrumahinfobank.org/article.php?id=355&c=51.

Nkrumah, K. (1973) *Revolutionary Path*. London: Panaf Books Limited.

Nnoli, O. (1981) *Path to Nigerian Development*. London: Zed Books

Noman, A., Botchwey, K., Stein, H. and Stiglitz, J.E. (eds) (2012) *Good Growth and Governance in Africa: Rethinking Development Strategies*. Oxford: Oxford University Press.

North, D.C. (1990) *Institutions, Institutional Change and Economic Performance*. New York: Cambridge University Press.

Nurkse, R. (1953) *Problems of Capital Formation in Underdeveloped Countries*. Oxford: Oxford University Press.

Nyerere, J. (1967) *The Arusha Declaration*. Ministry of Information and Tourism. Available at www.marxists.org/subject/africa/nyerere/1967/arusha-declaration.htm (accessed 20 April 2014).

Nyerere, J. (1969) *Freedom and Socialism (Churu Na Ujamaa): A Selection from Writings and Speeches, 1965–1967*. Oxford: Oxford University Press.

Nyerere, J. (1974) *Man and Development*. Oxford: Oxford University Press.

O'Brien, F.S. and Ryan, T.C.I. (2001) Kenya. In S. Devarajan, D. Dollar and T. Holmgren (eds), *Aid and Reform in Africa: Lessons from Ten Case Studies*. Washington, DC: World Bank.

Obwona, M. and Guloba, M. (2009) Poverty Reduction Strategies During Post-conflict Recovery in Africa. *Journal of African Economies*, 18 (suppl. 1): 77–98.

O'Connell, J. (1971) Political Constraints on Planning: Nigeria as a Case Study in the Developing World. *Nigeria Journal of Economic and Social Science*, 13.

Bibliography 179

Obasanjo, A.O. (2004) Foreword to National Economic Empowerment and Development Strategy (NEEDS) September, 2004, Abuja: Nigeria.

Obasanjo, A.O. (2004) Speech to the Nigerian Houses of Senate and Representatives to Present the Report of the Committee for Public Sector Reform. Abuja, May.

Obikeze, O.S. and Obi, E.A. (2004) *Public Administration in Nigeria: A Developmental Approach*. Abingdon: Bookpoint.

Obioma, E.C. (2010) An Examination of the Relationship between Government Obuasi Mines in Ghana. *International Research Journal of Library, Information and Archival Studies*, 1(3): 68–80.

Odinga, A.O. and Odinga, O. (1967) *Not yet Uhuru: The Autobiography of Oginga Odinga, with a Foreword by Kwame Nkrumah*. London: Heinemann.

Odukoya, A.O. (2006) Oil and Sustainable Development in Nigeria: A Case Study of the Niger Delta. *Journal of Human Ecology*, 20(4): 249–258.

Ofosu-Mensah, A.E. (2011)Gold Mining and the Socio-economic Development of Obuasi in Adanse. *African Journal of History and Culture*, 3(4): 54–64.

Ogbuagu, C.S. (1983) The Nigerian Indigenization Policy: Nationalism or Pragmatism? *African Affairs*, 241–266.

Oguntoyinbo, J., Areola, O., Filani, M. (eds) (1983) *A Geography of Nigerian Development*, 2nd edition. Ibadan: Heinemann Educational Books Ltd, pp. 296–310.

Ogwumike, F.O. (2002) An Appraisal of Poverty Reduction Strategies in Nigeria. *CBN Economic and Financial Review*, 39(4): 1–17.

Ohno, I. and Ohno, K. (2012) Dynamic Capacity Development: What Africa Can Learn from Industrial Policy Formulation in East Asia. In A. Norman *et al.* (eds), *Good Growth and Governance in Africa: Rethinking Development Strategies*. Oxford: Oxford University Press, Ch. 7.

Ojo, F. (2012) Constraints on Budgeting and Development Plan Implementation in Nigeria: An Overview. *European Journal of Sustainable Development*, 445–456.

Okereke, C. (2014) A changing climate and African development. In V. Dessai and R. Potter (eds), *The Companion to Development Studies*. Routledge: Abingdon, pp. 346–351.

Okereke, C. (2011) Governance and sustainable development in Africa. In I. Agyeman-Duah (ed.), *Pilgrims of the night: development challenges and opportunities in Africa*. Banbury: Ayebia Publishing, pp. 16–27.

Okereke, C. (2008) Culture, climate change and environmental conflict in the Niger Delta, Nigeria. In R. Dasgupta (ed.), *Cultural practices, political possibilities*. Cambridge: Cambridge Scholars Publishing, pp. 260–277.

Okereke, C. (2006) Oil Politics and Environmental Conflict: The Case of Niger Delta Nigeria. In B. Gokay (ed.), *The Politics of Oil*. London: Routledge, pp. 110–118.

Okereke, C. and Yusuf, T. (2013) Low carbon development and energy security in Africa. In H. Dyer and M.J. Trombetta (eds), *International handbook on energy security*. Cheltenham: Edward Elgar, pp. 462–482.

Okojie, C.E. (2002) Development Planning in Nigeria Since Independence. In M.A. Iyoha and C.O. Itsede (eds), *Nigerian Economy: Structure, Growth and Development*. Benin City: Mindex Publishing.

Okonjo-Iweala, N. and Osafo-Kwaako, P. (2007) *Nigeria's Economic Reforms, Progress and Challenges*. Global Working Papers. Washington, DC: The Brookings Institution.

Okonjo-Iweala, N. and Osafo-Kwaako, P. (2007) Improving Health Statistics in Africa. *The Lancet*, 370(9598): 1527–1528.

180 *Bibliography*

Okonjo-Iweala, N. (2012) *Reforming the Unreformable: Lessons from Nigeria*. Boston, MA: MIT Press.

Okoye, M. (1980) African Venture in Self-reliance: Preface. In E.U. Ikoku (ed.), *Self-Reliance African's Survival*. Enugu: Fourth Dimension Publishers, pp. 5–6.

Okupe, D. (2014) *Priorities and Progress in Nigeria: Imperatives for Stability and Growth*. Chatham House Lecture Series, Royal Institute of International Affairs, London, 24 July.

Olugbenga, T., Jumah, A. and Phillips, D. (2013) The Current and Future Challenges of Electricity Market in Nigeria in the Face of Deregulation Process. *African Journal of Engineering Research*, 1(2): 33–39.

Oluwasanmi, H.A. (1966) *Agriculture and Nigerian Economic Development*. Ibadan: Oxford University Press.

Onuoha, G. (2008) *Contemporary Igbo Nationalism and the Crisis of Self-Determination in the Nigerian Public Sphere*. Dakar: CODESRIA.

Oomen, B. (2000) *Tradition on the Move: Chiefs, Democracy and Change in Rural South Africa* (Vol. 6). Amsterdam: Netherlands Institute for Southern Africa.

Oosthuizen, M. and Cassim, A. (2014) The State of Youth Unemployment in South Africa. *Africa in Focus*. Available at www.brookings.edu/blogs/africa-in-focus/posts/2014/08/15-youth-unemployment-south-africa-oosthuizen.

Orilade, T. (2007) *PTDF Scandal: Senate Indicts OBJ, Atiku: Impeachment Motion Looms*. Sahara Reporters. Posted March 1 2007. Available at http://saharareport ers.com/2007/02/28/breaking-news-ptdf-scandal-senate-indicts-obj-atiku-impeachme nt-motion-looms.

Ostrom, E. (1990) *Governing the Commons: The Evolution of Institutions for Collective Action*. Cambridge: Cambridge University Press.

Ostrom, E. (1996) Crossing the Great Divide: Coproduction, Synergy and Development. *World Development*, 24(6): 1073–1087.

Ostrom, E. (2008) Institutions and the Environment. *Economic Affairs*, 28(3): 24–31.

Ostrom, E. and Gardner, R. (1995) *Rules, Games and Common-Pool Resources*. Ann Arbor: University of Michigan Press

Otobo, E.L. (2011) *The Challenges of Realizing Nigeria Vision 2020*. Address delivered at the annual convention of the Government College, Ughelli, Old Boys Association in North America.

Oversea Development Institute (ODI) (2004) *Achieving Food Security in Southern Africa: Policy Issues and Options*. Synthesis Paper. Forum for Food Security in Southern Africa. London: ODI.

Padayachee, V. and Sherbut, G. (2007) Ideas and Power: Academic Economists and the Making of Economic Policy: The South African Experience in Comparative Perspectives (1985–2007). *Cahiers d'Etudes africaines*, 2 (2011): 202–3.

Pahad, E. (1990) The Media Are too Important to Be Left to the Professionals to Plan. *Journalism Review*, 1(1): 52–53.

Perales, J.A.S. (2004) Consensus, Dissensus, Confusion: The 'Stiglitz Debate' in Perspective: A Review Essay. *Development in Practice*, 412–423.

Philips, A. (1987) A General Overview of Structural Adjustment Programme. In A.C. Philips and E.C. Ndekwu (eds), *Structural Adjustment Programme in a Developing Economy: The Case of Nigeria*. Ibadan: NISER, pp. 1–12.

Plange, N. (1979) Underdevelopment in Northern Ghana: Natural Causes or Colonial Capitalism? *Review of African Political Economy*, 15/16: 4–14.

Bibliography 181

Porter, M.E. (2000) Location, Competition and Economic Development: Local Clusters in a Global Economy. *Economic Development Quarterly*, 14(1): 15–34.

Porter, M.E. (2011) *Competitive Advantage of Nations: Creating and Sustaining Superior Performance*. New York: The Free Press Simon and Schuster Inc.

Pye, L.W. (1966) *Aspects of Political Development*. Boston, MA: Little, Brown and Company.

Qian, Y. and Xu, C. (1993) Why China's Economic Reforms Differ: The M-form Hierarchy and Entry/Expansion of the Non-state Sector. *Economics of Transition*, 1(2): 135–170.

Rahman, M.M. (2012) The 'Guided Ownership' Revisited: An Agenda for Independent Policy Making in Bangladesh. *Journal of Public Administration and Policy Research*, 4(5): 84–92.

Randall, D.J. (1996) Prospects for the Development of a Black Business Class in South Africa. *The Journal of Modern African Studies*, 34(4): 661–686.

Ray, D. (1998) *Development Economics*. Princeton, NJ: Princeton University Press.

Rodrik, D. (2000) Growth Versus Poverty Reduction: A Hollow Debate. *Finance & Development*, 37(4).

Rodrik, D. (2006) Goodbye Washington Consensus, Hello Washington Confusion? A Review of the World Bank's Economic Growth in the 1990s: Learning from a Decade of Reform. *Journal of Economic Literature*, 44(4), December: 973–987.

Rodrik, D., Subraminian, A. and Trebbi, F. (2002) *Institutions Rule: The Primacy of Institutions over Geography and Integration in Economic Development*. CEPR Discussion Paper, No. 3643. London: CEPR.

Rodrik, D., Subraminian, A. and Trebbi, F. (2004) Institutions Rule: The Primacy of Institutions over Geography and Integration in Economic Development. *Journal of Economic Growth*, 9(2): 131–165.

Roemer, M. (1982) Economic Development in Africa: Performance since Independence and a Strategy for the Future. *Daedalus*, 125–148.

Roemer, M. and Gugerty, M.K. (1997) *Does Economic Growth Reduce Poverty*. Technical Paper. Harvard Institute for International Development.

Romer, D.H. and Frankel, J.A. (1999) Does Trade Cause Growth? *American Economic Review*, 89(3): 379–399.

Romer, P.M. (1986) Increasing Returns and Long Run Growth. *Journal of Political Economy*, 94: 1002–1037.

Rosenstein-Rodan, P.N. (1943) Problems of Industrialisation of Estern and South-eastern Europe. *The Economic Journal*, 53(210/211): 202–211.

Rostow, W.W. (1960) *The Stages of Economic Growth: A Non-Communist Manifesto*. Cambridge: Cambridge University Press.

Rowden, R. (2013) The Myth of Africa's Rise: Why the Rumors of Africa's Explosive Growth Have Been Exaggerated. *Foreign Policy*, 4 January. Available at http://foreignpolicy.com/2013/01/04/the-myth-of-africas-rise.

RSA (2011) *Report on Dropout and Learner Retention Strategy to Portfolio Committee on Education*. Department of Basic Education, Republic of South Africa.

Rugumamu, S.M. (1997) *Lethal Aid: the Illusion of Socialism and Self-reliance in Tanzania*. Trenton, NJ: Africa World Press.

Sabatier, A. (2006) *Theories of the Policy Process*. Boulder, CO: Westview Press

Sachs, J.D. (2001) *Tropical Underdevelopment*. National Bureau of Economic Research Working Paper No. w8119.

182 Bibliography

Sachs, J.D. (2003) *Institutions Don't Rule: Direct Effects of Geography on Per Capita Income*. National Bureau of Economic Research Working Paper No. 9490.

Sachs, J. D., Warner, A., Åslund, A. and Fischer, S. (1995) Economic Reform and the Process of Global Integration. *Brookings Papers on Economic Activity*, 1: 1–118.

Sachs, J.D., McArthur, J.W., Schmidt-Traub, G., Kruk, M., Bahadur, C., Faye, M. and McCord, G. (2004) Ending Africa's Poverty Trap, *Brookings Papers on Economic Activity*, 1: 117–240.

Sandbrook, R. (1986) The State and Economic Stagnation in Tropical Africa. *World Development*, 14(3): 319–332.

Sandbrook, R. (2000) Closing the Circle: Democratization and Development in Africa. *Canadian Journal of African Studies/Revue Canadienne des Études Africaines*, 36(2): 405–408.

Sandbrook, R. and Oelbaum, J. (1999) Reforming the Political Kingdom: Governance and Development in Ghana's Fourth Republic. *Critical Perspectives* No. 2. Ghana Center for Democratic Development.

Schwab, K. (ed.) (2013) *The Global Competitiveness Report 2013–2014*. Geneva: World Economic Forum.

Scott, D. (1956) *Epidemic Disease in Ghana 1901–1960*. London: Oxford University Press.

Scott, J. (1999) *Seeing Like a State: How Certain Schemes to Improve the Human Condition Have Failed*. New Haven, CT: Yale University Press.

SekgomaG.A. (1994) The Lagos Plan of Action and Some Aspects of Development in Sierra Leone. *PULA: Botswana Journal of African Studies*, 8(2).

Sen, A. (1999) *Development as Freedom*. Oxford: Oxford University Press.

Senor, D. and Singer,S.(2011) *Start-up Nation: The Story of Israel's Economic Miracle*. New York: Random House LLC.

Shillington, K. (1992) *Ghana and the Rawlings Factor*. New York: St Martin's Press.

Simon, D. (1992) *Cities, Capital and Development: African Cities in the World Economy*. London: Belhavan Press.

Sklar, R. (1963) *Nigerian Political Parties*. Princeton, NJ: Princeton University Press.

Sklar, R. and Whitaker, C.S. Jr (1966) *Nigeria*. In J.S. Coleman and C. Roseberg Jr. (eds), *Political Parties and National Integration in Tropical Africa*. Berkeley, CA: University of California Press.

Solow, R.M. (1956) A Contribution to the Theory of Economic Growth. *Quarterly Journal of Economics*, 7: 65–94.

Southall, R. (2004) The ANC and Black Capitalism in South Africa. *Review of African Political Economy*, 31(100): 313–328.

Stewart, F. and Wang, M. (2004) *Do PRSPs Empower Poor Countries and Disempower the World Bank, or Is it the other Way Round?* QEH Working Paper Series S108.

Stiglitz, J.E. (1989) Markets, Market Failures and Development. *The American Economic Review*, 79(2).

Stichter, S. (1982) *Migrant Labour in Kenya: Capitalism and African Response, 1895–1975*. Harlow: Longman.

Stiglitz, J.E. (1996) Some Lessons from the East Asian Miracle. *World Bank, Research Observer*, II(2).

Stiglitz, J.E. (1998) More Instruments and Broader Goals: Moving toward the Post-Washington Consensus, Wider Annual Lecture.

Stiglitz, J.E. (2002) *Globalization and Its Discontents*. New York: W.W. Norton and Company Inc.

Bibliography 183

Stiglitz, J.E. and Hoff, K. (1990) Imperfect Information and Rural Credits: Puzzles and Policy Perspectives, in *The World Bank Economic Review*. Oxford: Oxford University Press.

Stiglitz, J.E. and Uy, M. (1996) Financial Markets, Public Policy And The East Asian Miracle. *The World Bank, Research Observer*, II(2).

Stolper, W.F. (1996) *Planning Without Facts: Lessons in Resource Allocation from Nigeria's Development*. Cambridge, MA: Harvard University Press.

Sutton, J. and Kpentey, B. (2012) *An Enterprise Map of Ghana*. London: International Growth Centre and London Publishing Partnership.

Svensson, J. (2000) When is Foreign Aid Policy Credible? Aid Dependence and Conditionality. *Journal of Development Economics*, 61: 61–84.

Swainson, N. (1980) *The Development of Corporate Capitalism in Kenya*. Berkeley: University of California Press.

Tangri, R. and Southall, R. (2008) The Politics of Black Economic Empowerment in South Africa. *Journal of Southern African Studies*, 34(3): 699–716.

Temin, P. (1988) Product Quality and Vertical Integration in the Early Cotton Textile Industry. *Journal of Economic History*, 48(4): 891–907.

Terreblanche, S.J. (1999) *The Ideological Journey of South Africa: From the RDP to the GEAR Macro-economic Plan*. Paper presented in a special ME99 workshop on Globalisation, Poverty, Women and the Church in South Africa.

The Economist (2011) A More Hopeful Continent: The Lion's King? 6 January. Available at www.economist.com/node/17853324 (accessed November 2014).

The Economist (2012) Africa's Impressive Growth. Available at www.economist.com/blogs/dailychart/2011/01/daily_chart.

Thompson, W.S. (1969) *Ghana's Foreign Policy, 1957–1966: Diplomacy, Ideology and the New State*. Princeton, NJ: Princeton University Press.

Thugge, K., Ndung'u, N. and Otieno, R.O. (2011) Unlocking the Future Potential for Kenya: The Vision 2030. Nairobi, Kenya. Available at www.csae.ox.ac.uk/conferences/2009-edia/papers/509-owino.pdf (accessed 11 April 2013).

Tisdell, C. (2009) Economic Reform and Openness in China: China's Development Policies in the last 30 Years. *Economic Analysis and Policy*, 39(2): 271.

Tomlinson, B. (2011) Democratic Ownership and Development Effectiveness: Civil Society Perspectives on Progress since Paris. *Reality of Aid 2011 Report*. Quezon City: IBON Books.

Tsikata, Y.M. (2001) Owning Economic Reforms: A Comparative Study of Ghana and Tanzania. (No. 2001/53) WIDER Discussion Papers/World Institute for Development Economics (UNU-WIDER).

UNCTAD (1969) *Liberalization of Tariffs and Non-tariff Barriers*. Geneva: UNCTAD DocumentsTDIB7C.2/83;TDIBIC.2/R.1,UNCTAD.

UNCTAD (1970) *Liberalization of Tariffs and Non-tariff Barriers*. Geneva: UNCTAD Documents/B/C.2/R.2;TD/B/C.2/R3,UNCTAD.

UNCTAD (1973) *Inventory of Non-tariff Barriers, Including Quantitative Restrictions Applied in Developed Market Economy Countries*. Geneva: UNCTAD Report.

UNDP (2010) *Human Development Report Nigeria 2008-2009. Achieving Growth with Equity*. Geneva: United Nations Development Programme.

UNDP (2013) *The Rise of the South: Human Progress in a Diverse World*. Human Development Report South Africa UNDP.

UNDP (2014) *Sustaining Human Progress: Reducing Vulnerabilities and Building Resilience*. Human Development Report. Available at http://hdr.undp.org/en/data.

184   *Bibliography*

UNECA (2001) *Compact for African Recovery Operationalizing the Millennium Partnership for the African Recovery Programme.* Addis Ababa, Ethiopia: United Nations Economic Commission for Africa (UNECA).

UNECA (2009) *The Status of Regional Integration in Africa.* Addis Ababa, Ethiopia: United Nations Economic Commission for Africa (UNECA).

UNECA (2014) *Dynamic Industrial Policy in Africa: Innovative Institutions, Effective Processes and Flexible Mechanisms.* Economic Report on Africa 2014. Addis Ababa, Ethiopia: United Nations Economic Commission for Africa (UNECA).

UNESCO (2012) *Education for All Global Monitoring Report.* Paris: UNESCO Publishing.

UNILEVER (2008) *It's Onwards and Upwards for SA's Black Diamond Women.* TNS Research Surveys Press Release. Cape Town UCT Unilever Institute of Strategic Marketing.

Usoro, E.J. (1977) Colonial Economic Development Planning in Nigeria, 1919–1939: An Appraisal. *The Nigerian Journal of Economic and Social Studies,* 19(1).

Van de Walle, N. (2001) *African Economies and the Politics of Permanent Crisis, 1979–1999.* Cambridge: Cambridge University Press.

Varvasovszky, Z. and Brugha, R. (2000) A Stakeholder Analysis. *Health Policy and Planning,* 15(3): 338–345.

Walsh, J.I. (2000) When Do Ideas Matter? Explaining the Successes and Failures of Thatcherite Ideas. *Comparative Political Studies,* 33(4): 483–516.

Wamai, R.G. (2009) The Kenya Health System – Analysis of the Situation and Enduring Challenges. *International Medical Community,* 134–140.

Waldman, C. (2008) *China's Educational Performance: Implication or Global Competitiveness, Social Stability and Long-Term Development.* Virginia Manufacturing Alliance/MAPI.

Wangwe, S.M. (2002) *Aid Reform in Africa: The Conceptual Framework. African Report: Assessing the New Partnership.* Ottawa: The North South Institute, pp. 17–36.

Ward, J.R. (1994) The Industrial Revolution and British Imperialism, 1750–1850. *The Economic History Review,* 47(1): 44–65.

Wasserman, G. (1976) *Politics of Decolonization: Kenya Europeans and the Land Issue, 1960–65.* Cambridge: Cambridge University Press.

Watkins, T. (n.d.) *Political and Economic History of Ghana.* San José State University Economics Department. Available at www.sjsu.edu/faculty/watkins/ghana.htm.

Weeks, J. (1999) Stuck in Low Gear? Macroeconomic Policy in South Africa 1996–1998. *Cambridge Journal of Economics,* 23: 795–811.

Weeks, J. and McKinley, T. (2009) The Macroeconomic Implications of MDG-Based Strategies in Sub-Saharan Africa. In T. McKinley (ed.), *Economic Alternatives for Growth, Employment and Poverty Reduction: Progressive Policy Recommendations for Developing Countries.* London: Palgrave.

Weissman, S.R. (1990) Structural Adjustment in Africa: Insights from the Experiences of Ghana and Senegal. *World Development,* 18(12): 1621–1634.

Whitfield, L. (2005) Trustees of Development from Conditionality to Governance: Poverty Reduction Strategy Papers in Ghana. *The Journal of Modern African Studies,* 43(4): 641–664.

Whitfield, L. (ed.) (2009) *The Politics of Aid: African Strategies for Dealing with Donors.* Oxford: Oxford University Press.

Bibliography 185

Whitfield, L. and Fraser, A. (2009) Negotiating Aid. In L. Whitfield (ed.), *The Politics of Aid. African Strategies for Dealing with Donors.* Oxford: Oxford University Press, pp. 27–44.

Whitfield, L. and Jones, E. (2008) Ghana: Breaking Out of Aid Dependence? Economic and Political Barriers to Ownership. In L. Whitfield (ed.), *The Politics of Aid: African Strategies for Dealing with Donors.* Oxford: Oxford University Press, pp. 185–215.

Williamson, J. (1989) What Washington Means by Policy Reform. In J. Williamson (ed.), *Latin American Readjustment: How Much has Happened.* Washington, DC: Institute for International Economics.

Williamson, O.E. (1975) *Markets and Hierarchies, Analysis and Antitrust Implications: A Study in the Economics of Internal Organization.* New York: Free Press.

Williamson, O.E. (2000) Ronald Harry Coase: Institutional Economist and Institution Builder. *Journal of Institutional Economics,* 1–6.

Wilson, M. and Thompson, L. (1969) *The Oxford History of South Africa: South Africa to 1870.* Oxford: Oxford University Press.

White, E. (2003) Kwame Nkrumah: Cold War Modernity, Pan-African Ideology and the Geopolitics of Development. *Geopolitics,* 8(20): 99–124.

Wolpe, H. (1972) Capitalism and Cheap Labour-power in South Africa: From Segregation to Apartheid. *Economy and Society,* 1: 425–456.

World Bank (1992) *World Bank Structural and Sectoral Adjustment Operations: The Second OED Review.* Operations Evaluation Department Report No. 1087. Washington, DC: World Bank.

World Bank (2012) Kenya at Work Energizing the Economy and Creating Jobs. *Kenya Economy Update Edition 7.*

World Bank (2013) *Growing Africa: Unlocking the Potential of Agribusiness.* Washington, DC: The World Bank.

World Bank Report (2014) *GDP per Capita, PPP (Current International $).* World Development Indicators database, World Bank. Available at http://data.worldbank.org/indicator/NY.GDP.PCAP.PP.CD?order=wbapi_data_value_2013+wbapi_data_value+wbapi_data_value-last&sort=desc.

Yeung, H.W. (2003) *Chinese Capitalism in a Global Era: Towards a Hybrid Capitalism.* London and New York: Routledge.

Zhao, Z. (1987) *Advance along the Road of Socialism with Chinese Characteristics.* Report Delivered at the 13th National Congress of the Communist Party of China on 25 October.

Ziblim, A. (2013) *The Dynamics of Informal Settlements Upgrading in South Africa: Legislative and Policy Context, Problems, Tensions and Contradictions.* A Study Commissioned by Habitat for Humanity International/EMEA Office. Bratislava, Slovakia.

Zimmerman, F. (2008) Home-owned and Home-grown: Development Policies That Can Work. OECD Development Centre Policy Insights No 75.

Index

Accelerated and Shared Growth Initiative for South Africa (ASGISA) 108–9, 112, 117–20, 129, 131
Adapted Development Strategies (ADS) 148 – 9
Adopted Development Strategies (AoDS) 148 – 9, 151, 153
Africa as a commodity exporter 18, 19
Africa Development Bank (AfDB) 16, 65, 144 – 5
Africa is rising 144, 160, 161
African National Congress (ANC) 110, 113
African Personality 2; *see also* Negrititude
African Renaissance 1, 3, 13, 26, 28, 75, 161
African ruling class 18, 20; relationship with African masses 20
African socialism 2, 13, 49, 91–4
African solutions 3, 46, 152–3
Africanization 15, 23, 73
Afrikaner political party 109
aid: and homegrown development 156; conditionality 6, 133, 149, 156, 161; effectiveness of 3,101; politics of 5, 140
Ake, Claude 1, 12, 17, 18, 21, 24, 38
Algeria 19, 26
ANC Charter 138
Angola 137, 160
apartheid 9–10, 108–116, 119, 123–8, 154
Arusha Declaration 1, 14
Asian Tigers 29, 60, 106
autarky 6

Balewa, Tafawa 14
bamboo capitalism 36; *see also* state capitalism

Bantu 110; Self-government Act 110
Berg Report 16
big push development 2, 13, 47, 48; *see also* Nkrumah, Kwame
Black Economic Empowerment (BEE) 109, 114
Black Economic Empowerment Commission (BEEECOM) 117
Blair, Tony 80 – 1
Botswana 36
Bouteflika, Abdelaziz 26
Brazil 37, 143, 146 – 7
Bretton Woods 3, 24, 26, 29, 82, 95, 114, 158
BRICS 108
broad-based stakeholder participation: as a feature of homegrown development 37–40; comparison of cases 131; controversies 138–42; in Ghana 58–60; in Nigeria 77–78; in Kenya 97–99; in South Africa 117–19
Broad-based Black Economic Empowerment 114, 131
Burkina Faso 20

Cape Town 138
capital accumulation 20–21, 40
cappuccino effect 124
China 3, 36, 39 – 40, 42–4, 143, 146–7
Chinese model 36, 42, 44; see also Bamboo capitalism
colonialism 5, 10, 22, 130–1; legacy of 17, 59, 71, 160
Comprehensive Development Framework 25, 126
Comprehensive Lagos Action Plan 16
Congo 19, 20, 157
Congress of South Africa Trade Unions (COSATU) 111

Index 187

Co-ordinated Programme of Economic and Social Development Policies (CPESDP) 52
Côte d'Ivoire 13, 15, 58
cotton ginning 2
cotton mills 15
country ownership 4–5, 29–30, 33, 65, 141; comparison of cases 131–35in Ghana 65–66; in Kenya 101–12; in Nigeria 81–82; in South Africa 121–22

dark continent 161
debt reliefs 3
decentralization 53, 63 – 4, 72, 122, 156
dependency theories 23
Diamond 36, 109, 130
donor agencies 4, 6, 25, 34 – 5, 44, 77, 82, 88, 90, 140, 159
donor countries 3, 5

East Africa Community (EAC) 16
Easterly, William 29
Economic and Social Action Programme (ESAP) 25
economic decolonization 1, 13, 20
economic diversification: as a feature of homegrown development 37–40; comparison in Africa 131; 1355–58; in Ghana 58–60; in Kenya 97–99; in Nigeria 77–78; in South Africa 117–19
Economic Recovery Strategy, Kenya 10, 91, 95; see also Kenya
endogenous growth18, 20, 58, 120, 150, 152–3
Equatorial Guinea 144–5
Ethiopia 12, 149, 160
export – oriented production 22

Foreign Direct Investment (FDI) 43, 84, 85

G77 and China 24
Germany 36, 56, 65
Ghana: development policies since 1990s 51–52; economic diversification and local imperatives 58–60; homegrown development after independence 46–51; homegrown development rating 130–46; public participation in development 56–58; social development 60–63; national health insurance scheme 61; local capacity and institutions 63–65; country ownership of development 65–66; implementation of development strategies 66–69.
Ghana Poverty Reduction Strategy 10, 52, 55, 132, 138
Ghana Shared Growth and Development Agenda (GSGDA) 52
Ghana Vision 2020 47, 52
Gold 47, 58, 109, 130, 135
Gold Coast 47
Gowon, Yakubu 73
Greene Kirk 9, 46–7
Groundnut production 2, 18, 86, 136
Growth Employment and Redistribution (GEAR) programme 108, 138
Guggisberg, Gordon 47
Guinea 137, 144–5

Harambee 92 – 4, 104, 107
Hayek, von 127
Hegemony 20, 22, 28
Highly Indebted Poor Countries (HIPC) 46, 55, 82, 154
HIV/AIDS 79, 85, 91, 126, 144
Homegrown Development (HGD): as a tested development strategy 42; conceptualization of 5, 7, 10, 32, 44, 148, 152; definition of 31; essential features of 36; not a magic bullet 150; pyramid of 148, 153; the core of 32, 36, 44, 131, 150
Hong Kong 29
Horticulture 98, 136
hybrid capitalism 36; see also Bamboo capitalism

import substitution 21, 23, 71, 93
Imposed Development Strategy (IDS) 150, 153
India 7, 35, 40, 143, 146–7,
indigeneity 4, 8, 56, 70, 91, 115, 130, 152
indigenization 15, 20, 24, 73 – 4
indigenous growth 5, 23
industrialized countries 16, 18, 27, 38
innovation 39–42, 80, 88, 99, 136, 145, 156
institutions: as a feature of homegrown development 39–40; comparison of cases 131, 145–47; in Ghana 63–65; in Kenya 99–100; in Nigeria 79–81; in South Africa 120–21
institutional capacity 40, 82, 89, 134, 139, 145, 155
international capitalism 20

188 *Index*

International Financial Institutions (IFIs) 3, 26, 57, 60, 132, 153
International Labour Organisation (ILO) 124
International Monetary Fund (IMF) 127
Israel 40

Japan 35–6
Jonathan, Goodluck 70
Jubilee Debt Campaign 157–8

Kagame, P. 159
Kaunda, K. 1, 13, 134–5
Kenya: Business Process Outsourcing (BPO) 97; Land Alliance 104; National Bureau of Statistics 98,

Road 2000 programme 96; economic diversification and local imperatives 97–99; homegrown development at independence 91–95; homegrown development rating 130–46; post 2020 development policies 95; public participation in development 96–97; social development 100–101; local capacity and institutions 99–100; country ownership of development 101–2; implementation of development strategies 102–3.
Kenyatta, Jomo 13–4, 92, 104
Kenyatta, Jomo 13, 92
Keynesianism 10
Khan, Mohsin 29
Kibaki, Mwai 91, 95–6
Kufuor, John 46

Lagarde, Christine 161
leather tanning 2
Lewis, Arthur 15, 48
Local Economic Empowerment Development Strategy (LEEDS) 76
lost decades in Africa 2
Lumumba, Patrice 20

Malaysia 44, 93
Mandela, N. 111, 116
manufacturing sector growth in Ghana 60
mass consumption 21
Mauritius 146
Mbeki Thabo 3, 26, 108
Medium – Term Expenditure Framework (MTEF) 54

Medium Term Plan (MTP) 52, 98, 101
Mensah, Joseph Henry 47
MERG 116, 121
metropolis 19, 21
Millennium Development Goals (MDGS) 25, 126
mixed economy 13, 113
Mkandawire, Thandika 38, 41
Mo Ibrahim Foundation 68, 145
modernization theory 2, 10, 13, 18, 21–22, 48, 56, 72, 94
Monitoring and Evaluation Directorate (MED) 102
Monrovia Declaration 16
Mozambique 144, 160
Muganda, Anna 29

Nasser, Abdul 14
National Cohesion and Integration Commission 100
National Development Policy Framework (NDPF) 52
National Economic Direction (NED) 70, 74
National Economic Empowerment and Development Strategy (NEEDS) 70, 74–5, 136
National Economic Social Council (NESC) 96, 101, 139
National Economic Social Council 96, 101, 139
National Planning Commission (NPC) 75–6, 78, 80, 82 – 3, 85, 87–9, 155
National Rainbow Coalition (NARC) 95, 101
Nationalization 23, 73, 93, 111, 114
Negritude 2; *see also* African Personality
Neo-colonialism 50
Neo-patrimonial politics 21, 54
NEPAD 3, 27, 29
New Growth Path (NGP) 108, 112, 117, 131
New International Economic World Order (NIECO) 24
New partnership 3, 27, 29, 75
New Patriotic Party (NPP) 52
Nigeria: Budget Monitoring and Price Intelligence Unit 84; Corrupt Practises and other Related Offences Commission (ICPC) 84; due process in 84, 156; Economic and Financial Crime Commission (EFCC) 84; Joint Planning Commission (JPC) 72;

Index 189

National Orientation Agency 80;
National Youth Service Corps 74;
the crippled giant 85; Ten Year Plan
of Development and Welfare for
Nigeria 71
Nigerian Development Policies; colonial
legacy 71–72; country ownership of
programme 81–83;
economic diversification 77–78; homegrown development after independence 72–74; homegrown
development rating 130–46; recent
national development polices 74–76;
public participation in development
56–58; social and human
development 78–79; institutions
79–81; implementation of
development strategies 83–85
Nkrumah, Kwame: big push
development 2, 14, 47, 47; battle cry
13; independence speech 12; policies
14–20; overthrow 23
Non-traditional export 24, 137
Nyerere, Julius 1, 13–4, 20, 150

Obasanjo, Olusegun 3, 26, 74
Odinga, Oginga 94
Okonjo-Iweala 76–7, 81–2, 84, 88, 134
Okupe, Doyin 87
OMEGA Plan 26
Organization of African Unity (OAU) 3,
16
Ostrom, Elinor 38–40
Overseas Development Institute (ODI)
133

palm oil 2, 15, 18, 73, 86, 136
parallel development 36
Paris declaration 3
policy autonomy 3, 6–7, 68, 134,
149–50, 154, 160
Post – Washington Consensus 31
post-apartheid reconstruction policies 112
post-structuralism 10
Poverty Reduction Strategy Papers
(PRSPs) 4, 10, 25, 31, 46, 52, 81, 133,
149, 153
prebendalism 74
privatization 75, 77, 80, 84, 89–90, 106,
143, 158 – 9
protectionist policies 24
Rawlings, Jerry 51
Regional Coordinating Council (RCC)
53

Rostow 21
Rwanda 34, 90, 146, 149, 159, 160

Sankara Thomas 20
Scientific socialism 2, 47–8 (*see*
Nkrumah)
Sector Wide Approaches (SWAP) 25
Self-reliance 1–2, 13–5, 22, 24, 32, 40,
73, 94, 104, 146, 150, 152, 160
Self-rule 2, 20
Senegal 26
Senor, Dan 40
SERVICOM 80
Shacks 108, 112, 119, 123, 126, 128
Singapore 29, 40, 44, 52
Singer, Saul 40
Sirte, Libya 27
Social and human development: as a
feature of homegrown development
40–42; comparison of cases 131,
142–45; in Ghana 60–63; in Kenya
100–101; in Nigeria 78–79; in South
Africa 111–20
Soludo, Charles 82
South Africa: country ownership of
policy 121–22; economic
diversification 117–19;
homegrown development after
independence 72–74; homegrown
development rating 130–46; human
and social and development 119–20;
ideology contestation 16, 125;
implementation of development
strategies 122–25; institutional
capacity 120–21; Macroeconomic
Research Group 116; political
history 109–12; post–apartheid
development 112; public
participation in development 115–17;
recent national development polices
74–76;
South African Communist Party
(SACP) 111, 127, 131
South Korea 29, 44, 93
Soviet Union 42
state capitalism 36 *see also* bamboo
capitalism
State Economic Empowerment
Development Strategy (SEEDS) 76
Stiglitz, Joseph 30
Structural Adjustment Programme 3–9,
24, 54, 126–7, 153
Sudan 12, 15
Sunil Sharma 29

190 *Index*

Sustainable development 1, 5–6, 36–7, 129–38, 145– 6, 150–3

Taiwan 29
Tanzania 2, 13, 15, 20, 23, 93
Technical assistance 1, 19, 94
Technological innovation 39–40, 80, 88
textile industry 23, 35, 59
The Brandt Report 24
The Freedom Charter 111
The Millennium Partnership for the African Recovery Programme 26
The Start-up Nation 40
Thompson Wendy 80
Tom Mboya 13, 92–4
tourism 40, 58–9, 97–8, 102, 104, 136, 155
Transparency International Corruption Perception index 146
Tunisia 19
two nations legacy 108
tyranny of participation 39

UHURU 8, 23, 92, 105
Ujamaa 2, 23
Umkhonto we Sizwe 110

UNESCO 143, 146
UNICEF 144
UNILEVER 124, 125
United Nation Commission for Africa (UNECA) 34, 75, 137
Universal Basic Education 79
US Jubilee Debt Campaign 157
USAID 141

Vietnam 137
Vision 2030 10, 91, 95–106, 139
Volta River Project 49

Wade, Abdoulaye 26
Washington Consensus 30–1, 90, 158
Wood, Angela 158
World Bank 3–9, 24–5, 29–30, 139–40, 141–2, 153–6
World Economic Forum 138

Xiaoping, Deng 42–4

Yar'adua, Musa 70

Zambia 1, 13, 134, 149, 157, 159
Zulus 109

CPSIA information can be obtained
at www.ICGtesting.com
Printed in the USA
BVHW040538241119
564611BV00004B/26/P